52 True Stories about Successful Witnessing

Nellie Pickard

Foreword by Joseph M. Stowell

Baker Books
A Division of Baker Book House Co
Grand Rapids, Michigan 49516

© 1996 by Nellie Pickard

Published by Baker Books
a division of Baker Book House Company
P.O. Box 6287, Grand Rapids, MI 49516–6287

Compiled from *What Do You Say When* . . . (© 1988), *What Would You Have Said?* (© 1990), and *Just Say It!* (© 1992), published by Baker Book House

Printed in the United States of America

Library of Congress Cataloging-in-Publication Data

Pickard, Nellie.
    52 true stories about successful witnessing / Nellie Pickard ; foreword by Joseph M. Stowell.
       p.   cm.
   ISBN 0-8010-5704-3 (pbk.)
    1. Witness bearing (Christianity) 2. Pickard, Nellie. I. Title. II. Title: Fifty-two true stories about successful witnessing
   BV4520.P493   1996
   248'.5—dc20   96-8863

Contents

Foreword

During baseball season, televised games are interrupted by spectacular moments of baseball history. They capture the thrill and essence of America's favorite pastime. As the promo draws to a close, the words blaze across the screen, "Baseball Fever . . . Catch It."

Nellie Pickard has a certain fever for evangelism, and those of us who enjoy her friendship have found it contagious. Evangelism is indeed more caught than taught. My own witness for Christ has been stimulated by the author's creative approach to loving the lost. For her, evangelism is not a project; it is a passion. The lost that she encounters are for her an opportunity to express the life-changing love of Christ.

You will be intrigued, challenged, encouraged, instructed, and enabled after reading these glimpses of the power of God unto salvation. Nellie Pickard's effective use of personal encounter will open new vistas of awareness and sensitivity.

I am delighted that you are reading this book. The author reinforces my prejudice that evangelism comes from the overflow of a loving, gracious heart. I am delighted, as well, for the sake of the gospel.

While some will not be able to relate to others exactly as Nellie does, since she is the ultimate people-person, these episodes will teach us to see others in terms of their need and the precious gift of Christ.

While effective evangelism is done in many different ways, this book will add an important arrow to your quiver. *Catch it!*

Joseph M. Stowell
President, Moody Bible Institute

Introduction

hy is it so hard for Christians to share their faith with unbelievers?" I've asked that question over and over again as I speak at seminars and retreats. The answers are generally the same all over the country.

I'm afraid people will laugh at me.
People will think I'm weird.
I may not be able to answer their questions.
I don't have the gift of evangelism.

Yes, people might laugh and think you're weird. Don't let that stop you. I remember a neighbor who laughed at me and thought I was weird. Then one day she knocked on my door and said, "We have a serious illness in our family. I know you are a woman of prayer." She hesitated a little then said, "Will you pray for us?"

You don't have to be a theologian to witness. But you can't witness with an empty head either. If you read a portion of Scripture on a daily basis, you'll gain knowledge. And Jesus promised that the Holy Spirit will bring to your remembrance the things he has said (John 14:26).

You may not be able to answer all the questions people ask. You don't have to. Tell them, "That's a good question. Let me look up the answer." Then ask your pastor or Sunday school teacher to help you. When you find the answer, call them back. They will be happy and respect you for taking the time to look up the answer.

You may not have the gift of evangelism. But Jesus said in John 20:21, "As the father sent me, so send I you into the world."

I've discovered that over 90 percent of Christians are timid when it comes to sharing their faith. You need to know that witnessing is on-the-job training. The more you do it the easier it becomes. I'm not talking about collar grabbing. That's of the flesh. But being available to the Lord to speak a word for him when the opportunity affords itself.

Part of the problem is fear, and fear paralyzes. It is never productive. "God did not give us a spirit of timidity, but a spirit of power, of love and of self-discipline" (2 Tim. 1:7).

As you read my stories, you'll discover how easy and natural it is to witness. Give God a chance to use you in this way. It's an exciting experience.

1

Not Predestined
for Such Faith

A new mall had just opened, and I was eager to take advantage of the bargains. It was Christmastime and the window section of one of the stores was beautifully decorated. The manger scene with angels hovering above was the main attraction. I enjoyed looking at all the details and listening to the carols being sung.

I wonder if the people are hearing the words, I thought.

I was grateful to the management for the beautiful music and mentioned this fact to several of the salespersons and to the manager. Then I noticed that little round tables for two were set up and that free coffee and cookies were being served, so I sat down to enjoy the holiday atmosphere.

As I looked around, I noticed a woman loaded down with packages. She seemed very tired and dejected and was looking for a place to sit. I gave her a big smile and motioned for her to come and sit with me.

She seemed relieved and sighed heavily. "Oh, me, I sure don't have the spirit of Christmas. Do you?"

"What's your problem?" I asked.

"Well, my son isn't going to be home for Christmas. Life changes so much when the children leave home. Christmas this year won't be fun like it used to be." She arranged her packages beside her on the floor. A woman brought coffee and a plate of cookies to our table.

11

"I would just like to skip Christmas this year," said my new friend after we exchanged names. "But I suppose I should consider my husband. I guess I'm feeling sorry for myself and shouldn't be going on like this in front of a perfect stranger."

"I understand," I said. "It just isn't the same without one's children around. My son won't be home either. Where is your son?"

"He's taken a job in Florida. And yours?"

"He's in Vietnam," I told Mary.

"Oh, I'm sorry. I have no right to complain."

"That's all right," I said. "You see, my son has invited Jesus Christ into his life. My husband has and so have I, and that's really what Christmas is all about."

I could hardly believe I said that. I was actually witnessing! God had taken me up on my offer.

"You are so fortunate," Mary said. "But I wasn't predestined to have such faith."

"Oh, but that's not what Christianity is all about. The good news of Christmas is for everyone. You see, God lets *you* choose. The Bible says in Joshua 24:15, 'Choose for yourselves this day whom you will serve.'"

"But how do you do it?"

Excitedly, I reached into my purse and pulled out a little booklet.* "This will tell you how. It gives the basics of how to become a Christian."

My first impulse was to just give it to her and run. But I mustered my courage and said, "Why don't you take this home and, if you want to discuss it further, give me a call."

"But couldn't we read it right now?" she asked.

Well, I thought, *if she doesn't care that people at the next table are looking at us, I guess I don't either.* So there we sat in the middle of the bustle of the holiday season, discussing the true meaning of Christmas.

---

*The booklet I use is *The Four Spiritual Laws* distributed by Campus Crusade for Christ. I like it because it forces people to face their spiritual condition. The booklet begins, "God loves you and has a wonderful plan for your life." I qualify that by saying that plan is salvation from sin. If I didn't qualify it, an eighty- or ninety-year-old might say, "But my life is almost over."

Together we read about God's love for mankind (I used John 3:16, Rom. 3:23, Rom. 6:23) and how sin has separated man from God. We read that Jesus Christ was God's only remedy for sin (Rom. 5:8, John 14:16). We read Revelation 3:20, where the Lord Jesus says, "Here I am! I stand at the door and knock. If anyone hears my voice and opens the door, I will come in and eat [fellowship] with him, and he with me."

I took a sip of my coffee, which had now gotten cold, then said, "Christianity is a relationship with Jesus Christ. It's something like a marriage relationship. We love and respect our partner. We speak to and delight in one another. If one does all the talking and the other just listens, it's a lopsided relationship. It has to be a two-way street."

"I pray all the time, but I never read the Bible," Mary confided.

I nodded. "That's what I mean. The Bible is God's Word. He speaks to us through it. That's really the best part of the relationship. Through his Word, he tells us how to live and what pleases and displeases him. The wonderful part is that he created us to have fellowship with him."

I gave Mary the booklet and, being too timid to press the issue, I asked, "Would you call me and let me know if you decide to invite Christ into your life?"

"I'll be in touch," she promised.

When Mary and I parted, I was so happy to have had my first experience of being available to the Lord in that manner.

I finished my shopping and was on my way out of the mall when I felt a tap at my elbow. It was my new friend, Mary, who was saying, "I just wanted you to know that I have invited Jesus Christ into my life."

I could scarcely believe my ears. I thanked God for the privilege of leading Mary to Christ.

Some time later, she confessed to me that before she accepted the Lord Jesus into her heart she had had periods of depression; but since then, the depression has never returned. Her whole personality has changed. She has become a happy and radiant Christian.

Reflection

That morning I said to my husband, "I told the Lord that I want to be available to him and asked him to please lead me to anyone he wants me to speak to. Still, I'm a little nervous about it."

"Why?" he asked.

"I'm afraid God will take me up on it."

I am continually overwhelmed at God's love and mercy. Here was Mary, a needy soul. She had attended church all her life but never had been given the Bread of Life. There was I, desiring to share a bit of my spiritual food. So God brought us together.

From that time on, I have practiced being available to God. I started noticing people and became more friendly in general. God guides me to people he wants me to witness to. He is faithful to his promises.

He has told us through Moses in Deuteronomy 31:6, "Be strong and courageous. Do not be afraid or terrified because of them [your enemies], for the LORD your God goes with you; he will never leave you nor forsake you."

God has said in Isaiah 55:11, "So is my word that goes out from my mouth: It will not return to me empty, but will accomplish what I desire and achieve the purpose for which I sent it."

Almighty God has promised these things. He will never go back on one thing he has promised. It is our responsibility to walk in the good of every word of God.

Wanting to End It All

*E*ighth-grade Sunday-school girls generally bubble over with either constant excitement or mischief. My friend Ola and I team-taught a class one year and had a wonderful time individually. But sometimes it did take both of us—especially to pray.

Katy was different from the rest of the girls. It was hard to get a word out of her. She came to class every Sunday, but she just sat there, kind of sad-looking. Ola and I prayed for her and went out of our way to be kind and pay special attention to her.

"We've decided," I announced one day in class, "that those of you who have perfect attendance for the next three months will be treated to dinner at Howard Johnson's. Our husbands will pay the bill, and you can have anything you want to eat."

They were delighted with the prospect.

And then I reminded them, "A little less talking and a little better behavior in class will be greatly appreciated, too, I might add." I said this with a twinkle in my eye so they would know I wasn't upset with them.

They smiled back. They had gotten the point and did make a slight effort afterwards.

Ola and I loved the girls and had already decided that their behavior was normal for their age. Perhaps not amazingly, their attendance and decorum records for the next three months were very good.

"Ola and I are very pleased with your attendance," I told them. "It looks like our husbands are going to have to work overtime to pay for this crowd's dinners."

15

The girls loved that.

"What I need to know is whether your parents will be able to bring you to the church. Does anyone need to be picked up?"

Katy raised her hand. "I have no one who will be able to drive me to the church." She hesitated. "I would like to come, though."

"No problem," I said. "It's practically on my way."

I was glad I picked her up. It gave me a chance to meet her mother. I had wondered what she would be like. Actually, she was just like Katy, quiet and withdrawn.

During the outing, as the girls in the class began to tell jokes and relate funny stories, we all laughed. They were so funny that even Katy had a faint smile on her face. She seemed to be enjoying herself. After dinner and a few more hilarious jokes and lots of giggles, it was time to leave.

"We've had loads of fun and good food," I said to them all. "And I believe our friendship and love for each other has grown. We probably won't be meeting like this any more, since you'll all be graduating into another department." I loved it when they groaned, since I felt it meant they had accepted Ola and me. We needed that because we wondered many times if we had ever gotten through to them that we loved them.

As Katy and I drove home together, she opened up and became surprisingly talkative. "I had such a good time tonight. I want to thank you for picking me up," she told me. Then it was as if a torrent had broken loose. "I wish my mother was like you. In fact, I wish you were my mother."

"Why, Katy, you surprise me. You have a mother who loves you, I'm sure."

"She never talks to me unless she's scolding. I never do anything right. She's been like that ever since my brother committed suicide."

"Oh, Katy. I didn't know that. I'm so sorry. Your mother must really be hurting. She needs you to love her."

"She doesn't want my love," Katy said. "She wants me to go to live with my aunt for a while. I guess I'll go. I think my aunt likes me."

My heart ached for this young girl.

"Katy, have you ever invited Jesus Christ into your heart?"

"I'm not sure. When the minister preached and asked people to come forward, I was too scared to go up in front. But I wanted to."

"Would you like to be sure you're a Christian?" I asked her.

"Yes, I would."

I knew that she had heard the plan of salvation many times, but it was the application to her life that I questioned. So, in a very simple way, I explained to Katy about God's great love in sending his Son to die for her. If she would receive him as her Savior and Lord, she would then be a child of God.

Timidly, she whispered, "Would you help me pray?"

I prayed the sinner's prayer a sentence at a time, and she repeated it after me.

When we finished, I said, "Katy, I sense you have lots of needs. But now you can talk them all over with your heavenly Father. He really cares for you. When you go to live with your aunt, take your Bible with you and read a portion of it every day. It will be a great help and comfort to you."

Soon after, Katy left town to live with that aunt in another state, and it was several years before I saw her again. When she appeared at church one morning, I hardly recognized her. Katy was extremely thin and hard-looking and no longer the shy, quiet, little girl I remembered.

"How about coming home with us for dinner?" I asked, wanting to get some meat on her bones and spend some time with her.

"I won't be able to today," she said. "May I come during the week?"

"Anytime," I answered. And Katy did begin coming any time she felt like it.

I was really shocked at the change in her. Where she had once been quiet and shy, now there was an air of aggressiveness about her. I also noticed that she became very demanding of my time. "I'm jealous of your children," she told me.

My children had gone out of their way to be kind to her. They invited her to our game time, but she refused, saying, "Thanks, but I'd rather go for a walk with your mother."

I went along with her at first, until it was apparent that she was trying to shock me with her lifestyle. She told me things like, "I've taken up smoking. Of course, I can quit any time I want to," and "I'm thinking of getting a job as a nightclub dancer." Once she said, "There are a lot of men who want me. I just can't keep them away."

"Katy, you've committed your life to Jesus Christ," I said. "You know what you're telling me is wrong. It hurts me to hear this; but more than that, you're grieving the Holy Spirit."

"I know. But when I quit, he'll forgive me."

"You're playing with fire. I wouldn't want to be in your shoes."

Katy seemed defiant and unresponsive to my words. She seemed determined to go her own way. My husband and I prayed for her, but we finally decided we couldn't allow her to disrupt our family time anymore.

One night, Katy called and said, "I hate my life. I've decided to commit suicide."

Ordinarily, I would have panicked; but I was very calm when I asked, "Why do you want to kill yourself?"

"My life is such a mess. I just want to end it all."

"How do you wish to do it?" I asked in a steady voice.

"I'm going to eat a whole bottle of aspirin."

"Katy, that won't kill you. It'll only give you a terrible, terrible stomachache. Why don't you come over and we'll talk." I don't know what made me say that. It scares me every time I think about it. But it worked, and I was grateful to God.

When she arrived at the house, I put my arms around her and said, "I love you, Katy. I'm glad you changed your mind. Whatever made you even think of such a foolish thing?"

"I'm pregnant. I have no money. I hate the father. I won't marry him, and I want to keep my baby."

"You can't keep your baby if you take your life. Actually, you'd be taking two lives, yours and the baby's."

"I'm so confused and mixed up. I don't know what to do," she admitted.

Then we prayed together and I assured Katy of our love and support. Later we found a Christian counselor through our church. He helped her deal with her situation.

Katy insisted on keeping little Debra after she was born, and she truly loved that baby. But she had so many struggles. Her health was failing. She never ate properly (her main diet was Cokes and hamburgers), and she wasn't able to get rid of her smoking habit, though she had tried.

About nine o'clock one evening, she called. "I went to the Bible bookstore tonight. I bought a picture of Jesus talking to the little children. I'm going to hang it over Debra's bed. Mrs. Pickard, I want you to know that when I saw that picture, I realized that I don't want my baby to have the kind of life I've had. I want to raise her to know about Jesus, and I want to be a good mother. I want to help her all I can to be an obedient Christian. I've been so rebellious, and I'm so very sorry. I don't know how the Lord can ever forgive me, but I got on my knees tonight and asked him to take me back and help me live the rest of my days for him. Now I'm asking you to forgive me. I know I've been a big disappointment to you and taken so much of your time—and your family's time."

"Oh, Katy," I said. "Of course we forgive you. That's what Christianity is all about."

"Thank you," she said. "I have such peace and love in my heart. Thanks for your patience."

I shared Katy's words with Paul, and together we gave thanks to God for the good news.

I was awakened the next morning by the ring of the telephone. My friend's voice sounded excited but strained when she asked, "Have you heard about the fire?"

"No, what fire?"

"Katy and the baby. They found her in the middle of the living room floor, holding the baby. She had tried to cover Debra with her own body."

The newscasters said the fire had started in the bedroom. They figured Katy was in the kitchen when she smelled the smoke and ran for the baby. But she couldn't get to safety.

It is such a bittersweet story—but I'm glad Katy called me that night. Perhaps it was God's mercy that took her home.

Reflection

Our family schedule was interrupted and inconvenienced by Katy many times. There were times when we felt our efforts were useless. "Why bother?" we would ask ourselves. Then the Spirit of God would remind us that we are not our own. We are bought with a price.

3

Changing Your
View of Life

O ne of the most exciting aspects about leading someone to
the Lord is that no two experiences are ever the same.
Every person is unique, and every situation involves a different set of circumstances. We must learn to be alert and sensitive
to the individual needs of the people we meet. It is usually these very
needs that provide an opportunity for us to witness for the Lord.

Take, for instance, my meeting with Fran, which happened one
afternoon at poolside. But let me start from the beginning. . . . My
husband and I had purchased a condominium in Florida, and we
were involved, as were many other new owners, in decorating our
vacation apartment. No matter how busy we were, though, we
always managed to take time for a daily swim or a walk on the beach.

One afternoon, while I was taking my break at the pool, I was introduced to Fran, an attractive, outgoing woman who was experiencing the same frustrations I was in dealing with broken delivery
promises from furniture companies. While we were comparing notes,
Fran mentioned that she had been in bed for several weeks. Naturally, I picked up on her comment and asked, "Have you been ill?"

"While I was swimming in the ocean," she said, "I was stung by a
Portuguese Man of War. That's a horrible, poisonous sea animal with
long tentacles; and the pain was so intense I had to stay in bed for
weeks. This is my first week out, and I'm so happy to be up and
around."

We talked about her unfortunate accident and got better acquainted that afternoon, but it wasn't until several months later that I actually had an opportunity to share my faith with Fran.

I met her on the beach one morning. Remembering how ill she had been after the Man of War encounter, I asked, "How are you feeling?"

To my surprise, she said, "Right now, I'm recovering from a cancer operation; but I'm really not concerned because, you see, I have faith."

Well, this was something to explore.

"Faith in what? Would you tell me about it?"

At this point, she became flustered and stammered, "Well—uh—ah—I really don't know exactly what to say, because I guess I don't know God. I was hoping you could help me. Someone at the apartments told me you had your head together about God, so I made the trip down here hoping to find you so you could help me."

She stopped for a moment and looked out at the surf. Then she said, "You see, having just had a brush with death, my thinking about life has changed." There was a quiver in her voice. "Knowing more about God is very important to me now."

I was both flabbergasted and pleased. I was flabbergasted because here was Fran asking me to share my knowledge about God, when normally I am the one searching for an appropriate opening. And I was pleased because I evidently had a convincing testimony and had sown the seed with someone at the apartments. God was using that seed in this experience. I silently thanked him for giving me what I call another "divine appointment."

I never know exactly what direction I will take with a person until the situation presents itself. Then I rely on the Holy Spirit to give me the wisdom to say and do the right thing. In Fran's case, the key was that she wanted to know about God, so I promptly began to respond to her need, knowing she was anxious to be helped.

"Do you have a Bible?" I asked.

"No," she admitted.

"Well, it's very important, when you want to know God, to read and study the Bible. One of the books in the Bible, Romans, says in the seventeenth verse of the tenth chapter that 'faith comes by hearing the message,' and this message is the Word of God. That means that if we want to have faith, we must listen to what God has to say in his Word, the Bible."

Fran was so eager to get started that we immediately left the beach, got dressed, and went together to purchase a Bible at a local bookstore. I suggested that she start reading in the Book of John, and then we could discuss the next day what she had read.

I thought she would read just a few chapters, but she told me the next day, "I stayed up reading until two o'clock this morning, and I read the entire Book of John." I felt she had a real desire to know the truth and that she wanted to make up for lost time.

Before we discussed her reading, Fran shared some things about herself. She was a very busy, financially secure woman who was involved in three different businesses. As she talked, I had an overwhelming desire to help her find the abundant life that Christ came to give.

"Do you remember reading John 3:3?" I asked. "Jesus says, 'I tell you the truth, no one can see the kingdom of God unless he is born again.'"

"I think I remember that verse," said Fran.

"Well, just as a baby is born into a human family, so must a person be born into the family of God. As a baby needs milk and food to grow physically, the Christian needs the Word of God in order to grow and mature spiritually. When a Christian neglects reading God's Word day after day, he begins to experience malnutrition just the same as a human being does when meal after meal is skipped."

Fran listened closely, but I sensed she needed more time to read and talk about God's Word, so I didn't press her for a decision.

The next day I was sitting on my balcony when I saw her on the beach below, reading her Bible. We had spent so much time together that I thought she might like to be left alone for a while. But she looked up and saw me and yelled, "Come on down!"

I quickly put on my bathing suit and went down to the beach.

"Before I saw you on the balcony," Fran said, "I asked God to please send you down. I really want to know more about the Bible. There's so much I don't know."

I sat beside her and we began with John 3:16. "Read it out loud," I said.

She read Jesus' words: "For God so loved the world that he gave his one and only Son, that whoever believes in him shall not perish but have eternal life."

When Fran finished, I explained: "You and I deserve to die for our own sins. But Christ willingly bore all of our sins on the cross for us. He actually took our place and died the death that we deserve. If we believe that and tell God the Father that we want to stand in the good of the death of Christ for us, he will grant our request and forgive our sins. He will give us everlasting life." I continued, "Look here at John 3:17, the next verse: 'For God did not send his Son into the world to condemn the world, but to save the world through him.' We make the choice either to receive Christ as our Savior or to reject him."

Fran took in everything I said, as if each word was a precious gem. She said she had a lot to think about. "Why don't you and I go out to dinner tonight?" she suggested.

I sensed she was very close to making a decision for Christ. "I'd love to," I said.

We went to a restaurant overlooking the ocean. The sun was beginning to set, and the view was breathtaking. *Only God could paint such a scene as this*, I thought, knowing also that only God could perform a miracle in Fran's life that night.

Though the waitress approached our table several times to see if we were ready to order, each time Fran would tell her we were not. She was filled with questions about God and Jesus and was so eager to know the answers that eating was hardly on her mind.

We finally ordered our dinner, but it took us almost two hours to complete it because of Fran's insatiable desire to know and understand God's Word. Our meal got cold as we got more and more involved, but neither of us cared, since we were both fulfilling our needs—mine to witness to Fran and Fran's to know God.

Returning to my apartment, I suggested we read that little "Four Laws" booklet I often use. It presents the plan of salvation in a simple, concise way. When we finished, I said, "Fran, would you like to accept Christ as your Savior?"

"Oh, yes!" she replied, as if there was not a doubt in her mind.

We bowed our heads and prayed, and Fran asked Christ to be Lord and Savior of her life. It was such an emotional moment for both of us that we cried tears of joy.

Before Fran left, I explained to her that she was now like a diamond in the rough. God would be chipping away to make her the kind of person he wanted her to be.

I received a letter from her a few weeks later. In it she told me she had gone to her jeweler and asked him to make her a ring with two stones—one a green, bumpy unfinished diamond and the other a white sparkling one. "I know that right now I'm like the green, bumpy one," she wrote, "But as God chips away at my life, I'll become more and more like the beautiful white diamond."

Reflection

I could never have dealt with Fran in this manner if I had unconfessed sin in my life. I'm learning to keep short accounts with my Lord.

Now, you might be frightened by the realization that Fran asked a lot of questions at dinner that I didn't include in my story. I'll expand on that conversation now, but I want to say first that you may not have all the answers to questions people ask you. When that happens to me, I simply tell them, "I can't answer that now, but let me have time and get back to you." This keeps me from giving a hasty answer I haven't thought through, and it also creates an opportunity to resume the conversation later.

Fran did say, "As a teenager, I attended the Jehovah's Witness Kingdom Hall. I went with my aunt. I didn't feel comfortable in that church. They don't believe you should salute the flag, and they don't believe in blood transfusions, no matter how desperately a person may need them. Do you know about the Jehovah's Witnesses?"

"The last time I talked to them," I said, "I told them I would allow them to come into my house if they would allow me equal time to share my faith. They said they would; but, when it was my turn to speak, they kept interrupting so much I finally had to ask them to leave. You see, they don't believe that Jesus is God in the flesh. When I showed them the first chapter of John, which says that Jesus is the Word of God that became flesh, and that he, Jesus, is God, they denied it and said that Jesus is *a* god.

But, Fran, that means they believe there are many gods—and that's idolatry."

(I might mention here that reading about cults in the light of Scripture helps us to "always be prepared to give an answer" to those who ask about our reason for hope [1 Peter 3:15].)

"But how can you be sure the Bible is the Word of God and that it's true?" she asked.

"There are many proofs," I said. "One is the changed lives it produces. Second Corinthians 5:17 and 18 says that if anyone is in Christ, he is a new creation. That's what happened to me. Actually, that's why some of the people in the condo say I have my head together about God. Another reason is that many predictions made in the Old Testament are fulfilled in the New. For example, prophecies about how Christ would die and that he would rise from the dead were recorded hundreds of years before they happened.

"It's interesting to read about those who have read the Bible with an open mind and have been convinced of the truth. Even some who have set out to prove that Jesus Christ is a fraud have fallen on their knees begging forgiveness after reading what the Bible has to say. One of these men is Lew Wallace, who was a famous general. After his conversion, he wrote the novel *Ben Hur.* Another is C. S. Lewis, who was a professor at Oxford. One of his post-conversion books is *Mere Christianity.* Both men were convinced that the Scriptures are authentic."

Fran was an eager listener. I had found a heart that was ripe for the Savior.

I saw Fran in Florida recently. She is a growing Christian who is sharing Christ with others. She is delighted that her daughter and son-in-law have also accepted Christ, and all of them attend church together regularly.

Not all of my witnessing experiences, of course, are as easy or as productive as this one with Fran. Sometimes I only get to sow a tiny seed by sharing a thought or giving a word of encouragement or asking a pertinent question. But I rest assured that, however far I am able to go with an individual, God knows and will honor my obedience in being faithful to him.

4

A Welcome Hug

One day I decided to ride my bike down Ocean Boulevard. When I got to the corner, a young man jumped out of the way as if he thought I was going to run into him.

"Don't worry," I assured him. "I saw you coming and was prepared to stop."

"I'm always careful when I see a bicycle coming," he said. "Where I went to school, there were more bicycle accidents than car accidents."

"Where did you go to school?"

"Michigan State."

"My son graduated from Michigan State," I told him.

"Are you here on vacation, or do you live in Florida all year?" he asked.

"We live here part of the year and part of the year in Michigan. This year, we came early because my father broke his hip. He's almost ninety-nine years old, and we felt he wouldn't have a lot of time left in this life. We want to spend as much time with him as possible."

The young man looked genuinely sympathetic. "I'm sorry about your father."

"Thank you," I said, "but you don't need to feel sorry. You see, my father is looking forward to going home to be with the Lord."

"Did I hear you correctly? Did you say he was looking forward to going home to be with the Lord?" He seemed stunned by my comment.

"Why, yes. He's ready and really excited."

Then the stranger surprised me by saying, "My name is Chuck. Could I hug you?"

I looked at this young man of about twenty-four years of age and said, "If you feel the need of a hug, go right ahead."

He gave me a bear hug. And then he said, "I needed that. I came to Florida feeling rotten. My wife left me three months ago. We had been married for only five months. It really put me in a slump. My uncle asked me to drive him to Florida to help him buy a condominium.

"'You need a change,' my uncle said. 'The trip will do you good.' But I still feel very depressed. You see, it isn't as though I didn't know my wife before we got married. I dated her for four years before I asked her to be my wife. We both joined a Bible study group. I became a true believer in the Lord Jesus Christ, and I thought my wife had, too. We got married and believed that our newfound faith would make our marriage extra-special. But a few months later, she announced to me that I was too religious and that she was going to go her own way."

"How sad," I said.

"I was absolutely devastated," Chuck admitted. "I've been getting some help from a Dr. Stringer up at State. If it wasn't for that, I don't think I could have survived."

"Are you talking about Dr. Ken Stringer?" I asked.

"Why, yes. You know him?"

"I've known him since he was a little boy. He's one of the finest young men I know. He and I are members of the same church."

Chuck was shaken. "I can't believe this! I simply can't—" Tears came to his eyes. "Our meeting was no accident," he said. "You know, I thought God had forgotten me."

"God never forgets," I said simply. "And I agree that our meeting was no accident. It was one of God's appointments. He arranged for you to meet another Christian, knowing you would be at the beach and that I'd be along. You see, I've told the Lord that I'm always available to him to use any way he wants."

"I suppose you thought it strange for me to ask you for a hug."

"Oh, yes, somewhat. But you looked safe enough. I guess I just followed my instincts."

"Well, I'd just been on the beach talking to a group of people. One of the women asked me if I was married. I told her my wife had just left me, but that I was praying for God's wisdom to work it out. 'How stupid,' she said. 'I suppose you don't believe in abortion either.'"

I interrupted him: "That was a strange thing to say. It sounds as though she realized that God wasn't in favor of abortion."

"Well, that kind of talk didn't make me feel any better," Chuck admitted. "I walked on down the beach and met a young man wearing earrings. He tried to solicit me. I couldn't believe it. Two days in Florida and this is what I run into! Then when you said that your father was looking forward to being with the Lord, I went from the slough of despond to sheer joy. I finally found someone on my wavelength. I just had to hug you."

I invited Chuck to have dinner with us and to meet my father. They became instant friends. Chuck felt free to share his heartache with him, and my dad prayed with him about his needs. The next time I saw Chuck, he said, "To see a man ninety-nine years old so full of the joy of the Lord—and at his age and in his condition to have a concern for others—is something I won't ever forget. I want to be a growing Christian and end up knowing God like your dad does."

Reflection

Chuck, a new Christian, had some wonderful things to learn about God's care for him. Remember that God promises, "Never will I leave you; never will I forsake you" (Heb. 13:5).

Psalm 139:2–3 says, "You know when I sit and when I rise; you perceive my thoughts from afar. You discern my going out and my lying down; you are familiar with all my ways."

Here again, as we tell God we are available to him to meet the needs of people, he will use us to minister to those who hurt.

(By way of note, I had a husband at home. I would never have invited Chuck to my home had I been living alone—nor should any woman, even when the aim is witnessing!)

5

Our Way or God's Way?

"I'm very concerned about Nicole, a friend of mine," Pam, a young lady I was discipling, said at one of our sessions. "Would you be willing to go with me to see her? I have already told her about our Bible studies and she would like to talk to you."

When I first met Nicole, she was the picture of despair. She wasted no time telling me about her problems: "Peter and I had been having an affair for over a year and planned to be married. I couldn't believe it when he said that he wanted to break off our relationship and return to his ex-wife. I begged him not to, but he acted as though we were never close. I've tried calling him, but he won't answer."

I sat in silence, listening to Nicole as she went on: "My life is such a mess. I don't know what to do. I feel like ending it all. Ever since I was a little girl, I've had nothing but one rejection after another."

"Well, then, I'm glad we got together today," I said, "because I'd like to tell you about the One who came into my life and who has kept his promise never to leave or forsake me. That person is Jesus Christ."

Her face seemed to cloud up, but I went on: "I confessed my sin of living my life without him and of going my own independent way. I had never once consulted the Lord about his will for my life. He lovingly forgave all my sins and made me a member of his family. It's the best decision I've ever made in my life. I now have peace and a life worth living. And you can have this life, too."

"I know all that," Nicole snapped. "It's not going to help me!"

I stood up and prepared to leave.

29

"Oh, please don't go," she pleaded. "I need help with my problem."

I wanted to stay, but it was obvious to me that Nicole wanted Peter back more than she wanted to understand the reason for her predicament. So I said, "I came to tell you that the Lord Jesus Christ is the very best help I can recommend. Without him, there is no real solution to your problem. But you say you 'know all that,' so I really have nothing else to offer."

I walked toward the door.

"Please, may I see you again?" I heard Nicole say.

I thought of my schedule. "You may come to my home next Thursday at eleven o'clock if you would like." I gave her my address and left.

During that week, I prayed that God would prepare her heart and give me the wisdom to know how to help her. I wasn't sure if she would even come. But she did arrive, and promptly at eleven. I was pleasantly surprised. We sat on my porch and relaxed over a cup of coffee. "Tell me a little about yourself and your family," I prompted.

Once again Nicole seemed eager to talk: "I spent my early years on a farm with my parents, two brothers and a sister. I was only nine when my mother died. My family fell apart. My sister and older brother moved out of the house, and my father, who was an alcoholic, married our housekeeper and left the farm."

"Did you go with your father?" I asked.

"No, my father took off without us. He actually left us on the farm to fend for ourselves. I was eleven and my brother was only nine at the time."

I was amazed. "How did you survive?"

"We lived on the food we found in the cupboard. I remember sitting under a tree, tears streaming down my face and thinking, *I hate grown-ups. I never want to be one.*"

"Someone must have come to your rescue," I suggested.

"Right. One day, my brother and I took a walk down the highway. We met Mrs. Smith, our neighbor, who kindly asked, 'How are things at home, Nicole?'

"'Not so well,' I told her. 'Bob and I are all alone on the farm. Dad got married and left with our housekeeper.'

"Mrs. Smith invited us to have dinner with her and later called the authorities. She arranged to have us live with her and became our foster mother for three years. A doctor friend of ours was also kind. He counseled me and saw to it that I got a good business education."

"Did things become a little better for you then?" I wondered aloud.

"Yes, life was much better for a while. Then one day I received news that my father had died from overconsumption of alcohol. He was only fifty years old. His death brought on emotions that I had experienced often as a child, feelings of loneliness and dejection."

I nodded my head in sympathy.

"Shortly after my father's death, I met a very successful businessman who made me feel good. He was wealthy and treated me like a queen. We were married and were happy at first. I soon became pregnant and we had a little girl. We enjoyed our baby, but our happiness didn't last long. My husband began to mistrust me. Every time I stepped out of the house, he would accuse me of having an affair. His jealousy became so intense that he would badger me all through the night. I wanted to cover myself up to rid myself of his accusations. We were soon divorced. Once again I felt alone and rejected.

"I lived quietly, adjusting to the change and caring for my daughter. Then Peter came along and showered me with attention. I felt accepted and loved again. He was the answer to all my problems—that is, until he decided to go back to his ex-wife. Loneliness and rejection seem to be the pattern of my life. . . ."

Nicole paused. "You know, when I was with Peter, we had a beautiful relationship. We even went to church every Sunday."

"Do you feel that going to church with Peter made your relationship right?" I asked.

She didn't answer my question, but instead told me, "I'm so afraid that, when I leave here, I'll go home and call Peter. I want to see him so very much." Nicole looked so wistful when she said that.

"Well, you can't have it both ways," I said. "You have to make a choice. It's either God's way or your way."

Quickly she said, "But I do want God's way—and I do need him."

"Would you like to tell him your choice?" I asked her.

She just sat there and looked at me. Then she nodded slowly and began to pray: "Lord Jesus, I confess I've gone my own way, leaving you out of my life. I need you and receive you as my Savior. Thank you for forgiving my sins and for opening the gates and letting me walk through."

That was a new beginning for Nicole, though the next few weeks were rough ones for her. She called me several times a week, crying on the phone. She was having a hard time putting her life back together again. The temptations of her old life were still strong, but God gave her strength. We met for Bible studies once a week for a while.

Her little girl has also received the Lord Jesus as her Savior, and the two of them read the Scriptures and prayed together. Nicole has joined a Bible-believing church and is now an active participant in its fellowship. She recently accepted a very good job and is already considered to be one of the top sales reps in her firm.

Nicole is a very attractive person, and she tells me she is often approached by men. "Do you know what I tell them?" she said one day. "I tell them I'm not interested, that I've been there. I now have a new quality of life in Jesus Christ."

Reflection

Nicole was miserable when I first knew her and hardly needed me to point a finger at her. To her, life was not worth living without Peter. She wanted a fairy-tale ending, but sin had robbed her of that possibility. I gave her the only solution I knew—a right relationship with Jesus Christ. But she wasn't ready for that at first.

I had nothing more to say to Nicole at that point. She needed time to reflect on what I had said and time for the Holy Spirit to do his perfect work in her heart. Though I knew she was hurting, I couldn't comfort her in her unrepentant sinful condition.

I was glad when Nicole wanted to see me again. That meant she had not shut the door entirely and that I had another opportunity to bring to her attention that her lifestyle was a complete offense to God and that she would have to make a choice—her way or God's. Nicole learned that her way led only to despair, but God's way brought her peace. It was a hard lesson, but she learned it.

We had many good times together after that. We played tennis and she came to our home for dinner many times. We had Bible studies together. She learned quickly. Now, Nicole is no longer the picture of despair. She's a beautiful, radiant Christian.

As 1 Corinthians 10:13 says, "No temptation has seized you except what is common to man. And God is faithful; he will not let you be tempted beyond what you can bear. But when you are tempted, he will also provide a way out so that you can stand up under it."

Let us point out to hurting people that guaranteed way of escape!

6

As Long As You're Sincere

ometimes I can scarcely believe the situations in which God places me. Take, for example, what happened one day when I was purchasing supplies to make a decoupage purse. That's exactly how I met Shirley . . . but I'm getting ahead of my story.

One Sunday at church, I had seen my friend Sally's latest decoupage purse and remarked with a slight tinge of envy, "Sally, your purse is beautiful! I would love to have one just like it." Sally is very gifted in arts and crafts. She makes enamel flowers, tole paintings, and many other beautiful craft items. Her decoupage purses are simply exquisite. Many of her friends and I had often prodded her to teach us.

A couple of days after that Sunday conversation, Sally called. "Nellie, I would be willing to teach an arts and crafts class if you think we could use it as an outreach to win some neighbors to Christ." I agreed at once that it was a great idea, so we began planning for our class.

Our church has a Christian day school, and we were able to obtain the use of the art room for our project. Sally would teach decoupage and I would give devotions. We spread the word and the class started. About twenty-five women came.

I, too, wanted to make a purse as part of the class, so I went to a nearby arts and crafts store to get my supplies. Only one other customer was in the store besides myself, which I later found was quite unusual. The other customer was a rather elderly woman. As I was looking through the supplies, I heard the owner of the store, whose name was Shirley, say to her, "Harriet, your work is superb! It is absolutely beautiful!"

I turned to see Harriet smile. In fact, she beamed as she said, "This is quite a day for me. I'm going to receive an award today from my church for all the good work I've done."

My ears perked up. This was interesting. Since I was a brand-new customer and had never been in the store before, I didn't want to intrude on the conversation. But then Harriet added, "You know, it really doesn't matter what you believe, as long as you're sincere." To my surprise, she turned to me and asked, "Don't you agree with me?"

I reached over and touched her arm gently and said, "I'm sorry. I can't agree with you. You see, that isn't scriptural. The Bible tells us that salvation is not by works, but by grace, which means it is unearned favor. It's a gift from God. We receive it by faith."

"Now, what is that all about?" Harriet asked.

"I have a little booklet [*Four Laws*] in my purse that explains God's requirements for a right relationship with him. Would you like to take it home and read it?"

Shirley, the owner, had been listening and suggested, "Why don't you read it to us?" And I did.

I read of God's great love in sending his Son to die on the cross for our sins and of the purpose in Christ's coming—to give us abundant life. I read how our sins have separated us from God and that only Jesus Christ could bridge the gap between man and Holy God—not our works, not a good life, nor even being "religious." I read how each individual had to receive Christ and that when we receive Christ by inviting him to come into our lives to cleanse us and to forgive us and to take control and guide us, we then experience the new birth.

I looked at the women and asked if they would like to receive Jesus Christ as their Savior.

Shirley said, "I can't believe that you're standing there and I'm standing here. You're answering a need I've had in my life for months. Two years ago, I was asked to demonstrate decoupage at a Christian Women's Club. When I was finished, I told the hostess I needed to get back to the store and asked if she minded if I left.

"She said, 'Yes, I do mind. I think you ought to stay and hear the message.' What could I do? So I stayed and heard the same thing you've told me today. I didn't take it too seriously because I didn't feel the need for God in my life. Then, three months ago, my father had a stroke. Now he can't walk and he can't talk. He was such a handsome man and an active golfer. He was a dentist and now he can't do a thing except sit in his wheelchair and be waited on. It breaks my heart. On top of that, my husband lost his executive position in a large advertising firm. For some time I have wanted to reach God, but I couldn't remember what the speaker had said. And now you've come here and told me the way."

Shirley bowed her head and asked Christ to come into her life, to forgive her sin and make her his child.

When I turned to Harriet and asked her if she would like to receive Christ, she looked at me and said, "I'm not going to give up eighty years of good works for this." Then she left, having made her choice.

But my contact with Shirley did not end that day. Often, when I witness to someone, I am given the opportunity to meet and reach other people in that person's life. So it was with Shirley; this was just the beginning.

For a year I met with her for Bible study on Tuesday mornings before her shop opened. It wasn't always easy. The phone would ring or a customer would knock on the window, hoping to get in early. The interruptions seemed endless, but it was thrilling to watch Shirley grow as a young Christian.

Shirley's business was very good, but the emotional strain of her father's illness and her concern about her husband's job finally made her decide to sell the shop. An added burden was her increasing worry about her mother's spiritual condition. Her mother, Ella Foster, had told Shirley she thought Christians were pushy. She wasn't interested in listening to her daughter tell her one thing about her newfound faith in Christ. Then one day Shirley asked me if I would be willing to visit her folks.

"I'll do it," I said, "but it might take a year before I'll be able to talk to your mother about Christ. Remember, you told me about her saying Christians are pushy."

And it did take exactly a year before Mrs. Foster came to Christ. I visited her about once every two weeks. I would bring her flowers from the garden or something I had baked. I would sit and listen as she poured out her heart. She and her husband had shared such a good life together. They had had so many friends, but now only one of his colleagues ever came to visit. They found life very hard.

One day Mrs. Foster said, "I've been doing most of the talking. Please tell me something about yourself and your family."

I told her some of my delightful stories about my children—the nice things mothers tuck away in their hearts. Then I told her that my younger daughter, Greta, had come down with an illness called lupus when she was a senior in high school.

"The doctor told me it was treatable but not curable," I said. "I couldn't believe it. She had been such a healthy child and this had come on so suddenly. I fell flat on my face, but it was only momentarily. You see, I knew that God made every cell in Greta's body and had counted every hair on her head. He loves her more than I possibly could. Together, my husband and I committed this situation to the Lord and we have had peace.

"One day, as I visited Greta in the hospital, we talked about her condition and I told her she had a choice to make. She could either become bitter and say, 'Why should this happen to me?' or she could use this experience as opportunity to grow. And you know what she said? She said, 'That's what I want to do, Mom. I want to grow. You see, I believe in God because you told me about him. But now I've had my own experience, and I know he's with me.'"

I could see that Mrs. Foster was moved by my story, so I went on: "Through the kindness and tutoring of her teachers, Greta was able to finish high school at home, where she stayed in bed for three months. She had been accepted by Gordon College before being hospitalized, but now we thought she wouldn't be able to attend college—especially Gordon, which was eight hundred miles away. Greta was very excited about going and would talk constantly about her plans, but there was no way of explaining to her that she just wasn't well enough.

"We talked with the doctor about this. He said, 'If she were my daughter, I would let her go. But be prepared to pick her up in about six weeks. At least she can say she went to college.'"

"So Greta attended college—not for six weeks but for four years. There seemed to be an epidemic of flu every year in her dorm, and we were concerned because the doctor had told her to be extremely careful about catching a cold or taking medication without consent.

But Greta didn't have the flu or even a cold in her four years at Gordon! We had prayed that God would put a hedge about her, and he did."

Mrs. Foster threw her arms about my neck and wept. Then she said, "I'm so tired and I have so many needs."

"Perhaps I can help you," I offered. "I believe I can, if you will let me." I told her I would see her soon and then left.

As I visited her from time to time, I told her about some of the people I had met and led to Christ. I shared with her exactly how each situation developed and told her what Scripture I had used. She seemed to listen very carefully and was quite interested. Then she told me one day, "I think it's wonderful that you are able to help so many people."

Shirley had given her mother a Bible, and each time she visited she noticed the Bible was open, so she knew her mother was reading it.

During this time Dr. Foster became too difficult for his wife to handle and was taken to a nursing home. While on my way to visit him one day, as I approached his room I noticed his door ajar. I heard him calling, "God, oh, God," over and over. I entered the room and found him very distressed. When I asked him if he wanted a nurse, he shook his head, so I stroked his forehead and tried to comfort him the best I knew how.

I explained how he could reach God through Jesus Christ, saying that if he would invite the Lord Jesus into his heart, he would be forgiven of his sins and God would accept him as his very own. Dr. Foster just groaned and seemed more distressed. He tried to talk, but I couldn't understand him.

Next I called Shirley and said, "I think you need to go and tell your father what Jesus Christ has done for you and that you are now in God's family. Tell him you are concerned that he know the Lord as his Savior."

She did just that. Later she told me she had taken his hand and said, "Dad, I've been going to Bible class and we've been studying the Book of John. I've learned so much about Jesus Christ, and I've accepted him as my Savior and confessed him as my Lord. Would you let me read to you some of the things I've learned?" He squeezed her hand as a sign of agreement. He began to relax; his daughter was relieved.

Shirley visited him day by day after that and read to him from John. One day she said, "Dad would you like to receive Christ as your Savior?"

He took her hand and nodded "Yes." And then he had peace. Shortly after that, he died and went to be with the Lord.

Mrs. Foster, who by then had asked me to call her Ella, asked if it would be possible to have a little memorial service just for the immediate family and a doctor friend who had been faithful in visiting her husband during his illness. She also wanted me to be there, as well as our mutual friend, Sally Roost, and asked me if I thought the pastor of my church would say a few words. I felt that now was the time to ask Ella about her relationship with the Lord.

"Tell me, Ella," I said, "we've talked a lot about how some of the people I've met along the way have come to know Christ. What about you?"

"Oh," she said to my delight, "when you first told me how, I accepted Christ as my Savior."

I have known Ella for some time now. She has a hunger for the Word and truly loves the Lord. Every time I was asked to speak someplace, Shirley and her mother would be there, constantly learning and still excited about the Word of God.

All of this happened because I visited an arts and crafts store as one of my scheduled errands for that day and took the time to respond to a human need. But the story does not end even here.

My husband and I spent Christmas in Florida that year. Before we left, Shirley asked us to stop in to see her widowed aunt in West Palm Beach if we were in that vicinity. Shirley loved her aunt and was very eager for her to meet us. "She's attended church all her life, but I know she's not born again."

We visited Shirley's Aunt Ann on Christmas Day. She was all alone and, despite the fact that she was almost blind and had a difficult time moving about, she had an outgoing personality and welcomed us warmly into her home. We introduced ourselves as Shirley's friends and told her how we had become friends, including how Shirley had come to know Christ. I explained that her niece was now in the family of God, that she had been born again.

"Would you explain to me about being born again?" Aunt Ann asked. "I've listened to Billy Graham talk about it many times, but somehow I didn't think it was for me. You see, I attended my church for forty years, and they never told me about it. The minister visits me from time to time, but he never mentions it. Please tell me more."

I told Ann about Christ's purpose in coming to earth. I told her that God's love is so great that he gave his Son to pay the penalty for our sins. When we accept the fact that he died for us because of love, and when we receive him as our Savior, we are born again.

"Would you like to receive Christ as your Savior?" I asked.

"Are you sure it's for me?"

I read Revelation 3:20 to her, then said, "Jesus invites you. It's up to you to accept his invitation."

"If it's for me, I want it," Ann replied. She prayed with me and invited the Lord Jesus Christ into her life. She was born again on Christmas Day.

Shirley was so very happy to receive a letter from her aunt, telling about her salvation experience. Six months later, Aunt Ann died and went to be with the Lord.

How marvelous that four people in that family became saints of God out of my one small visit to an art store!

Reflection

Witnessing and sharing the love of the Lord Jesus is not something mystical or scary, something reserved for a select few who feel called to the ministry. Neither is it homework that you do for church. Rather, witnessing can become a completely natural part of your everyday life. It can be as common and routine as the daily functions of eating and sleeping. It can be as life sustaining and invigorating to our spiritual well-being as those functions are to our physical lives. As we are earnest, ready, and willing to practice witnessing, God will instruct us and guide the process.

7

When I'm Sleeping, I'm a Saint

The shopper standing next to me, looking through the lingerie rack, pulled out a nightshirt and started to laugh. "How would you like to wear this?"

My ears pricked up at the woman's beautiful British accent, and I turned to see what she was looking at. On the front of the shirt was written, "When I'm sleeping, I'm a saint."

We both laughed, and I felt the freedom to speak after we introduced ourselves. "It's interesting how many people think that if a person's sleeping or doing nothing or merely behaving himself, this automatically makes him a saint. That's not what the Bible says a saint is."

"I know," Debbie said. "A person is made a saint after he or she dies, by a group of bishops or religious higher ups." Since her voice implied a question mark, she didn't seem to be quite sure about that.

"Well, in the New Testament, the apostle Paul wrote letters to people he called saints," I commented. "Sometimes he called them 'believers,' but those people were alive and serving God. Today, when we become members of God's family, we, too, become saints. We may not always act very saintly, but that's what God calls us."

"Well, if you don't act saintly, why does God call you a saint?"

"He does demand perfection," I agreed, "and none of us is perfect. But Jesus Christ is. We come to God through Christ. Christ serves as the bridge between the sinner and the God who demands perfection. In John 14:6 Jesus says, 'No one comes to the Father but by me.'"

"I have some very nice friends who are Christian Scientists. You make me think of them. Are you one?" Debbie asked.

"Oh, no," I said gently. "I'm not. You see, a Christian Scientist doesn't believe that Jesus is God. But the Scriptures say that Jesus is God in the flesh."

"Hmmm. That's interesting," she said. "Tell me where you go to church."

I told her and added, "My husband and I are presenting a series of films on 'The Holiness of God.' It's a six-week study. My husband first reviews the previous week's lesson, and I lead the discussion after the film has been shown."

"May I come to your class?" she asked.

"We'd love to have you come." I gave her directions. Before she left, she said, "I believe God meant for us to meet today."

I prayed for Debbie during that week. I didn't know whether she would actually come to church, but on Sunday morning, as I was helping my husband arrange the chairs, I felt a tap on my shoulder and heard a familiar voice saying, "Can you tell me where I can find Nellie Pickard?"

It was Debbie—and I was delighted to see her there.

The film shown that day was "Holiness and Justice," part of the series produced by Dr. R. C. Sproul. First, the story of Nadab and Abihu was read from Leviticus 10, where God destroys Aaron's sons for failing to follow the letter of the law in the matter of the Holy of Holies, that part of the tabernacle where only the High Priest could go once a year. A second story, from 2 Samuel 6, told of Uzzah, who was struck dead when he reached out and touched the Ark of the Covenant, which God had forbidden anyone but the priests to touch.

These were not easy passages to deal with, though they did help us understand the sovereignty of God and that we—as his subjects—cannot tell God how to run his kingdom. He gives the orders. The lesson also showed what rebellious creatures we are.

I wondered how my friend would receive the message.

When we finished class discussion and ended the meeting with prayer, Debbie called across the room, "Nellie, may I talk to you before you leave?"

"I'll be there in a minute," I said. "Just let me put my papers away."

When I reached her, she said, "I have some questions I want to ask you. When we talked at the store, you said that God demands perfection. Am I right?"

"Yes, I said that. The Bible says none of us can reach God's standards. We just can't make it on our own."

"You also said that I could come to him through Jesus Christ. Is that correct?"

"That's correct," I said. "Now would you like to hear the rest of the story?"

"Very much," she said.

We found a couple of chairs and sat down to discuss God's wonderful plan of salvation. We talked about sin and how it separates us from God, and I explained how we don't have to stay in that condition of being a sinner. God has provided a remedy, the Lord Jesus Christ, the Perfect One. We read from 1 Corinthians 15, which tells us that Christ died for our sins, was buried, and that he was raised on the third day and was seen by his disciples and later by more than five-hundred people.

"You know, Debbie," I said, "Jesus died for the sins of the whole world. That includes you. He died for you as an individual. That means that you as an individual need to receive him as your Savior and Lord. It says in John 1:12, 'Yet to all who received him, to those who believed in his name, he gave the right to become children of God.' Another thing the Bible says is that our salvation is by grace. We don't work for it. We can't work for it. It's a gift. That's what it says in Ephesians 2:8 and 9. If we could work for it, we would have a tendency to brag about what we had done.

"You told me in the store, Debbie, that you felt God meant for us to meet. Perhaps this is the reason, so that you could find out how to be in the family of God."

"Probably," she said seriously.

"Would you like to pray and ask the Lord Jesus to come into your heart and forgive your sins?"

"I would like to do that." And she did.

Later, Debbie told me that she had planned to go to a religious retreat that weekend but told her husband that she felt it was very important for her to go to see a woman she had met at the store. "I felt such an urge to see you, and now I know why," she added.

We have met together several times since for Bible study and fellowship. I am delighted with her answers, especially since not too long ago she didn't know the Bible contained both a New and Old Testament. Now Debbie is learning to find the references quite well. Having gone to church most of her life, she had previously done some teaching, though she had never searched the Scriptures for herself.

God must have a sense of humor. After all, he brought us together over a silly nightshirt!

Reflection

Who would ever think a conversation over a store display could be an opener for witnessing? That, however, is part of the witnesser's mind-set. Any little casual circumstance can be a crack in the door, an opportunity we do not want to miss. We may not know where such a conversation will lead, but God does—and he uses our availability.

A few years ago, I probably would have laughed about the nightshirt along with the woman and let it go at that. Since I now have a better knowledge of the Word, I realize that, even though the statement on the nightshirt was funny, it wasn't true.

Here was my opening—my chocolate-covered cookie—and I went for it!

8

Happy in a Cultist Church

Maude seemed happy in the Christian Science Church. The members had been kind to her when she had a real hurt in her life, and she had many friends among them. Maude was a most gracious octogenarian. While visiting her sister-in-law, Joyce, in Florida, Maude attended services at our church with her. It was conference time, with two services four times a week, and going to all the meetings as well as the Saturday-night dinner and concert was no easy feat for an elderly woman.

This woman did not look her age, eighty-six. She dressed well, carried herself beautifully, and was "a lady" in every sense of the word.

When I met Maude, I said, "Are you enjoying your vacation in Florida?"

"Why, yes, I am. I'm especially enjoying these meetings and the speakers. It is all very good."

Joyce couldn't understand what Maude meant by that. The next time I saw her she said, "I'm really stumped. Maude is having the time of her life, and yet I know she isn't saved. Would you be willing to have lunch with Maude, her daughter Janis, and me, of course? Maybe you'll get a chance to talk to her about the Lord."

"I'd love to," I said. "And if the Holy Spirit provides an opportunity for a discussion, I'll certainly try to be sensitive to the situation. But we do need to be careful about pushing her into something she's not ready to accept. Let's all pray about it and see what comes."

I was rather surprised when another friend from church, Ruth, showed up at the restaurant. She had held Bible classes in the church and was well versed in the Scriptures. The thought came to me, *Four gung-ho Christians—and Maude. Poor soul, she doesn't have a chance!* But I prayed, "Dear Lord, please take charge."

The food was delicious, and we chatted for a while about the beautiful weather, the ocean, tennis, and how great it was to be in Florida. It didn't take long before our conversation got around to spiritual matters.

"You certainly have had some inspiring speakers at your church this week," Maude volunteered.

"Did you agree with their messages?" Ruth asked.

"Yes, pretty much."

"What do you think of the virgin birth?"

"I believe Jesus was born of a virgin," Maude said.

"Do you believe the Bible is the Word of God?" I asked her.

"Yes, I do."

No matter what was asked, Maude had a good answer, until I asked her if she believed that Jesus was God in the flesh.

"No, that I don't believe," she admitted.

"What about sin? Do you believe that Jesus died for your sins?"

"I believe Jesus died for the sin of the world. He already did that, so he didn't have to die for *my* sins."

On the one hand I felt sorry for Maude. One against four. On the other hand, I admired her. She did not seem one bit ruffled by our questions. She handled herself with dignity and composure.

When we finished our meal, Maude insisted on paying for all of us. "I've had such a good time and I want this to be my treat," she told us.

I walked Maude to her car. On the way, I said, "I have a workbook that is called 'The Uniqueness of Jesus.' There are questions to be answered, and the answers must be looked up in the Bible. You can learn a lot about who Jesus Christ is by studying these lessons. Would you be willing to spend some time on this book?"

She smiled and said, "Because I like you, I will do it." I was delighted. We drove to my apartment so I could get the book. "Maude, when you have completed these lessons, would you mind sending them to me and letting me know your conclusions?" I requested.

When she left, I thought, *How gracious she is.* Then I prayed that the Spirit of God would open her eyes and heart to receive the truth of the Scriptures as she began her studies.

Soon after that, Maude went back to her home in Tennessee. I learned that her daughter Janis called her from time to time and would always ask, "How are you doing on your Bible lessons?"

Once, Maude had answered, "I tell you, Janis, I'm not going to do those lessons, because I do not believe that Jesus is God."

"But you promised Nellie!"

"I don't care," said Maude.

"But does a Christian Scientist go back on her word?"

"Oh, all right, I'll do them," she agreed.

Janis herself was growing as a Christian and was very concerned that her mother would turn to Christ, too. After all, at eighty-six, Maude might not have many years left. So Joyce and Janis and I covenanted to pray for her.

When I arrived back in Michigan from Florida, I waded through the mail and to my delight noticed an envelope with Maude's return address on it. I quickly opened it and, sure enough, the workbook was completed. She had answered all the questions. I carefully read each one and it was incredible. The answers were perfect.

Paul looked at what Maude had done, commenting, "Do you think she just copied the answers from the Bible? Or do you think she really believes what she's written?"

"I sure hope she does. I'll call her." I couldn't wait. I picked up the phone and dialed.

"Maude? I got your lesson book. You did a beautiful job. The answers are perfect. Tell me now, what conclusions have you come to? Do you believe that Jesus is God?"

"Oh, Nellie, absolutely," she said. "Do you know that after doing my lesson, I went to my Christian Science study book, and it said that Jesus is a son of God. I said to myself that this wasn't enough. So I went back to the Bible and it said Jesus *is* God. If the Bible says it, it has to be true."

When I got off the phone, I told my husband what she had said. "There's only one thing I failed to mention," I said. "I should have asked her about sin. I wonder if she now believes that Jesus Christ died for *her* sin."

I started to write Maude a letter, then threw it in the wastepaper basket. I picked up the phone and called her instead. "Maude, I don't want to leave any stones unturned." I asked her that important question.

"Oh, yes," she said, "I've asked Jesus Christ to be *my* Savior, and I also know that he is the only way to God."

Reflection

The booklet I used with Maude was "The Uniqueness of Jesus." It is the introduction to *Ten Basic Steps Toward Christian Maturity*, published by Campus Crusade for Christ, San Bernardino, California. See how valuable it was in reaching an intelligent person who was steeped in the teachings of another doctrine? Sometimes, when our words seem to fail completely, we can refer a person to a workbook like this that will require her to study the Bible. The Holy Spirit works through the Word. As I have said, it's incredible! New birth is a spiritual matter, not something we work up or produce. Though a workbook will often help us find where an unbeliever is hung up, we must remember that coming to Christ is not an intellectual decision.

This story about Maude shows that "faith comes from hearing the message, and the message is heard through the word of Christ" (Rom. 10:17). We must remember also that "the word of God is living and active. Sharper than any double-edged sword, it penetrates even to dividing soul and spirit, joints and marrow; it judges the thoughts and attitudes of the heart" (Heb. 4:12). (Study John 1 for the heart of "the message.")

Maude has completed five workbooks on the different aspects of the Christian life. She's amazing!

9

Depressed about Life

My fellow patient was a pitiful sight. His head was completely swathed in bandages, except for two peepholes for his eyes and a slit for his mouth. His room was next to mine at Straith Memorial Hospital, where I was recuperating from a foot operation. I knew his operation couldn't have been life-threatening since that hospital does only elective surgery.

One afternoon as I hobbled down the hall I saw him coming toward me. We stopped and talked. We both laughed as we noticed the many bandaged heads and feet, most of them victims of an almost frivolous desire to enhance appearance.

"If I didn't know better, I would say that this is a place for the maimed and infirm," I said laughingly. Then, looking at his bandages, I asked, "What happened to you? Were you in an accident?"

"No, this was no accident," he told me. "This was on purpose. I had a face-lift, a nose job, and two hair flips for my receding hairline."

I thought it was quite unusual that a man would want a face-lift, especially one whose voice and gait suggested that he was quite young. We chatted casually over the next few days, and I sensed a loneliness and hurt about this young man, who had told me only his first name, Jim.

When the bandage was removed from his nose, I said, "It looks like they've given you a good-looking nose. I don't know what it looked like before, but it looks very nice now."

"It was very large before," Jim said. "I also had very deep lines in my face. I looked pretty bad. I want to improve my looks for my wife, but I don't think she really cares about me. In fact, I don't know what's going to happen to my marriage."

The day he was to leave the hospital, Jim came to my room. Even though most of his face was still bandaged, I could tell by his body language that he was still dejected.

"What's the matter?" I asked. By that time I felt he knew I was his friend.

"My wife just called me, and I feel awful. She's angry with me because I didn't pick a hospital closer to our home. She's a busy person and is annoyed that she has to drive five miles farther to pick me up."

I couldn't believe a wife would say that to her husband, though I noticed that he had not had any visitors.

Jim continued, "I'm really depressed about my life. But I do know one thing, that I couldn't make it without God."

"I'm glad to hear you say that," I said. "Have you been born again, and are you a member of God's family?"

"I don't know anything about that. I only know that I need God in my life."

My roommate and the nurses were walking in and out and making it difficult to talk, so I suggested, "We obviously can't talk here. Why don't you take this booklet to your room? It explains God's requirements for becoming a member of his family."

He held out his hand for it and turned to leave.

"When you're finished," I said, "please come back and let me know if it makes sense to you. By the way, there's a prayer at the end of the booklet. I suggest that you read it, think about it, and see if that meets your need."

Jim left and about an hour later peeked into my room and asked, "Could we talk?"

"Sure. Come on in."

He had tears in his eyes as he said, "Thanks for caring. That message is just what I needed. I prayed the prayer and received Jesus as my Savior."

Though Jim apologized for crying, his tears kept coming. Finally he went into the washroom at the end of my room and sobbed. When he had composed himself, he came back and thanked me again for caring. Then he was gone.

His name was Jim. That's really all I know about him, but I hope my witnessing helped him sort out his life.

Reflection

Helping a stranger who is hurting is rarely easy, but the love of God should constrain us to do it. If we stop to ask ourselves, "What am I getting into?" we are like the priest and the Levite who saw a man lying half-dead after he had been stripped and beaten by robbers. They passed by on the other side of the road, not raising a finger to help.

I am glad the Samaritan stopped and helped that man. We—following the pattern of our Lord Jesus—are to be Samaritans, too. We need to be inconvenienced at times, to be reminded that we are not here to serve ourselves but to serve others. In doing that, we serve God.

Since Jim was a married man and I am a married woman, it would not have been good judgment on my part to directly comfort him when he was weeping or to try to follow him up after we both left the hospital. However, I have prayed that God would send someone into his life to help him grow in the knowledge and love of his newfound Savior. Sometimes this is all we can do.

I wouldn't know Jim now if I met him on the street, but I'm comforted by the thought that he who knows the number of the hairs on our head certainly knows Jim and will provide for him.

10

Going Crazy

had just started to wash my hair and was thinking about the young people's meeting held in our home the night before, when the phone rang. A distraught voice at the other end pleaded, "I'm Laurie. I was at your home last night, and I need to talk to you. I'm desperate. I didn't sleep all night. I think I'm going crazy! Please, may I come over right now?"

"Give me an hour," I said as the water trickled down my neck. "I'm in the middle of washing my hair. Come over about eleven."

I hung up the phone and thought, *I don't even know this woman.* We had had quite a number of young adults at the house, and I couldn't remember her. I was even more perplexed by the fact that she said she was going crazy. I wondered whether her distress was mental or spiritual. Before I finished my hair, I made a quick call to my husband. "Paul, you need to pray for Laurie," I said as I explained the brief details and then felt reassured by his support.

When Laurie arrived at my door, I saw a very pretty young woman whom I vaguely remembered from the night before. Although she had said she was desperate, she now appeared to be in control.

"Hi, won't you come in?" I smiled and led her out to my favorite sunny porch. It was apparent that she was nervous and uncomfortable, so I quickly tried to put her at ease. "Would you like a cup of coffee?" I wanted to reassure her with my voice and my smile.

"Yes, please." She followed me into the kitchen.

"Do you work or go to school?"

"I'm going to school, and I'm in between jobs right now," Laurie replied.

Sensing her difficulty in telling me the real reason for coming over, I said, "Why don't we pray and ask for God's blessing and help as we talk together." And then I prayed: "Heavenly Father, you know all about us, even the deep secrets of our hearts. Thank you for sending Laurie here today; and I pray that, whatever her need, you will give wisdom and direction. May we honor Jesus Christ in whatever decisions are made. We ask in his Name. Amen."

I had barely finished praying when Laurie blurted out, "My big problem is that I don't have what you and some of the people who were here last night have. I feel I'm missing something in my life. Christ seemed to be a part of every aspect of your lives."

She barely stopped for a breath before she went on: "In fact, it was as though Christ was woven into the very fiber of everyone's life here, not just something added. I can't understand, for example, why Craig would spend hours talking to people about Christ on his vacation. That's what really got to me last night. I felt so uncomfortable. Outwardly, I was sitting here and listening, but inwardly, I was screaming. I don't know what you were all talking about!"

"Laurie, I don't think you've ever surrendered your life to Christ," I said. "You've ignored the only one who can give real meaning to life, the Perfect One who can cleanse you from your sin and make you a member of his family."

She looked at me with a sense of awe, then said, "It's as though you see right through me." Lowering her head and voice, she added, "You're so right. I've never surrendered my life to Christ."

"Would you like to do it right now?" Laurie's struggle was reduced to my simple question. The very thing she desperately needed was being offered to her.

She bowed her head and prayed out loud: "Lord, I give you my life and all of my problems. I trust you to work them out, and I want to live for you from now on. I confess that I've been playing at being a Christian most of my life, but now I really want Jesus as my Savior and Lord. I want to live for you."

When she finished praying, she began telling me her life story.

"Believe it or not, I was raised in a Christian home and an evangelical church. At the age of seven, going forward seemed to be the thing to do, so I said I wanted to be saved. I remember that day very clearly in terms of what I wore, but little else. I was too scared and upset to know what I was doing or why. In fact, I didn't say one word the whole time because I was crying so much. When I saw how pleased everyone was with my 'decision,' I decided that if they didn't know I was confused, I certainly wasn't going to tell them.

"As I grew older, I remember thinking how really empty my heart felt. The older I got, the less satisfactory my so-called conversion was for me. Since I knew the talk and walked the walk, I found that as long as I outwardly conformed, nobody bothered me about my heart—except for a small voice inside me. The louder it spoke the harder I worked. I played the piano, sang, taught Sunday school— you name it. And in time the voice got quieter. Then I didn't hear it any more.

"I hoped to find the security and happiness I longed for in another person, and I married after high school. I worked hard at being a good wife. I tried very hard to find meaning for my existence in the various roles I played and the things I did, but nothing satisfied for very long. I drifted along with no goals or purpose or hope. I certainly had enough to be happy and comfortable by the world's standards, but I was not.

"I guess that to admit I wasn't happy would have been too hard. To say that I was just going through the motions of being a Christian and, in fact, had no vital relationship with Christ would have destroyed the only world in which I knew how to function. I was frustrated and desperate, but I didn't know what to do. If I carefully broached the subject to someone else, I was reminded of all the blessings I had.

"After eight years of an empty marriage, I was divorced. If God was sovereign, why had he allowed the situation to turn out so badly? It was in the months that followed that I resolved to prove just what an ogre God really was. I quit church and all pretense of being a Christian. I had fun—the world's style—but something was still missing, and that nagging voice came back."

"Is that when you began attending our church?" I asked Laurie.

"Yes. I threw myself into church activities all the harder. I copied the actions of my new friends and read my Bible regularly. This time, though, the voice got even louder, and I saw genuine differences in the lives of these new friends. As I read the Bible, the Holy Spirit began to speak to me about a personal relationship with Christ. I had too much pride, though. What would people think? I was just too busy being religious and too stubborn to give in. At least till now.

"But God knew how important it was to get my attention, and he knew just how to do it. One by one, I saw the things that I had used as substitutes either pried out of my hands or lose their significance for me to the point I let go of them. One day I realized I didn't have much left, but I still resisted.

"Last night, when the class met at your home, I was very uncomfortable. Though I knew in my head what the others were talking about, my heart was confused. I went home to bed, but I didn't sleep. I was awake all night. My thoughts were jumbled, but I did some thinking. Could God really love me? Could I possibly have a relationship with him like the other people here last night? Could God possibly understand what I'm going through? I knew I had to talk to someone like you."

"I'm glad you felt that you could come here," I said. "But how did you get my phone number?"

"As soon as the church opened this morning, I called and asked for your number. I knew you would understand. I appreciated so much that you didn't ask me any probing questions, but simply invited me to come right over." She turned and looked out the porch windows. "Oh, the sun is shining. It's so beautiful!"

"The sun was shining when you came in, Laurie, but you didn't notice," I said, smiling.

Her entire countenance had changed. The *Son* indeed had come into her life!

Reflection

I am glad I didn't put Laurie off that morning because I was "too busy." She probably would never have called back, and I would have lost the opportunity to lead her to Christ.

As 1 Peter 3:15 says, "Always be prepared to give an answer." Laurie, without knowing it, had made those words a priority in my life that day. I had looked forward to a relaxed morning. I was in the middle of washing my hair and had a big clean-up job left over from the night before. Forty people can cause quite a stir in a house, and there were lots of dishes to do.

If one of my friends had called, and asked, "Nellie, how about going out to lunch today?" my answer would have been, "Please give me a rain check. I'm snowed under from the big gang we had over last night."

But Laurie was an emergency. She obviously needed help—now! I felt compelled to drop everything as I was reminded of my commitment to God when I prayed, "Lord, I want to be available to you."

As I continue to read, study, and memorize the Word of God on a daily basis, I am building on my knowledge of that Word. And then witnessing becomes a natural way of life—just as it was for me that day with Laurie.

11

The Biblical View of Homosexuality

J was standing on the balcony of the Florida condo that Paul and I had bought for investment or eventual retirement. Paul had been detained by unexpected work, but I didn't mind being by myself for a few days. I love the warmth and the ocean breezes, so I came on ahead.

While looking to see if the beach was crowded, I heard someone call my name. One of my neighbors was trying to get my attention from her balcony across the way.

"Is your husband with you?" she asked.

"Paul had to finish some work, but he'll be down in a couple of days."

"Dave won't be down until next week. How about going out to dinner tonight?"

"Sounds like fun."

I had known Elizabeth casually for a couple of years. We had been introduced by the Delrays, mutual friends and neighbors who were born-again Christians. I knew that Elizabeth had attended their church many times. Jim Delray, who is really up on Revelation, had talked a lot about it to Elizabeth and her husband, Dave. Jim found it fascinating and used it as an opportunity to warn them to be prepared to meet God.

I was pleased when Elizabeth asked me to have dinner with her and prayed for an opening to share the gospel with her. She knew I was a committed Christian and seemed not at all embarrassed when I suggested we say grace before our meal.

We had no sooner started to eat when Elizabeth asked, "Have you met Ed, the new single fellow in your building?"

"I know who he is."

"He's got to be the handsomest man I've ever laid eyes on—" Her voice sort of trailed off before she added, "He's a homosexual, you know."

"No, I didn't know that."

"If I wasn't married and he wasn't gay, I could really go for him," Elizabeth confided.

I didn't know how to respond, so I said nothing until she asked, "Nellie, what do you think about homosexuals?"

"I take the biblical viewpoint," I replied.

"What is that?" She seemed surprised at my answer.

"It's quite clear in the first chapter of Romans and also in the Old Testament that homosexual behavior is an abomination in the eyes of the Lord. He hates it and says that such acts are perversions. I'm committed to love what God loves and hate what he hates."

"Well, then, do you hate Ed?"

"Oh, no. I don't hate Ed—and neither does God—but I hate his lifestyle."

"Would you speak to him if he spoke to you?"

"Of course I would, and I'd be kind to him. God would want me to."

"I didn't know the Bible talked about things like homosexuality," Elizabeth remarked.

"The Bible talks about every aspect of our lives including relationships with other people—children to parents, parents to children, husbands to wives, and wives to husbands. The most important part, of course, is our relationship to God. Would you be interested in knowing what God requires of you to be in his family?"

"Why, yes, I would," she prompted.

"Well, just as Ed has a problem with homosexuality," I continued, "we all have a sin problem. We were all born sinners. We may not be homosexuals, but we haven't been able to live up to God's standard any better than Ed has."

"I understand that," Elizabeth said. "Dave and I hear all the time at church that everyone is a sinner."

"But do you know that God has a remedy for sin?"

"I've never heard it expressed exactly that way. What do you mean by 'remedy'?"

"Well, you know that God is a holy God and refuses to condone any sin. No unrepentant sinner can stand in his presence. In fact, the Bible says in Romans 6:23 that the wages—or the payment—of sin is death. But God has offered each one of us a gift. 'The gift of God is eternal life,' it says in that same verse. I have it here in a booklet if you want to see it," I said, as I opened my purse and pulled out my tool.*

"Oh, yes, I do," said Elizabeth.

I showed her where it was as I continued talking. "But most gifts are given for a reason. God's reason was love, though sin requires punishment and someone has to die. So God chose to die on our behalf. God the Son came into the world to pay the penalty for our sins. That same verse says that God's gift of eternal life is through Jesus Christ our Lord.

"The Bible tells us in Romans 5:8 that God demonstrated his love to us by having Jesus Christ die for us, even while we were still sinners. Jesus is the only way to God because he is the only one who could die for sinners. We cannot get to God by praying to any saint. The saints didn't die for us. Jesus himself said, 'I am the way and the truth and the life. No one comes to the Father except through me.' That's in the Gospel of John—John 14:6."

Elizabeth was very quiet. All she had said as I talked was, "Mmmmm."

"Do you believe the Bible is God's Word?" I asked her.

"Yes, I do. I just don't know it very well."

"Let me read you a couple of verses." I read from John 1:12: "'Yet to all who received him. . . .'" I paused and looked up. "Jesus," I explained

She nodded.

---

*I feel it is important to keep a tool handy at all times, in my purse or pocket. I can then leave it with the person I am talking to.

There are many booklets available at Christian bookstores, or you may wish to order from publishers. Navigators (Navpress, Box 6000, 3820 N. 30 St., Colorado Springs, CO 80934) has a bridge booklet; Dallas Seminary (3900 Swiss Ave., Dallas, TX 75204) has "How to have a full and meaningful life." "Peace with God" is published by the Billy Graham Evangelistic Association (1300 Harmon Pl., Minneapolis, MN 55403). Other booklets I have used are "Four Spiritual Laws" and "Have You Heard of the Five Jewish Laws?"

Use whatever is comfortable for you and easy to explain. A Bible in a restaurant may be a bit scary until a person realizes it is the book of life.

"'. . . to those who believed in his name, he gave the right to become children of God.'"

She nodded again.

"Now listen to this one," I went on. "'For it is by grace you have been saved, through faith—and this is not of yourselves, it is the gift of God—not by works, so that no one can boast.' That's Ephesians 2:8 and 9."

Once again, I heard her say, "Mmmm."

"Now this next verse you're going to have to respond to one way or the other. It's Revelation 3:20. Listen to what Jesus is saying: 'Here I am! I stand at the door and knock. If anyone hears my voice and opens the door, I will come in and eat'—or fellowship—'with him, and he with me.' What he is asking you is, 'Elizabeth, will you open your heart's door to me and let me be involved with you in everything you do? Will you repent of your sins and thank me for dying on the cross for you? Will you ask me to come into your life and make it my home?'"

She looked at me and broke into a smile. "Oh, yes, I want Jesus to come into my life."

"Would you like to tell him that?"

She nodded and we bowed our heads as I led Elizabeth in prayer. She repeated after me: "Thank you for dying on the cross for my sins. And I do want you to come into my life and be my Savior. Amen."

She got up from the table acting like a totally different person. She was excited as she said, "Let's go back to my place. I want to call the Delrays and tell them what happened."

As soon as Elizabeth opened the door of her apartment, she headed for the phone. "Come on up, you guys. I've got something exciting to tell you," she told them.

"What's all the excitement about?" Jim asked as he walked in the door.

"This is the first day of the rest of my life. I just asked Jesus Christ to be my Savior."

Of course, the Delrays were delighted.

Later on that evening, Jim got me aside and said, "I've been talking about our faith to Elizabeth for a long time. Why couldn't I lead her to Christ?"

"I don't know, Jim. I know you've been emphasizing the end times, and I'm sure that prepared the way. But she just didn't know how to receive the Lord. You whetted her appetite and made it easy for me to present the gospel to her. We both need to remember that God's timing is always perfect."

Before Elizabeth returned to Florida the following year, she had read the entire Bible through. Then, when Billy Graham had his crusade in Florida, she went forward to let the whole world know she had taken a stand for Jesus Christ.

Reflection

When God wants us to witness to an individual, he always prepares the way and provides the openings.

I was rather surprised when Elizabeth began to talk in glowing terms about our homosexual neighbor. I didn't know what to say at first. My silence caused her to ask me, "What do you think of homosexuals?"

I had just read the Book of Romans, so I knew exactly what God thought—and I had to speak out and tell her that he hates such perversions.

When Elizabeth found out God's views on homosexuality she wanted to be on the Lord's side. That led naturally to a discussion of sin in general. Then I showed her the Scripture concerning salvation, and she had no argument. Her attitude was: If that's what God wants, that's what I want. It was refreshing.

Jesus said, "Whoever acknowledges me before men, I will also acknowledge him before my Father in heaven" (Matt. 10:32). Notice that when Elizabeth arrived home from our dinner, she immediately went to the phone to tell her friends that she had just been born into the family of God. She was very enthusiastic. Another good sign was that she wanted to go forward at the Billy Graham crusade to publicly identify with Jesus Christ.

It is a constant source of amazement to me to realize that God knows all about us. He knew that I would be in Florida by myself for a few days and that Elizabeth's husband would be detained, too. He knew that both Elizabeth and I would be on the balcony at the same time that morning. Above all, he knew how eager I was to be available to him. So he arranged our divine appointment. What marvelous timing!

12

Church Seems
Dull and Boring

*H*ow are the newlyweds today?" I asked Sue and Bill as we met on our morning walk one day.

"We couldn't be better," Sue said with a smile.

I remember thinking that it was good to see them so happy. Both of them had been married before, Sue had told me earlier. Her husband had been a psychiatrist and had committed suicide. I had also learned that Bill's first wife, on her deathbed, had asked her children and husband to come to her room. When they arrived, she started to scream, "Why aren't you praying for me? Can't you see I'm dying?"

Bill had told Sue that his late wife was "a very religious person. Every time there was something going on at church, she was there. If I didn't go with her, she would tell me I was committing a sin. I can't figure out why a religious person would die screaming and yelling. How come no peace?" Sue had no answer, but apparently she thought about it many times.

The next time I met them, Bill addressed me in a very sympathetic tone of voice: "I understand your father is failing rapidly. We're so sorry to hear that. Is he having a hard time?"

"Dad does very well, thank you," I said. "He's really anxious to go home to be with the Lord. He was able to come to the table Thanksgiving Day. We asked him to pray. I'll never forget it. He was very weak. But, when he prayed, his voice was strong and powerful. 'Oh, mighty God,' he prayed, 'you whose eyes circle the earth and keep track of all your children, I thank you for your mercy and loving-kindness all of my life.'"

"That's a beautiful prayer," Bill said. "How old is your father?"

"He's just had his ninety-ninth birthday."

"Remarkable." Bill shook his head in disbelief.

Some time later, after my father finally died, my neighbor Cathy had come to the funeral. When she got home, she told a group of other neighbors, "I just attended the most joyous occasion. It was a funeral. Actually, it was more like a celebration."

The neighbors looked at her as if she were out of her mind. "Joyous funeral? Celebration? I've never heard of such a thing," one of them said.

"Now, hear me out," Cathy had said. "The minister told how he visited Nellie's dad and said to him, 'Ole, the Lord is getting you ready to go home to be with him. Are you afraid?' Now Ole had no strength and no voice left, and he couldn't sit up in bed by himself, but on his own he sat up and said in a loud voice, 'Nooo!'" Cathy told me later how amazed the neighbors were.

Soon Sue and Bill had also heard the story, and I shared a bit more with them since they seemed genuinely interested: "Before Dad died, I heard him pray one day, 'Lord, have mercy on me, an old man, and take me home to be with you. I love you, Lord Jesus.' Dad could pray that way because he had a personal relationship with Jesus Christ."

"What kind of minister did your father have? Who is he?" Bill asked.

"David Burnham," I said. "He's a man of God who teaches the truth of the Scripture. He not only teaches from the Word of God, but he lives it. His gracious spirit and attitude were a tremendous influence on my father in the last few years of his life. Why don't you and Sue attend church with us next Sunday? Then you can hear for yourself."

"We'd like that very much, and perhaps we can have dinner together afterwards," Bill suggested. I was excited about their response, and my husband and I prayed much for them that week.

Bill and Sue really liked the pastor's sermon and wanted to talk to him after the service. "That's the best preaching I've ever heard," Bill said. "Why, you're as good as Billy Graham." Pastor Burnham laughed and thanked him for his words.

On the way home, Sue was still enthusiastic. "I'd really like to attend that church. I learned a lot this morning." To our surprise, Bill added, "I'd like to attend, too, but not every Sunday. Things come up, you know. We'll come once in a while though."

I was disappointed and Sue was, too. Later she said to me, "I'd love to attend church every week, but, since Bill and I are newly-weds, I'd better be careful not to alienate him. His first wife put such demands on him concerning church activities that he's a bit apprehensive."

"I think you're wise not to push him," I agreed.

Then Sue said, "I'm expecting a friend of mine in a few days and would like you to meet her. She'll be here all week. I don't think Bill will mind if I take her to church. He plans to play golf next Sunday anyway."

"I'd love to meet her," I said. As we parted, I added, "I'd like to stop over tomorrow if you'll be home. I've got something I'd like to share with you."

"I'd like that. Why don't you come over after lunch."

I was a bit nervous as I knocked on Sue's door the next day. Maybe it was excitement I felt. I had been praying for Sue's salvation for some time and felt that today would be a good time to talk to her about the Lord.

"Come on in," she said. "I want you to meet my friend Sylvia. She arrived two days earlier than I expected. We've already had a chance to talk and catch up on things." Sylvia was very friendly and had a beautiful smile. I liked her instantly. After a few minutes of small talk, I prepared to leave.

"Didn't you say you had something to share with me?" Sue asked.

"I'll wait until your company leaves," I said, not wanting to put her on the spot until we were alone.

"Oh, Sylvia is such a good friend of mine that I don't mind if she hears what you have to say. I'm anxious to hear it myself."

"Well," I hesitated, "you seemed to be so interested in our pastor's message that I wanted to be sure you knew how to be in the family of God."

Sue and Sylvia both looked at me in disbelief. "You won't believe what we've just been talking about," Sue said. "I was just telling Sylvia that I was happy in my marriage and had enough money to live comfortably, but there's something missing in my life. I told her I think my problem is spiritual. Sylvia feels her problem is spiritual, too, and then you knocked on the door. It's absolutely amazing!"

I thought, *Amazing, yes, but it's God's timing.*

Sylvia said, "We've both attended church most of our lives, but we don't get much out of it. It seems dull and boring."

"Having a relationship with Jesus Christ is anything but boring," I said. "You see, he came to give us abundant life. He speaks to us through his Word, the Bible, and we speak to him through prayer. It's really very exciting."

"Oh, I believe in Jesus, but I don't know the Bible very well," Sylvia said.

"But believing facts about him can be like knowing facts of history that don't really affect the heart. A personal relationship with Jesus Christ involves a commitment to him. It involves admitting that we are sinners who need a Savior, sinners who cannot save ourselves. It means repenting of our sins and receiving Christ as our Savior."

I opened my purse and took out my Bible, turning to Romans 6:23. "The Bible says that 'the wages of sin is death'—we deserve to die because we're sinners—'but the gift of God is eternal life in Christ Jesus our Lord.' He died the death we deserve for being such sinners. He actually became our substitute. John 3:16 says, 'For God so loved the world that he gave his one and only Son, that whoever believes in him shall not perish but have eternal life.'"

Tears came as both Sue and Sylvia admitted they were sinners and that they needed Christ as their Savior. We prayed together and each one asked the Lord to come into her life.

"It's strange," Sylvia said. "I feel like a new person, like a load is off my back." Joy had replaced her tears.

Sylvia left for home a couple of days later and we helped her find a good Bible-teaching church in her area. Sue and I began having Bible studies together. Her desire to learn was delightful and refreshing.

About that time, Bill developed a severe eye infection and was extremely concerned about it. "Please ask the people at your church to pray for me," he said. "If my eye gets better, I'll start coming to church."

"You can't bargain with God," I replied. "You serve him because you love him, not to get his favor. But of course, I *will* ask our church members to pray for your physical and spiritual healing."

Bill's eye got better, but he didn't come to church.

Some time after that, he and Sue went on a trip. They were to be gone for several months. As they were leaving, Bill promised me, "Things will be different when we return. I'll start coming to church."

That never happened. I later got a card from Sue saying, "I have sad news. Bill passed away in his sleep."

Reflection

Sue and Sylvia were honest about their spiritual condition and responded to the work of the Holy Spirit in their hearts.

Bill, on the other hand, wanted God's benefits with no strings attached. He had the witness of my father who died triumphantly, the witness of Sue's conversion, the witness of his own healing as the probable result of prayer, and the witness I gave him. Though God had answered his questions about life and death time after time, Bill never saw the truth.

We can never fully know what is in another's heart—the condition of the soil upon which our seed will fall. But our responsibility is to sow nonetheless, trusting in God that we have sowed "good seed." It is to be our hope that the Lord's timing will allow the seed to root in fertile soil, so that the person to whom we witness will hear and understand the Word. (Read Matthew 13.)

Though we can never know what tomorrow will bring, anyone "who knows the good" must do it. (Read James 4:17.)

13

I'm Manic Depressive

J knew that woman in the audience didn't like me. I could tell by her body language. She sat with her arms folded and had a hostile look on her face. She might as well have worn a sign that said, "What do you think you can teach me that I don't know already?"

I had accepted an invitation to hold a series of morning Bible classes at a church on the east side of our city, about thirty miles away. Since this was the first women's Bible class they had had, I was excited. Our study would be of the Book of Galatians.

When I arrived, I was surprised to see men in the audience. "I thought this was a women's Bible class," I said to Edith, my hostess. "I didn't know there would be any men here. And they look so serious!"

"They're just deacons," she told me.

"Mmmm, I bet they're checking me out. I really don't blame them. After all, I'm a Baptist and this is a Lutheran church."

Edith laughed as she patted my shoulder. "Don't worry."

I wasn't worried, but I did feel somewhat uneasy. I wanted to be a blessing to these women, so I prayed and asked God to break down any barrier that might stand in the way.

After I was introduced, I began by saying, "I'm not a theologian. I'm a homemaker who has had good Bible teaching all my life, and I love to study and share the Scriptures. I hope we will all learn from each other as we study the Book of Galatians together."

I spoke for half an hour on the first chapter, contrasting the pure gospel of Jesus Christ with "a different gospel—which is really no gospel at all" (Gal. 1:6–7). The Galatians were trying to add to the gospel by putting unnecessary burdens on believers. I mentioned the importance of being biblical and not accepting "every wind of teaching" that came along (Eph. 4:14).

That was the problem in Galatia, I said. I referred to the Bereans, who had received the message with eagerness but "examined the Scriptures every day to see if what Paul said was true" (Acts 17:11). I also brought out the point that in Paul's greeting he said, "Grace and peace to you . . ." not "peace and grace" (Gal. 1:3). We first have to experience God's grace before we can have his peace.

We then had a coffee break. During the break, one of the deacons came up, put his two hands on mine, and said, "Lady, you've got it all together!" What a relief! The barrier was broken.

Standing behind the deacon, a woman waited patiently to speak to me. She was the one who had sat, arms folded, with a "show me" look on her face. She introduced herself as Yvonne and asked, "Would you be willing to talk to me after the meeting is over? I need help in several areas of my life."

I was amazed. Sweetness and humility had replaced her hostility. Her attitude had completely changed.

When we talked later, Yvonne said, "I'm a very confused person. I've gone to church for years, but I don't think I've experienced God's grace like you talked about this morning. I know because I don't have peace."

I looked at this attractive, well-groomed woman and wondered what her problem might be, since she seemed outwardly composed. She said, "I'm a teacher, but I'm having problems keeping my job. I sometimes go into deep depression and have had to be hospitalized several times. They tell me I'm manic depressive."

Disturbing thoughts flooded my mind. She needed a doctor. I was not equipped to handle this.

Then she went on. "I have highs and lows. I go on spending sprees that are very exciting. But, when I can't pay my bills, I get very depressed and anxious. I try to borrow money and that makes me feel worse. I like beautiful things and want to look as nice as the other women in this group, but I feel like a nothing compared to them.

You might say that I have a poor self-image. I don't feel accepted. I hear about the abundant life that Christ came to give, but I certainly don't have an abundance. I'm always struggling to pay my bills. Can you help me?"

"Well, first of all," I said, "the abundant life does not mean an abundance of things. It means a life full of joy and peace and contentment. When we recognize the fact that Jesus died for our sins, took our place on the cross and paid our penalty, we have an overwhelming desire to commit ourselves to him. When we do that, we realize we are free from guilt and the awful burden of sin. Then and only then can we understand what the abundant life is all about."

"Then what is grace all about?" Yvonne asked.

"Grace means unmerited favor. We can't get Brownie points from God by doing good deeds or by trying to turn over a new leaf without his help. Ephesians 2:8 and 9 says, 'For it is by grace you have been saved, through faith—and this not from yourselves, it is the gift of God—not by works, so that no one can boast.' We need to understand that God is holy and that everything he does is right. Sin is completely offensive to him. We all have offended our Holy God.

"The good news is that God loves us and demonstrated this by sending his Son, Jesus Christ, to die for us. He didn't do this for so-called good people, for 'while we were still sinners, Christ died for us.' That's in Romans 5:8. In the light of this, all we need to do to be accepted by God is to confess that we are sinners and want to receive Jesus Christ as our personal Savior. He paid the penalty for our sins. Then God not only forgives us; he accepts us into his family."

Yvonne shook her head. "I've never done that—that is, confessed my sins. And I haven't received Jesus as my Savior. I always thought the important thing was to attend church on Sundays."

"Oh, it's important to attend church and to be with other believers," I agreed, "but the most important issue of all is acknowledging Jesus as your Savior from sin. You need to invite him into your life. Unless you do, you'll be separated from God forever. When you commit your life to him, you will experience peace and can begin a brand-new life. It's called being born again."

"I really need to do that," Yvonne said as she bowed her head and began to pray: "Dear God, I know I sin. I think it's the cause of all of my problems. I think it's wrong of me to buy perfume I can't afford and expensive clothes I can't pay for. That's why I'm so miserable and don't have peace. I confess this and the other sins I've committed, and I receive Jesus as my Savior. Thank you for dying on the cross for me and for giving me a way out of my misery."

When she looked up, she smiled shyly and said, "With God's help, I'm going to lick this problem. I really want to."

During the discussion period the next week, Yvonne stood up and said, "Today, I can say for sure that I am a Christian. I don't just try to do Christian things. Our lesson today says that we are not justified or saved by keeping the law or by doing good things, but by placing our faith in Jesus Christ. I placed my faith in Jesus last week after class, and I'm beginning to understand what is meant by the abundant life. It's not an abundance of things but an abundance of peace. Today I can truthfully say that I have peace."

The following week, Yvonne showed me a budget she had made for herself and told me, "I thought you would like to know that I'm working on my priorities. I made a list of things I thought I needed. Then I crossed off the things I couldn't afford. The surprising thing was discovering that the items I crossed off weren't *needed* at all. They were only things I *wanted*.

"I feel so good about it. I believe God is helping me to get my life under control. I'm so much more relaxed, and I have a peace that I never experienced before. Another thing that is helping me out of my confusion is reading small portions of Scripture and thinking about them."

I agreed with her. "It's good to hide God's Word in our hearts," I said. "The Bible says it keeps us from sinning. Psalm 119:11 says, 'I have hidden your word in my heart that I might not sin against you.'"

Each week Yvonne had something new to share about the working of the Spirit of God in her life. It was interesting to watch her growth as the weeks passed. As we studied the fifth chapter of Galatians, concerning the acts of the sinful nature in contrast to the fruit of the Spirit, it was obvious that Yvonne was aware of the transformation taking place in her life. She was a joy to behold and a cause of praise to the Father.

When the women ended the series of Bible studies with a luncheon, I asked Edith, our hostess, "Would you allow Yvonne to tell the group about her new job? I think it will mean a lot to her." I also knew that everyone was deeply interested in the change that had taken place from week to week right in front of their eyes.

Yvonne spoke about working the past month for a company that sends out representatives to help women with their grooming. "I show them how to fix their nails and hair and how to choose clothes and the proper accessories. Some women don't know where to start and just need a little direction. I give them low-cost, budget-conscious tips for self-improvement. My job is to make a completely new person out of each one of them, at least on the outside."

While she was talking, I couldn't help but think of the transformation in Yvonne's life. The dark clouds were gone from her face. Instead, there was a beautiful smile and a confidence that God had given her. I was excited for her and thanked God for allowing me to witness the change, as she continued her story:

"I just finished with a woman who was very happy with her new appearance. I told her, 'I've done the best I can to make you look beautiful and I think you do. I've completed my part, but there is another part of you that needs changing before we can say we're done.'

"My client looked puzzled. 'What is that?' she asked.

"'That is something only God can do,' I told her. Then I said, 'Let me tell you how God changed me from the inside and how it affected the outside of my life.'"

What an ending to our Bible-study series! I wanted to give Yvonne a standing ovation. Instead, I sat there and cried tears of joy.

Even though Yvonne lives a distance away, I have seen her several times in the past years. The last time I talked to her on the phone she was still growing as a believer.

"When I first met you," she said, "I was full of fear and mistrust. I felt anxious and frightened, though I may have looked hostile. I really looked up to you as a role model and came for help. I was seeking and searching, and God has taught me to replace fear with love. He has brought me peace and helped me forgive those I once mistrusted. I'm learning so much and have a lot more to learn. I have so much to thank God for."

Reflection

Yvonne came to Christ when the Word of God was explained to her. I added verses of Scripture to my conversation, letting the Holy Spirit use them and work in her heart.

I was wrong to judge her attitude initially by body language and facial expression. Man looks on the outward appearance, but God looks on the heart. Looks are deceiving and often cause us to make wrong judgments. Our job is to be faithful and not put up barriers between ourselves and the person to whom God wants us to witness.

We must also have full confidence that God will use his Word in people's hearts. Yvonne picked up on the salutation of Paul and the little lesson I drew from it—that we must first experience grace before we can have peace. That hit her problem head-on and drew her to the Savior. I had no way of knowing that God would use that little truth to bring Yvonne to himself. How important for us to be full of the Word and full of trust that the Holy Spirit will bring people to Christ by using the little things that spill from our lips.

And talk about fulfillment! What perfect joy it is to see one whom we have pointed to the Savior in turn point someone else to him. Yvonne did this and, to my knowledge, is still winning others.

14

I Don't Know How to Pray

M y husband and I always look forward to September, the time of year we visit our married daughters in New England. Greta lives in Connecticut and Karen in Massachusetts. En route, we usually stop at Rockport, a quaint little Massachusetts town nestled by the ocean. We stay at a favorite motel, which has all the facilities we enjoy—tennis courts, a swimming pool, a sauna and whirlpool tub.

One year, during our annual stopover, I decided to swim after a game of tennis with Paul. He chose to sit on the pool deck and catch up on his reading—a choice that would play an important part in the incident that followed.

I was feeling so refreshed and relaxed by the water and so caught up in my own little world that I barely noticed the one other person—a woman—in the pool. She appeared to be enjoying her swim just as much as I. Eventually we got close enough to speak to each other, and she introduced herself.

"Hi, I'm Evelyn," she said.

"Hi, I'm Nellie Pickard."

"Where are you from?"

"I'm from Michigan. My husband and I are out here visiting our daughters. Where do you live?"

"Oh, I live in Essex, just a few miles from here."

I wondered what she was doing in a motel so close to home; and, of course, with my innate curiosity I couldn't resist asking her.

"I recently injured my back," she said, "and my doctor prescribed swimming and the whirlpool to strengthen my muscles. I have an arrangement with the motel management, and for a yearly fee they let me swim here whenever I want. Unfortunately, I missed Sunday and Monday and can really feel the difference."

"I suppose you went to church on Sunday and did your house-work on Monday and got your back out of whack again," I prompted.

"Oh, no, I didn't go to church on Sunday. In fact," she said, "I have a problem—I don't know how to pray."

Now why would someone say to a perfect stranger, "I don't know how to pray"? I was immediately aware that this was one of God's divine appointments for me. Right there in that swimming pool, he had arranged an opportunity for me to share my faith with Evelyn. I've learned over the years that effective witnessing involves being alert, responsive, and sensitive to the people I meet—even in swimming pools. It also means looking for "openers" that will help me make a smooth connection to share the love of Christ. Evelyn had given me a fantastic opener. I could hardly believe it. She even repeated it: "I just don't know how to pray. I try, but it just seems to hit the ceiling."

"Perhaps I can help you," I said. "I teach a women's Bible class, and I often meet women who don't know how to pray. I might even be able to tell you what your problem really is."

"How can you possibly tell me what my problem is?" she asked. "We've only known each other for a few minutes."

"Tell me, Evelyn, when you pray, do you go directly to God?"

"Of course."

"That's your problem," I said. "You see, God demands perfection. We can't approach him in our imperfect condition (see Reflection, p. 76). We need a mediator (1 Tim 2:5; John 4:6)."

"Well," she said, "I keep the Ten Commandments, and I'm really good to my neighbors."

I responded very kindly, "You look like such a nice person, and I'll bet you *are* good to your neighbors. But, you see, no one has kept the commandments perfectly. God's Word says that everyone has sinned. God demands perfection, so that's your problem."

I wasn't sure how she would accept this truth but she asked anxiously, "What in the world can I do?"

"Fortunately, God didn't leave us to flounder," I said. "He provided a way. He came to earth himself to die for our sins and in our place. The Bible says that the Lord Jesus is standing at your heart's door, knocking and desiring that you will open the door of your life, repent of your sins, and receive him as your Savior."

"I had a maid," Evelyn said, "who tried to tell me about Jesus Christ many times. Because she was my maid, I didn't pay much attention. Now you're telling me some of the same things."

Usually, when witnessing, I take out copies of a little booklet that presents the plan of salvation in a simple, precise manner. With the other person following along, I read it aloud. I have found this an important tool that has been invaluable to me in many situations. It also gives the person I'm talking with a chance to look away from me for a while. A change of eye contact allows a more relaxed feeling. Then I give the book to the person to keep. However, here I was standing in a swimming pool with no booklets!

We decided to go to the whirlpool and continue our conversation there. On the way, I stopped by Paul and asked him to please go and get me two copies of the booklet. God had *him* there for a purpose, too! When Paul brought them, I gave one to Evelyn and invited her to follow along as I read aloud. As I finished, I confronted her with a direct question: "Is Christ running your life—or are you?"

"I've definitely been running my life," she said.

"Do you want to continue to run your life? Or would you like Jesus Christ to come into your life and take control?" I held my breath, praying that her answer would be yes.

"I would very much like Christ to come into my life and take over," she said. "How can I tell him that?"

I explained that God looks at the heart and is not concerned with the specific words we say, and then I helped her pray. Right there in the whirlpool with the warm, soothing water swirling around us, Evelyn joyously received Christ as her Savior.

I told her it was important to tell someone she had accepted Christ as her Savior, as a means of reaffirming her faith and sharing it with someone else. "I have a friend named Julie Kerr," I said, "who lives in Hamilton, about twenty miles from here, and she's a Christian. It would be good for you to tell her of your experience."

"I know her!" Evelyn laughed. "She sells real estate and showed me some houses just two weeks ago. My husband and I buy homes that need fixing and then sell them."

Neither of us said, "It's a small world," but I'm sure we both thought it. If I ever doubted that God has prearranged appointments for me, my doubts vanished right then and there.

Evelyn returned to the pool to finish her workout. I watched her as she glided through the water effortlessly. When she was finished, she said happily, "I prayed every stroke of the way."

I smiled. "I thought you didn't know how to pray."

"I didn't, but I do now!" She was radiant.

Over the years, I have kept in touch with Evelyn by letters and phone calls and have had the privilege and joy of seeing her grow as a Christian.

Reflection

Evelyn is just one example of how opportunities for witnessing occur everywhere. Sometimes, as she did, a person will begin the conversation; other times, I have to ask a question or make a comment to get things going. I use something that is available and would obviously be of interest to both of us.

In Evelyn's case, I was able to attract her attention with the protocol of prayer. She found it difficult to understand why she couldn't go to God except through Christ. That offered an excellent opportunity to explain to her that God is holy and demands perfection. Since we are not holy, we cannot approach Holy God in and of ourselves, any more than we can on a human level walk directly into the President's office.

When a person tells me, "I have a problem, I don't know how to pray" or "I try to pray and I feel as though my prayers hit the ceiling," I can usually identify their problem.

If I start out by saying, "You can come to God only as a repentant sinner," he or she would become defensive. We need to know that no one can reach God's standard (Rom. 3:23). God's standard is perfection.

Evelyn knew she could not keep God's commands—perfectly—and immediately asked, "What can I do?" That is what I was waiting for.

I was then able to tell her that the Lord Jesus Christ is the answer to that dilemma. When we accept him as our Savior, we can come to God in his name—we are clothed in his righteousness, and now God the Father will hear us.

I use John 14:13–14, where Jesus says, "And I will do whatever you ask *in my name*, so that the Son may bring glory to the Father. You may ask me for anything *in my name*, and I will do it." Or I might also use Jesus' words in John 16:23: ". . . I tell you the truth, my Father will give you whatever you ask *in my name*" (italics mine).

"In my name" means all that Christ's character stands for. We receive an answer to our requests because we ask according to his righteousness. Of course, we must not be careless about praying to our heavenly Father in the name of the Lord Jesus and in the power of the Holy Spirit (Jude 20).

Last year, while attending a Bible study in Massachusetts with my daughter Karen, I saw a little slip of a woman who caught my attention. We looked at each other and our eyes locked in recognition.

"Evelyn!"

"Nellie!" We both spoke at once.

We hadn't seen each other in several years, and that was in the swimming pool. We both looked different in street clothes.

What a time we had catching up! Evelyn was so excited about the things she was learning. "Nellie," she said, "I'm trying to make up for lost time. I attend two Bible studies every week, I have so much to learn. Oh, how I wish I hadn't wasted so much time. All my life I've been attending Unity and it was such a waste. I didn't learn about the Bible at all."

We sat together in class, and I told everyone about our meeting in the swimming pool several years before, when Evelyn had come to know Christ. What a difference salvation makes in a life!

15

Still Searching

I was sitting in the overflow room of our church one Sunday when I noticed a young woman coming in to take a chair. I smiled at her and she smiled back. Then I saw her take a visitor's brochure from an usher as my husband whispered to me, "You be sure to talk to her."

I slipped over to the newcomer and introduced myself. I said, "Visitors are invited to the library for a cup of coffee after the service and an opportunity to meet the church staff. I hope you'll come. It's a good place to get acquainted. I'd like to meet you there."

"I'd love to," she whispered, after telling me her name was Mary Beth.

When she came into the library, I asked her, "Do you live in the area, and have you ever visited our church before?"

"I live nearby, but I've never attended your church. I'm not too happy with the church I belong to. I just don't get anything out of it. I asked the boy I ride to school with if he knew of a good church. He said Highland Park Baptist was a good church."

"Does your friend attend this church?" I asked.

"Oh, no. He isn't interested in religion."

I found that amusing and asked, "Tell me, are you a full-time student or do you work?"

"I attend Wayne State University, but I have Fridays off," she told me.

"How about having lunch with me on Friday? Then I'll tell you about our church and the young people's activities and anything else you'd like to know."

"Sounds like fun. Give me directions to your house, and I'll be there."

When Mary Beth arrived on Friday, I felt as though I was welcoming one of my own children. She greeted me with a big smile and a hug. As we enjoyed our lunch together, I asked, "Do you have any brothers and sisters?"

"Lots," she said, laughing. "There are eleven children in our family. My father is a doctor, and he and my mom have taken good care of us. One of my brothers is an attorney, and I have a sister who goes to law school." Mary Beth seemed proud of her family, and I enjoyed hearing about them.

Then she said, "I have another sister and brother-in-law who were invited to a Christian businessmen's meeting and there they found the Lord. Their lives are so different since they've—" she hesitated, "—found the Lord. They're so happy. I wish everybody could find the Lord. The world would be a better place to live in."

"Have you found the Lord, Mary Beth?" I asked.

"I'm searching, and I know about him, but I don't think I've found him yet."

"It's not enough to know about him," I said. "We need to confess that we have sinned against him and need his cleansing and forgiveness. We need to receive him as our Savior. Knowing about the Lord is a matter of the head. Receiving him is a matter of the heart. It's a commitment to him and becomes a relationship. We then become a member of the family of God. Look what it says here in the Bible—"

I turned to Revelation 3:20 and explained, "You see, Jesus is waiting for you to invite him into your life. Is there any reason why you wouldn't want to ask him to be your Savior and Lord?"

To my delight she said with a big smile, "Not a reason in the world."

We bowed our heads and Mary Beth prayed, "Lord, I know that I'm a sinner. Never before have I invited you to take charge of my life. I ask your forgiveness. I now ask you to be my Savior and to take control of my life."

When she looked up, her face was radiant. "I'm so glad I took this step today," she said. Tears filled her eyes. When she left, she hugged me again and said, "I'll see you on Sunday."

Mary Beth and I have had Bible study together since then, and she attended the college-age Sunday-school class the very next Sunday. I took her to the room and introduced her to the members, suggesting that she tell everyone what had happened to her the previous Friday.

"I asked Jesus Christ to come into my life," she said.

The class hadn't expected to hear that and said in unison, "Ahhhhhh!"

Reflection

Look around. You never know who is sitting next to you in church. Just because a visitor is all dressed up and sits listening attentively to the sermon is no reason to believe she or he is saved. Mary Beth was a person whose heart was ready. Her sister and brother-in-law had done the sowing and watering. Their happy lives had proved to her the reality of salvation. All I did was give Mary Beth a nudge.

Again, let me say that it's important to use our homes for witnessing. If you open the door and invite these very needy people in, you are showing them that you are interested and available. In 1 Peter 4:9 we are admonished to practice hospitality. It pleases the Lord—and we get the blessing.

16

Put on the Spot

"I believe we have a couple of newcomers in our class today," I said during a women's Bible study I was leading. "Let's take a few minutes to get acquainted before we get into the lesson. Each of you tell two things about yourself. If this is your first time here, tell us what circumstances brought you."

I was especially interested in a tall, blonde woman who came by herself, but I didn't have a chance to speak to her before class except to nod and smile. "My name's Penny Wilson," she said when it was her turn. "A woman in our car pool invited me to come. I'm really concerned about the drug situation in the public schools, so I put my children in a private school. Since my husband isn't willing to pay any of the tuition, I'm working in my home as a hairdresser to pay for their schooling."

I decided I wanted to know more about this industrious young woman. I also wondered what her religious background was and watched for little clues as I taught. She seemed tense. She listened but never volunteered to answer any questions.

After the third week, Penny was a bit more relaxed, and I was delighted when she spoke up in class. "Would it be all right if I brought my sister-in-law to class? I think this is what she needs. You see, she has an incurable disease and needs something that will give her peace." She turned and looked at the others in the group. "Don't misunderstand me. She's deeply religious, but she doesn't have what you have."

"We encourage all of you to bring your friends to our class," I said.

Things are unfolding, I thought. Penny was concerned about her sister-in-law, but I was concerned about Penny. I didn't like the way she said, "She doesn't have what *you* have," so I asked the Lord to give me wisdom to know how to handle the situation. Though I didn't want to rush things, neither should I wait too long to speak. I asked God to let his Word work in her heart.

The next week, Penny brought both her mother and sister-in-law to class. We were studying the Book of John, and I began by review-ing the first three chapters. Since we had visitors, I decided to read the first twelve verses of chapter one aloud.

> In the beginning was the Word, and the Word was with God, and the Word was God. He was with God in the beginning.
>
> Through him all things were made; without him nothing was made that has been made. In him was life, and that life was the light of men. The light shines in the darkness, but the darkness has not understood it.
>
> There came a man who was sent from God; his name was John. He came as a witness to testify concerning that light, so that through him all men might believe. He himself was not the light; he came only as a witness to the light. The true light that gives light to every man was coming into the world.
>
> He was in the world, and though the world was made through him, the world did not recognize him. He came to that which was his own, but his own did not receive him. Yet to all who received him, to those who believed in his name, he gave the right to become children of God.

Then I asked some questions.

"What do we know about this 'Word' who created the world, turned the water into wine, and told a member of the ruling coun-cil that unless he was born again he could not see the kingdom of God?"

Betty, one of our regular members, raised her hand. "The four-teenth verse says, 'The Word became flesh and made his dwelling among us. . . .' Since the Word is God, we're talking about Jesus Christ here. The rest of the chapter makes that very clear."

"Thank you, Betty," I said. "It's extremely important that we under-stand this first chapter. I believe it's the answer to the cults that don't believe that Jesus is God in the flesh but merely a good man. A Jehovah's Witness told me once that Jesus was *a* god. This meant that she believes in several gods and that's idolatry." I got a little preachy and ended up saying, "If Jesus is God, we'd better listen to what he has to say and obey him."

That seemed to stimulate the discussion. We talked about how we could share with friends and neighbors who Jesus Christ is.

I was just about to close with prayer when Penny spoke up: "I told my husband that the Bible was true."

"I'm glad you were able to discuss that with him," I said. Then I gently turned the question back on her. "Tell me, Penny, do you believe the Bible is the Word of God?"

Her answer shook me to the core. "Shut up!" she muttered.

There was dead silence in the room, and I thought, *I must have asked the wrong question.* Finally, I gained my composure enough to say, "Let's just close in prayer."

I felt absolutely awful. Though I wanted to apologize to Penny for putting her on the spot, she was gone before I could reach her. I had been invited to a luncheon afterward but decided to call Penny as soon as I got home.

I arrived at my friend's home with a heavy heart. Serious concerns were running through my mind: *Penny will never come back to class. I've ruined everything. How could I have been so insensitive?*

Small tables had been set up for the luncheon, to which my friend had invited eleven guests. I looked across the room and there was Penny! When I learned she had been placed at my table, I prayed an S.O.S. *"Lord, I need wisdom."*

As soon as I sat down, I said, "Penny, I'm truly sorry I put you on the spot today. It was so insensitive of me. Will you forgive me?"

She apologized to me for her hostile reply. She had been flustered, she explained, by having her mother there. And she hadn't known the answer to my question. "I have a problem," she confided. "I don't know why I can't believe. I'd like to talk to you about it sometime."

"Why don't I stop over to your house next week and we'll lay all your problems on the table and see if we can come up with some solutions."

"I'd like that. It's keeping me awake nights. I've got to settle this thing once and for all."

The following Saturday morning I had coffee at Penny's home. We talked in general terms for about an hour before she seemed settled enough to discuss the problem that concerned us both. "You told me the other day," I said, "that you were having difficulty believing. What exactly is hard for you to believe?"

"I struggled with my unbelief all during the week, but now I'm as ready as I'll ever be to accept Christ as my Savior." I could hardly believe what I was hearing. I had been prepared for some arguments, but Penny was full of surprises.

Then, rather shyly, she said, "All I need now is to have you pray with me."

I prayed and thanked God for the work of the Holy Spirit in Penny's heart in the past few days. Then Penny prayed and thanked him for sending his Son to die for her sin and for accepting her as his child. She ended with, "Please help the rest of my family to believe in you, too."

There was a definite change in Penny's life after that. She told the class about the decision she had made and began entering into our discussions. She seemed very concerned about her family and friends. Her in-laws owned a family restaurant, and Penny invited the waitresses to attend our Bible study. Several were able to come, since Tuesday morning was not a busy time at work. Penny had a big station wagon and filled it to capacity. She brought as many as thirteen people at a time. It was great!

Tammy, her sister-in-law, had been attending for about six weeks before she spoke up in class: "I've been feeling guilty coming to this class because I've always been taught that it was a sin to attend any other church but my own. But the memory verse for this week helped me to see that my former teaching has not been correct. You see, it says in 2 Timothy 3:16 that 'All Scripture is God-breathed and is useful for teaching, rebuking, correcting and training in righteousness.' What I'm learning here is Scripture, and it's good for me. I haven't learned that in my own church."

I love to watch the expression on the faces of the rest of the class when someone for the first time discovers the truth of God. Now everyone was grinning from ear to ear. They had been praying for these newcomers and were very interested in their responses.

After class, I asked Tammy if she could stay for a few minutes. Penny, who was driving, overheard my question. "No problem," she said. "Plenty of time." So Tammy and I had time for a little chat.

"Have you ever received Jesus Christ as your Savior?" I asked.

"But I'm not worthy," Tammy replied.

"None of us are worthy. There's nothing we can do to make ourselves worthy of the salvation Jesus came to give. He wants us to have it as a gift. Ephesians 2:8–9 says, 'For it is by grace you have been saved, through faith—and this not from yourselves, it is the gift of God—not by works, so that no one can boast.'"

This was new to Tammy, who had been trying to work for her salvation, yet had no peace.

"Would you like to receive this gift God offers you?" I asked her.

"Oh, yes. If it says that in the Bible, I believe it."

Tammy bowed her head and thanked God for the gift he had offered her. "I now understand I can't work for it," she prayed, "so I'll accept Jesus Christ as my Savior and say thank you."

Soon after that, Tammy became concerned for her family, especially her son. After lengthy talks, prayers, and finding notes from her on his dresser, he too became a believer.

Penny and Tammy next became interested in getting the rest of their sisters and sisters-in-law to the Bible study. There was a problem, however, because some of them worked. Penny asked me, "Would you be willing to come one evening a week to teach a class at my sister-in-law Lillian's home? Everyone will be family except one—a close friend."

Even though it was a distance from my home, I was delighted for the opportunity. The first night, there were eight of us seated around a large table. They seemed excited to learn. Penny and Tammy had told them about the Book of John and that's what they wanted to study.

First we had an overview. Though their religious background had included some scriptural facts, none of them had read the Bible for themselves. As we went through John's Gospel over the next several weeks, I drew their attention to the many times Christ's enemies had sought to kill him. But "his time had not yet come," I read in John 8:20. (See also 2:4; 7:6, 8, 30.)

The women were fascinated. "Sounds like God really is in control of things," one of them said.

"Yes, God is certainly sovereign," I said. "His enemies couldn't take his life until he was ready to lay it down. It was for each one of us that Jesus died. He is waiting for our response to take him as our Savior."

"I'd like to," Sandy (Penny's sister-in-law) said, "but I wonder whether I will have this great emotional experience I hear people talk about. I read about Pat Boone and his wife. They were overwhelmed with emotion when they were converted."

"Some people do have a great emotional experience," I said, "and some don't. But, later, as they fully realize what Christ has saved them from, they have a gratitude to God that many times stirs them to the point of tears. To put the emotional experience first is like putting the cart before the horse, if you know what I mean."

I prayed for Sandy that week. I prayed that she would be convicted of sin and of her need for the Savior.

The following Thursday night we met again. I opened with prayer and then the flood gates opened. "I had my emotional experience," Sandy said. "It was awful. I feel like such a sinner. What can I do? I've got to get rid of this awful guilt."

"Sandy, that's why Jesus died. He took your guilt and now he offers you salvation as a gift. How about it? Are you ready to receive him as your Savior and Lord?"

I helped her pray the sinner's prayer. I thought, as we did it, that I heard another voice, faintly. When we finished, Peggy, who was the only non-relative there, said, "I prayed, too."

You should have heard the sounds of excitement! We were all so happy!

Then Peggy, with a smile coming through her tears, said, "There's another miracle that has occurred here tonight—something that you, Nellie, probably aren't aware of. But Sandy and I haven't spoken to each other for more than ten years, and tonight—at the same time—we prayed to God together to forgive us our sins and for Jesus to be our Savior. God took care of two things at once. Our neighbors will certainly be surprised," she added. "You see, we live across the street from each other."

Reflection

It is not easy to know how far to probe in a class discussion. Sometimes it is better to approach a person on a one-on-one basis. We have to depend on the Spirit of God to lead us. Because of Penny's reaction to my direct approach I felt it was my fault.

I believe God allowed this incident to occur. That is evidenced by the results. We both apologized and became instant friends. The incident also opened the door for further opportunity to talk and resulted ultimately in her decision to accept Christ.

This total experience, which started with Penny, was almost like a replay of the incident in the first chapter of John, where Andrew found his brother Simon Peter, and told him, "We have found the Messiah." And Philip found Nathanael. Here, Penny brought Tammy, and Tammy brought her son to Christ, and then Sandy and Peggy came.

We need to be sensitive to the leading of the Holy Spirit, be willing to be his tool, and most of all desire to glorify God's name.

17

Letting a Child Die

As she came to retrieve her tennis ball from our court, Barbara said, "If you ever need a substitute for a tennis game, I'd sure like to play. Maybe we could fill in for each other. How about it?" I didn't know her very well, but Barbara's doubles team had been playing on the court next to ours all season. We all agreed it would be fun subbing for each other. That way, we could get in a little extra tennis.

One day, while both of us were waiting for a court, Barb and I struck up a conversation. "I feel kinda blue today," she said. "Maybe I should say 'bitter.'"

"What's the matter?"

"I was thinking about my son. He was killed in an automobile accident a few years ago and today would have been his birthday. He was only fifteen when he died. I've been wondering if I'll ever see him again." She turned away so I couldn't see her face. "Poor kid. He didn't even know his father, because my husband died when our son was only two-and-a-half years old."

"I'm so sorry," I said. "You've really gone through a lot, losing both a husband and a son."

"I just can't understand a God who would take an innocent child's life," she went on. "I never go to church any more, and I've lost all interest in religion."

"I'm sorry to hear that," I said. "When my youngest daughter came down with an incurable illness, I found that I needed God more than ever. Sickness, accidents, and other tragedies are all part of this life."

Before I could say another word, Barbara snapped, "I'm really not interested in religion, and I'd rather not talk about it." Then she brightened. "I am remarried, though, to a wonderful man. Cal and I have three children together. He's a Christian Scientist, but I don't buy that line."

We played tennis together from time to time, and neither of us referred to that conversation. I prayed for Barb whenever she came to mind but felt that since she had made it plain that she didn't want to hear what I had to say about God, it would be wrong to push.

One day I heard that Barbara had been operated on, and the doctor had found cancer. She seemed to recover quite well and was soon back playing tennis with an air of confidence, and certainly showing no sign of self-pity. I still was concerned but did not feel free to talk with her about the Lord.

About a year after Barb's surgery, my friend Marge called. "Barb's in the hospital again. She went in because she's having a lot of pain. I'm afraid they've discovered more cancer."

For days I debated with myself about calling Barbara. I would wake up in the middle of the night, thinking about her. Then I would pray for wisdom and guidance as to what to do. Finally, since I couldn't get her out of my thoughts, I took this as from the Lord. After further prayer, I called her. "Do you remember the talk we had a couple of years ago?" I asked.

"I most certainly do."

"Barb," I said, "would you be willing to get together? I have something to share with you—something too good to keep to myself. Will you hear me out?"

"Well—"

"If, afterwards, you're not interested, I'll never broach the subject again."

She hesitated but finally consented to see me.

I went to her house, knowing she might be a little nervous. She was dealing with an emotional issue—her cancer; and I was dealing with an eternal issue—her salvation. I knew she would resist being pushed, so I started telling her about some of the troubled people I had met over the years. I told her how they came to Christ.

"I once met a woman, named Evelyn, in a swimming pool. She was there because of severe back damage. She confided in me that she felt her prayers hit the ceiling and that God didn't hear her. And, you know, Barb, Evelyn's problem was not only her back but a heart condition before God. She needed to come to God through Christ. As we sat by the pool, Evelyn prayed and confessed her sin of leaving Jesus Christ out of her life."

"Well," Barb admitted, "I'm just like Evelyn. You might not believe it, but I've been trying to pray. But my prayers seem hollow and empty."

"Would you like to talk to God?" I asked.

"But I don't know how," she cried as tears ran down her face.

I helped Barb see that when she prayed, she could not bypass Jesus Christ, who had died on the cross for her sins. In order to get to God, she had to come through his Son Jesus. And she did!

"Lord Jesus," she prayed, "I confess my rejection of you. I need you and ask you to come into my life and to forgive my sins. Thank you for dying on the cross for me." When she looked up, a radiant smile broke through her tears.

Six months later, Barbara had finished four of a series of basic Bible-study books. She met other believers and enjoyed fellowship with them. Recently she came to visit and, while I was preparing some food, she remarked, "You know, Nellie, if I hadn't become ill with cancer, I probably would never have come to know the Lord."

Barbara and many friends prayed she would be restored to health.

"I want to live to honor the Lord," she said one day. "But if God doesn't choose to let me recover, I'm ready to do his will."

God did choose to take her home to be with himself. But through her death, her husband, Cal, came to know the Lord. I had the privilege of praying with Barb two hours before God called her home. It was at that time that Cal confessed his faith in Jesus Christ as his Savior.

I had just arrived home from the hospice when the phone rang. It was Cal's voice saying, "Barb's been healed at last. She's with her Maker."

Reflection

Barbara had a real problem coping with the tragedy of her son's death. Job 5:7 is so true: "Yet man is born to trouble as surely as sparks fly upward." But the words of Jesus that Paul quotes in 2 Corinthians 12:9 are just as true: "My grace is sufficient for you, for my power is made perfect in weakness." What security we bring people when we tell them that neither they nor their loved ones will perish when they trust Christ as their personal Savior (John 3:16).

And, like Barbara, with some people you must simply wait and wait and wait until they are ready. With a cancer victim, it would seem to be natural to push, because we don't know how much time that person will have. But knowing *when* to present the cross will come as we ask and pray. Prayer is an essential part of evangelism. It is the cord that hooks us up to God's lifeline. Our part is to bring sinners into the immediate presence of the Savior—to bring them face-to-face with the Lord, so that he can press his claims on them and draw them to himself.

In John 12:32 the Lord Jesus said, "But I, when I am lifted up from the earth, will draw all men to myself." It is our business to tell others about him. It is his business to draw people to himself. It is only when we try to "touch the glory"—to put our own imprint on this holy transaction, to witness in the strength of our carnal religiosity—that things fall apart. Salvation is of the Lord. It is his, not ours.

We play our part by knowing the Lord and his Word, walking in obedience, praying faithfully, and speaking and acting in love.

18

Beyond Redemption

ost of the people I pass on Ocean Boulevard are fast walkers. I try to walk fast, too. It's my daily health project. But Sam is a slow walker. He just trudges along. He never smiles or says "Hello" but just looks down at the ground. Sam is quite a contrast to the rest of the walkers, all of whom are very friendly.

I had seen him several years in a row on my brief trips to Florida. One year we spent five months in Highland Beach because of my father's illness. It bothered me to pass this man, day after day, and not even get a smile from him when I passed.

I was able to get Sam's attention one day, though. I simply stopped and talked. "I've seen you walking down Ocean Boulevard for several years now," I said. "How far do you walk?"

"I walk seven miles every day, come rain or shine," he answered, with a note of pride in his voice. "It takes me all morning, but it gives me something to do."

"Do you have any other projects?"

"I play bridge with my friends a couple of times a week. I've done a lot of traveling, and I read a lot. Right now, I'm reading a book on the problems of apartheid in South Africa. I'm also into Dante, Virgil, and Homer."

"Have you ever read the Bible?" I asked Sam.

"Oh, yes, a couple of times."

"That's my favorite book," I said. "It has the answer to life. I read it every day, and it's always fresh and new. I find it very exciting."

"I can see that you do. But me, I'm beyond redemption."

"Why do you say that?"

"I just know I am."

"But God doesn't turn anyone away who truly seeks him," I prompted.

He laughed. "I have a friend who's a nun. She says she prays for me every day. If *she* can't convert me, I'm sure you can't."

"Only God can convert you, but I'll put you on my prayer list. I'll see you again. Bye-bye." We then walked off in opposite directions.

The next time I saw Sam, he actually smiled and greeted me.

"How are you coming along with your reading?" I asked.

"I'm still at it." He mentioned again the books he was reading.

"Have you read the Book of Romans in the Bible?" I asked.

"Probably, but I don't remember what it's about."

"How about reading the first two chapters? I'd be interested to know what you think."

"I'll have to finish my other reading first," he said.

A week passed before I was able to get back to my walking routine and see Sam again.

"Haven't seen you for a while," he said.

"My father is failing fast. My sister and my husband and I take turns caring for him. He wakes up at night, and one of us has to be there for him."

"I'm sorry about your father. Is he going to die?"

"I don't think he has very long in this life, but he wants to go home to be with the Lord. I heard him pray this the other day. He said, 'Oh, mighty God, have mercy on me, an old man, and take me home to be with you. I love you, Lord Jesus.'"

"Do you think God heard him?" Sam wondered.

"Oh, absolutely."

Then Sam said, "I've talked to leading theologians all over the world, and none of them can answer my questions."

"What is so hard that they can't answer?"

He looked at me with a condescending smile and said, "Lady, if theologians can't answer my questions, I don't think you can."

"Try me," I suggested.

"Okay. You tell me how God could hear *me* pray—I, who am just a speck among millions and millions of people. It's impossible and ridiculous to even imagine such a thing."

"Sam, you've told me that you do a lot of traveling and that you have friends in Europe that you keep in contact with. Have you ever talked to anyone overseas by phone?"

"Sure, lots of times."

"You mean to tell me," I continued, "that you can pick up an instrument, dial a few numbers, and talk to a person who is thousands of miles away in a matter of minutes? That's impossible and absolutely ridiculous!" I said with a bit of teasing in my voice. "Isn't God—who made us—greater than man?"

"Well, I suppose so."

"Think about it, Sam. By the way, my husband and I will be heading for Michigan shortly. Maybe, when we get back, you'll have had time to read the first two chapters of Romans—unless you're afraid to read them."

"I'm not afraid," he said.

"Okay, then prove it. I'll see you in about seven months."

He laughed and waved good-bye.

Seven months later, Sam was still walking Ocean Boulevard. He was friendly when we met, so I was surprised when he said, "I read the Book of Romans, but I don't want to talk about it."

"I'm disappointed," I said. "I was hoping we could have a good discussion." I thought perhaps he was disturbed by what he had read. But I was glad he had read it, since God's Word is powerful and will do its work in time.

The next few days, as I passed Sam, I smiled and greeted him but didn't stop to talk. Then, one morning, I saw him walking a couple of blocks ahead of me. Since he was a slow walker, it didn't take me long to catch up. He seemed happy to see me and became very talkative. He talked about the Iranian situation and how the press was trying to "crucify the President." Then he talked about taxes and stocks and bonds, and I found him very interesting and knowledgeable. I learned a lot.

Finally he got a bit agitated and said, "I'm a very prejudiced person. I can't help it. I'm really very prejudiced." He kept repeating himself.

"Are you prejudiced against the Jewish people, for example?" I asked.

He looked at me and laughed. "I'm a Jew myself, but I do think they are stupid at times. Let me tell you what happened the other day, Nellie. I was playing bridge with my friends when they started to talk about former President Nixon. They tore him apart. They had nothing good to say about him and didn't give him credit for anything he had done. Then they started talking about King David, saying what a wonderful king he had been for Israel. They praised him to the skies. Now, how could they be so stupid? Why, David was a murderer. There's no comparison between what he did and Nixon's wrongdoings. I got up and left my friends. I couldn't stand hearing them talk."

"There's a difference though," I said. "You see, David repented. He was truly sorry for his sins. He actually agonized over them and everybody knew that. That's the difference. God knew his heart and forgave him. After that, David lived to honor God. In fact, God even called him a man after his own heart."

"How's David going to get punished for his sins?"

"David suffered remorse for his sin. He confessed his sin and was forgiven. You see, God looks at the attitude of our hearts. We can never fool him. You remember how in the Old Testament an animal had to be brought to the priest periodically as a sacrifice for the people's sin? The animal—a lamb or a ram—had to be perfect. The blood of the animal was sprinkled on the altar to make atonement for the Israelites. It was a covering for their sin."

"Yes, I know all about that," Sam agreed.

"The New Testament explains that Jesus Christ offered himself as a sacrifice for our sins. He was and is the Perfect Lamb who takes away our sin if we come to him and repent. Just as in the Old Testament the animal was the substitute for the sinner, so in the New Testament Jesus Christ is the substitute. The Bible says, 'He who knew no sin became sin for us.'"

"Jews don't sacrifice animals any more though," he said.

"I know. Jesus Christ was the final sacrifice. There's no need for any more sacrifices. He paid the ultimate price."

"Well, that's interesting. That's what you believe, huh?"

"Well, it's time for me to turn in," I said. "I enjoy these talks. Hope you do, too."

He smiled and continued his walk, and the next couple of days we just said "Hi" in passing. Then one morning, when I had reached the point where I turn around and walk back to my apartment, I heard a voice: "Wait and I'll walk with you." It was Sam. I was glad to see him.

"I have a present for you," I said, as I pulled from my shoulder bag a thin book called *The Reason Why*, by Robert A. Laidlaw. "With the way your mind works, I think you'll enjoy the way the author handles the arguments you come up with."

Sam seemed pleased and took the book. "Thanks. I'll read it."

Then he started to talk about taxes and investments. I listened and learned. At the same time, I waited for a crack to open in the door to his heart.

"My son is an attorney in New York," he said. "He's in business for himself. I told him that if he wanted to make money, he needed to know that there is no right, no wrong, and no justice. You do what you have to, and you'll get along in this world. And, you know, he's doing just great."

"I can't buy that philosophy," I said. "My son is an attorney, too. He has a strong sense of right and wrong and also has compassion for people. He was once doing some legal work for a migrant worker in his area. He knew the man couldn't afford large legal fees, so he charged him one dollar. The man was grateful and Tim, my son, was glad to help a fellowman in need."

"That's not being a good American," Sam said.

"What do you mean?"

Sam laughed and said, "Haven't you heard the philosophy of the old West? 'Don't do unto others as you would want them to do unto you.'" He admitted later that he was pulling my leg, and yet it appeared that he believed in looking out for Number One. "Now, here's something I've asked several people," he said, "but I'm not sure I've asked you. God is omnipotent. He knows everything, right?"

"That's right."

"God has also given man free will, right?"

"That's right," I agreed.

"Then how come he tempts people to do evil?"

"Yes, you've asked me that before. You must have forgotten my answer. You see, God doesn't tempt. Satan tempts. God tests. It's no different with your children. You would never tempt them or lure them to do evil. But you might *test* them to see if they can be trusted and if they've learned the things you've taught them."

"I see," Sam said, thoughtfully.

"By the way," I said, "you're talking about God. I thought you told me you were an atheist."

"No, I'm not an atheist. I believe in a supreme being."

"I'm glad for that," I said. "It makes as much sense to say there is no God or Creator as it does to say the watch you're wearing came into existence by itself."

"Yeah," Sam said.

I had found my talks with Sam very interesting. Three years earlier, he had told me twice as we were walking that he was an atheist. Yet, this day, he said he believed in a supreme being. I knew that God was working in him and that God was able to open Sam's heart.

Before he left, I said, "By the way, some time ago you told me you didn't mind going to hell because you would be with your friends. I thought I should tell you that the Bible says you would be cast into outer darkness and would not see your friends—ever."

"I don't believe the Bible."

I patted his arm and said teasingly, "Not yet, Sam."

He laughed as I turned to enter my apartment.

Reflection

I will probably see Sam again and again if God spares us. My job is to be a faithful witness and to be available to the Lord. We have a great God who is in control of all things, but it was important that I have answers for Sam. It was important that I knew the Word of God and could remind him of the atonement from both Old and New Testaments.

As witnesses, we must be transparent, open, sensitive, responsive. The minute we give the impression that we are tricky, we lose our credibility and our opportunity to bring someone to Christ. Answer with Scripture whenever appropriate. To do that, you must be a steady memorizer.

19

Idols on the Wall

*L*et me help you carry the groceries," my husband said as he greeted me at the door. "I'm starved. Hope you plan to have something good for dinner."

"Before I prepare something to eat, I have to tell you about the wall hanging I saw today. In fact, I brought it home—on approval, of course. It's in the trunk of the car, if you'd like to get it."

"Tell me about it while you fix dinner. I'll put the groceries away."

I was so excited I had a hard time concentrating on what I was doing. "Well, I saw this beautiful oriental rug at the import store on Woodward Ave. It will be just perfect for the living room."

We had been looking several months for the appropriate wall hanging for this particular room. I felt I had found it and hoped my husband would like it as well as I did.

I looked at him to see what his reaction would be. I couldn't tell, so I went on. "I talked to the manager, and he said I could take the rug home on approval. All I had to do was to sign a paper saying it was in my possession. They had other rugs too, but not nearly as nice as the one I brought home."

"Okay," he said, "but let's eat first. Then we'll take a look at it."

I was sure he would like it once he'd seen it. I ate my dinner hurriedly. I felt like a kid with a new toy.

"Why don't we go out for a hot-fudge sundae before we look at your prize?" Paul said with a twinkle in his eyes. He knew how much I liked hot-fudge sundaes but he also knew that was not important to me right then.

"Come on now, stop your teasing."

We hung the rug on the wall in a temporary fashion, and Paul seemed pleased. "It certainly goes well with the colors in the room. I like the oriental figures in it too."

"Can we buy it?" I asked.

"If you like it—go ahead and get it."

I could hardly wait until the next day. The carpet company was the first errand on my agenda.

The manager greeted me with a smile. "How did your husband like the wall hanging?" he asked.

"He liked it very much and said I could get it."

"By the way," the manager said, "I have papers that give the background of where the rug came from and the dynasty it represents. It tells quite a story."

"Now that will make it quite a conversation piece," I said. "I'm eager to get back home so my husband can hang it."

It had been a long time since I'd gotten such a lovely piece for our house. It would be the finishing touch for our new home. As my husband was preparing to hang the rug a bit more permanently, he said, "Read the papers that came with it. Let's see what kind of a story we will be able to tell our friends when they come to visit."

I eagerly started to read. "The figures on the rug represent five Chinese *idols*..." my voice trailed off into nothingness. "*Idols!* Who wants idols on the walls?" I asked. Then as if in defense I said, "But those idols don't mean a thing to us. We don't worship them."

"But, Nellie, that wall hanging is making a statement in our home. Do we want it to be about idols? And if our friends ask us what the figures on the rug are, what would you say? Would you feel comfortable telling them they are idols?"

I knew he was right but I was angry at the salesman. *If he hadn't given me those papers everything would have been just fine*, I thought.

I knew what I had to do but I wasn't happy about it. I reluctantly brought it back. In its place I bought another rug, very nice, but it couldn't compare with the oriental one.

When I got home, I noticed Paul was doing some calligraphy. He looked as though he was ready to frame it. "What are you doing?" I asked.

"As I was thinking about the oriental rug," he said, "it occurred to me, we should have a statement of faith in our home—something that represents *our* faith. Since this is close to the Fourth of July and everyone is celebrating the Declaration of *Independence* why don't we celebrate our *dependence* on God? Look, what do you think of it?"

I read:

Declaration of Dependence

Having been adopted by the most high and holy God into his family, through his Son who gave his life to redeem us from destruction, we hereby declare our desire to submit to the loving authority of Jesus Christ in all matters of faith and practice.

Because of who he is,

Paul E. Pickard
Nellie Pickard

"I'd like us both to sign it," he said.

"I agree. That will be our statement of faith for our home." I knew it was the right thing to do.

Our Declaration of Dependence was hung in the foyer of our home, where it can be easily seen by anyone who enters.

I was pleased with the plaque, but every once in a while I'd get a hankering for that beautiful oriental rug. I was still miffed at the salesman for giving me the papers telling me about the idols!

About six months later we had two young men come to clean our carpets. One of the men kept looking at our "Declaration of Dependence." He seemed a little hesitant; then as he shifted from one foot to the other, he said, "I like that." He then looked at the floor and repeated, "Yeah, I like that."

"It's our Declaration of Dependence on God. Do you have faith in God? Do you know Jesus Christ as your Savior?"

"Yeah, it just happened last week," he said nervously.

"Tell me about it," I said.

"Well, you see, it was like this. I was on drugs. I mean I was really gone on drugs. Life was worth nothing. My friend came to my rescue and told me how I could be forgiven of my sins. He introduced me to Jesus Christ. I asked him to come into my heart and forgive me. I believe in him now. That's why I like that [pointing to the plaque] 'cause that's what I want to do—depend on him."

I don't have a hankering for the wall hanging anymore. God showed me something better: doing that which honors him.

The interesting point is, I thought the oriental rug would be the conversation piece but it could never have stimulated the discussion that was started over the simple motto declaring our faith in God. Some have commented, "I would like something like that in my home."

Reflection

Many times since then I have thought, *If I could see as God sees, I'd make better choices in life.* But then I realize that's not living by faith. We must choose the best way in life while we have the chance to do so. I didn't deserve it but God allowed me to see the result of the more excellent way.

I now realize that my problem wasn't so much the idols on the rug—as it was the rug itself. It had become an idol. I wanted something I shouldn't have.

That night I prayed, "Oh, Lord, thank you for running interference for me, and causing the salesman to show us the papers on the oriental rug. Thank you for the wisdom you have given Paul and for his spiritual leadership in our home. I am so blessed."

20

Trusting God

I was surprised to see Marja, one of the officers of the bank, standing in line. She was waiting to get to the teller's window like the rest of the customers. I teased her a bit and asked her why such an important person had to take her turn to be waited on. "Why don't you go right up to the window?" I suggested. "After all, your time is valuable."

"Our customers' time is valuable too. I don't want to take advantage of them."

I liked this woman right away. *What an attitude*, I thought.

I was rather excited that day. My friends Ruth and Neil Duff had just had an autographing party for me. I had a number of checks in my hand ready to be deposited. Marja noticed and smiled.

"These checks will help pay for my new word processor, reams of paper I use, and the cost of having photocopies made."

"The word processor must be a great help to you," she commented. "What is the name of your book?"

"*What Do You Say When . . .*"

"That's an interesting title. What's it about?"

"It's stories about people I've met who don't know how to be in the family of God. I tell them what God's requirements are. The Bible is my authority, since that's the Word of God—not my church nor my opinions."

"Where can I get a copy?" she asked.

"It won't be in the bookstores for another two weeks but the publisher sent me some copies. I have them in my car."

"Would you be willing to sell me a copy?"

"I'd be happy to," I replied.

"Do you suppose I could have two? I'd like to send one to my father."

I went to the car and brought back the books. "The next time I see you," I said, "I'd appreciate it if you would give me an appraisal of the book. Let me know what you think of the message in it."

"Okay, I promise."

At the end of the week I had occasion to return to the bank. When I saw Marja, I walked up to her desk and asked, "Have you had a chance to browse through my book yet?"

"Both my husband and I have read it. The book has revolutionized our lives. I'll tell you about it if I get a chance the next time you come in," she answered as a customer approached her.

I saw her a week later. She motioned for me to come and sit down next to her desk. "Let me tell you what happened," she said in an excited tone of voice. "A few weeks ago, I was feeling very discouraged and very much alone. My husband, Ron, who is a diabetic, had been suffering with an ulcerated foot for almost three years. He has gone to several doctors but his foot would not heal. He has experienced many ups and downs with fevers and at times serious infections. The best the doctors could do was to keep the foot from being amputated. I was very upset, and began to ask, 'What next, Lord? Are you really there?' When you came into the bank, I was at a very low point in my life.

"After Ron and I read your book we realized other people had problems too, but God was always there. This encouraged us to put our trust in God. We then realized that for three years God had allowed Ron to keep his foot. It caused us to give thanks. We now want him to be in control of our lives."

I wasn't absolutely sure if Marja knew what it meant to trust Jesus Christ for her salvation, or if she understood what it was all about.

I then asked her, "Marja, have you ever accepted Jesus Christ as your personal Savior?"

"Oh, yes, I have, but I had allowed my problems to get in the way and lost touch with God. I wondered if he really cared about us, but now I know he does.

"We don't know what the future holds for us," she said, "but we're leaving it all in his hands. We are sure God has a purpose for allowing this to come into our lives. We know him better now, and things are just fine."

Marja's personality has changed. She is radiant. The love of Christ is evident in her life. One day she explained, "As I continue to read the Word and increasingly trust the Lord, everything seems to fall into place the way it should. Things seem to work out much better when God is in control. In the back of my mind, I knew this to be true, but the book brought it all into focus. I am so thankful for God's perfect wisdom in bringing this into my life during a 'valley' of my life. I hope I might spread the joy of the Lord by sharing this with others. I need four more books if you can spare them," she said. "We have some friends we want to encourage." I was delighted with the change in her life.

About a week later as I was transacting some business, Marja came up to the teller's window and said, "When you're finished come over to my desk. I have some very good news to tell you."

She seemed so excited. I wondered what it was all about. "What's up?" I asked, as I sat down near her desk.

"Ron has an appointment at the University of Minnesota's Wound Healing Clinic. He is to try a new miracle cure, one with a ninety-five percent success rate so far. What they will do is extract blood from Ron, mix it with a new drug, and apply it on the affected area of his foot. The healing process then begins. We are to be there on Saturday. I'm so excited, I can hardly wait. God is so good. The best part, Nellie, is that both Ron and I decided to trust the Lord before we heard about the cure."

I had read about the cure in the newspaper that very day and had hoped it would be available for Ron. I was delighted when I heard an appointment had already been set up.

Marja and her husband left for Minnesota the following Saturday, and in less than a week Ron was allowed to come back home. The rest of the treatments were done by his local doctor. Marja showed me pictures of her husband's foot as the healing progressed. The first pictures looked like a large, raw, T-bone steak. The last ones were of a completely normal foot. Success was 100 percent.

The last time I saw Marja, she and her husband were preparing to drive to Washington State, where her parents live—their first vacation in several years. Then after they return Ron will be allowed to go back to work. It had been a long illness. I rejoiced with her at the goodness of the Lord in their lives.

Reflection

Marja and Ron's attitude was not much different from the average Christian's. We get discouraged when we have problems. We pray and expect instant answers. Sometimes God does answer immediately; other times we must wait until his perfect work is done in us. It's a process that will bring rewards if we learn to trust him with our lives. I'm reminded of Romans 8:35, which says: "Who shall separate us from the love of Christ? Shall trouble or hardship or persecution or famine or nakedness or danger or sword?" Also verses 37–39:

> No, in all these things we are more than conquerors through him who loved us. For I am convinced that neither death nor life, neither angels nor demons, neither the present nor the future, nor any powers, neither height nor depth, nor anything else in all creation, will be able to separate us from the love of God that is in Christ Jesus our Lord.

21

One Step Forward, Two Steps Back

I've got so much to do today, I barely know where to start," I remarked to my husband.

"Make a list and then cross off each item as you complete it," he said.

I knew what his answer would be. He's an engineer and always well organized; but he's also very patient and generally goes along with my strange ways. He knows I'll eventually learn.

"What I really wanted to do first was give my hair a good treatment. I was sure I had some conditioner left but I can't find it. I'll have to go to the drugstore and get some. I'll never get anything done at this rate," I complained.

As usual, Paul came to my rescue. "Let me help you look," he said. "I know it's hard to find things around here. Being in Florida part of the year can pose a problem at times. You may have left it in Michigan."

We both looked in the usual places without success.

On the way to the store I began planning my day. I had some thoughts in my head that needed to be transferred to paper. I needed to make a tape. The house needed touching up, and then there was the banquet in the evening. I wondered if I would ever get these things done.

When I arrived at the drugstore I discovered it wouldn't be open for another half hour. There I go spinning my wheels again. *Why didn't I check on the time the store opened?* I thought.

Feeling utterly frustrated, I decided to wait. I'd only waste more time if I returned later.

While I stood *patiently* waiting, a woman walked up and asked, "Isn't the store open yet?"

"No," I answered, "not until nine o'clock."

"This town!" she said in a disgusted voice. "Things take forever to get going."

"Where are you from?" I asked.

"Actually I've lived here for twenty-two years, but I'm from Bloomfield Hills, Michigan."

"That's interesting. I'm from Birmingham."

We discovered we lived only a few miles apart.

"Are you planning to move to Florida?" she asked.

"Not for a while. It's a hard decision to make. My son and his family live about eighty miles from us. We get to see them oftener when we are in Michigan. And we attend the church where I was raised. We get excellent Bible teaching, which means a lot to me. It's really the only authority we have for our belief in God."

"What is the name of your church?" she asked.

"Highland Park Baptist. It's in Southfield. Did you attend church when you lived in Michigan?" I asked.

"Yes, I attended a Presbyterian church," she said.

"Well, whether it's Baptist or Presbyterian, as long as the Bible is the authority, it's pretty safe."

She made no comment but I sensed she wasn't sure about what I had just said.

"You know," I said, "I meet people all over who don't know how to be in the family of God. I love to tell them what the Bible has to say about that. In fact I just recently wrote a book about people I have met and shared the gospel with. I got acquainted with a woman in a swimming pool who confided in me that she didn't know how to pray. She needed to talk to God but didn't know how. Another young woman was suffering from guilt and needed God's forgiveness. Many people are looking for answers to life."

"What is the name of your book?" she asked. "I need to get it right away."

"Why do you need to get it right away?" I asked.

"Because yesterday my sister was diagnosed as having terminal cancer. She doesn't know it yet. Her husband died a couple of years ago. He was an atheist, and my sister hasn't gone to church for years. I need to read that book to her."

"I have some books in the car. I'll go and get you one."

Just then the store opened. "I'll go and order my prescription. I'll be at the back of the store," she said.

When I returned, I heard the pharmacist say, "Your prescription will be ready in about twenty minutes."

"Let's sit down and talk while you're waiting," I suggested.

"Can you afford the time?" she asked. (I had told her about my busy schedule for the day.)

"I'll take the time," I answered.

Yes, I had plenty to do that day but I sensed that this woman had a need greater than any of mine. This was now my priority for the day.

"By the way, my name is Nellie. What is your name?" I asked.

"My name is Florence. I'm just wondering was it coincidence that we met today? I feel as though this was meant to be."

"I call these meetings 'God's divine appointments.' I believe he arranges them. Both of us were impatient about the store's opening so late, and yet God knew all about it. Rather amazing, isn't it?"

I discovered that even though Florence had attended church for many years, I didn't know if she had a relationship with Jesus Christ.

"Florence," I asked, "do you believe that you are a sinner and that God sent his Son Jesus Christ to die for you?"

"Yes, I know that I'm a sinner."

"Have you ever received Jesus Christ as your Savior from the guilt and penalty of sin?"

"No, I've never done that," she said with her head bowed.

"Would you like to do that?" I asked.

"Yes, I would." Then she turned to me and asked, "Will you help me pray?"

"When you pray, it isn't so much the words you say that are important; it's the attitude of your heart that God sees."

I helped her and she prayed. "Lord, I confess I'm a sinner. I've pretty much done things my own way. I want to receive Jesus as my Savior. I thank you for accepting me into your family and making me your child. Thank you for forgiving all my sin. Help me to walk in your way. In Jesus' name I pray, *Amen*."

"Florence, you are now in the family of God. In one way it was fairly simple. You acknowledged you were a sinner and received Jesus Christ as your Savior. Isn't it incredible when we realize the price Jesus Christ paid for our salvation? We deserved to die for our own sins, but Jesus opted to be our substitute. He paid the penalty, and we went scot-free. To me that is overwhelming."

I gave her a booklet that gives the basics of salvation so she could understand what had transpired that day. I also suggested she start reading the Gospel of John.

I knew Florence would be completely tied up with the needs of her sister for the time being, so I didn't try to make arrangements for Bible studies. I felt we could keep in touch by phone.

I went home very excited about my experience. I could hardly wait to tell Paul. I was able to get my radio taping done, put my house in order, get some writing done, give my hair a good treatment, and had a wonderful time at the banquet that evening. Somehow everything fell into place!

The following morning I opened the door of the medicine cabinet in the bathroom. I couldn't believe my eyes. There it was, the bottle of conditioner I had been looking for! There were only a few items in the cabinet. How could I have missed it? How could Paul have missed it? He has eagle eyes. He doesn't miss a thing. I called my husband and said, "I want to show you something. You won't believe it. Look." I opened the door of the medicine cabinet and showed him the bottle of conditioner. "Why didn't we see that yesterday?" he asked. Then he added, "I guess the Lord wanted you to be at the drugstore so you could meet the need of a hungry heart." He gave me a big hug and said, "Isn't God amazing?"

I'm back in Michigan now, and while talking to Florence on the phone one day, she said, "I'll never get over the way God arranged for us to meet in front of the drugstore. It met a tremendous need in my life. Most of my time is taken up with caring for my sister but someone from hospice comes twice a week and that is a great help. Things are pretty much under control now."

Reflection

Every once in a while I picture myself dashing to the store that March morning in Florida. I didn't want to waste a minute. I was so concerned about the heavy schedule I had imposed on myself. I hadn't taken time to read or pray before I left. I figured I would do that while sitting under the hairdryer. Not a very good way to start the day. And yet in spite of myself, God used my frustrations to remind me that he, God, is in control of my life. I love it!

> Oh, the depth of the riches of the
>   wisdom and knowledge of
>   God!
>   How unsearchable his judgments,
>   and his paths beyond tracing out!
> "Who has known the mind of the
>   Lord?"
>   Romans 11:33–34

22

Being Ignored

Paul and I were house hunting. We had seen some townhouses advertised in the paper and decided to check them out. We wanted to see if they were as nice as the artist's sketch.

I was impressed with the beauty of the saleswoman assigned to us. Her dark hair and eyes contrasted with her flawless light skin. Her perfect figure caused me to admire her.

I was not impressed, however, with the wiggle in her hips and shoulders when she walked. And I was not impressed when she didn't even look at me but turned to my husband and in a sultry voice asked, "And how are you today?"

I looked at Paul to get his reaction. He gave me a knowing smile. I knew he understood. "I think I'd better hang onto you," I whispered. His eyes twinkled as he smiled.

The first model we entered looked bright and cheerful. We liked the size of the rooms. Patricia, our salesperson, then asked, "Do you have any specific need as far as a home is concerned?"

"Well, yes. My wife needs a place for her word processor. She is doing some writing. A small den or alcove would do just fine."

"Oh," she said turning to me, "what do you write about?"

"I write about people who are searching for the meaning of life. Many of them have had success in the world as far as money and careers are concerned. After achieving what they went after, there is still a longing for something better. They don't find it satisfying or fulfilling. Others thought they would find fulfillment in marriage, but something was missing. I tell them about Jesus Christ, who came to give them abundant life—the Bible being my authority. I tell them what God's requirements are. I don't tell them the beliefs of a particular church or my opinion. I tell them what the Bible says since that is God's Word."

"That sounds great," she said. "Have you ever heard of Bible-town?"

"Why, yes, we are associate members. We spend our winters here in Florida and are very active in that church," I said.

"My daughter attends their school," she said. "Boca Raton Christian School. I would work my fingers to the bone so she can attend. It's really a wonderful school."

"Where do you attend church?" I asked.

She hesitated for a moment and then said, "I don't attend church." She sounded apologetic.

"That surprises me," I said. "Do you mean to tell me that you send your daughter to school to get a Christian education and yet you don't attend church at all?"

"It wouldn't do any good," she answered.

"Why?" I asked

"My priest said that when I die, I will go straight to hell."*

"Why?"

"Because of my great sin," she answered.

"But that's why Jesus Christ died—for your great sin and mine."

She shook her head in bewilderment and seemed to dismiss the subject for the time being.

We looked at a few more models and then headed back to the office.

Her mind must have been on our previous conversation because on the way back she said, "Part of my daughter's homework is to memorize Scripture. I'm learning some of the verses too. I'm also reading the Book of Proverbs. It's great. I get a lot out of it."

How can I go back to Michigan tomorrow without telling her how she can know Jesus Christ as her personal Savior? I thought.

---

*I recognize that not all priests agree with this extreme position, but Patricia's priest was emphatic about her punishment.

When we arrived at the office I turned to Patricia and asked, "Do you have five minutes to spare? I would like to tell you why Jesus Christ died on the cross and how you can have your sins forgiven."

"Yes, I can take a few minutes."

"Patricia, I don't know what your particular sin is but Jesus Christ died on the cross for that sin. He paid the ultimate penalty. In fact the Bible says in Romans 5:8 that 'God demonstrates his own love for us in this: While we were still sinners, Christ died for us.' The Bible also says in Romans 3:23: 'for all have sinned and fall short of the glory of God.' There isn't a person in the world that has met God's standards. But the good news is that God will acccpt you into his family if you confess that you are a sinner and need his son, Jesus Christ, to be your personal Savior. You must ask Jesus to be Lord of your life."

She seemed to hang on to every word I said.

"Just think, he who knew no sin became sin for you and for me. We deserved to die but he chose to become our substitute.

"You must have been living a miserable existence, thinking you were doomed to hell," I said.

"Well, even though the priest said I was going straight to hell when I die, I determined in my heart that my daughter would have a chance. That is why I'm sending her to a Christian school."

"You don't have to go to hell, Patricia. Jesus said, 'I have come that they may have life, and have it to the full' (John 10:10). He wants that for you. He wants you to trust him and believe everything he says. Hc also said, 'I am the way . . .'"

Bufore I could finish she interrupted and said, "'. . . the truth and the life. No one comes to the father except through me.' That's one of my daughter's memory verses. I learned it too."

"That's just great." I was excited. *Maybe there's a chance for Patricia*, I thought.

"We haven't talked very long," I said, "but would you be ready and willing even now to confess to God that you are a sinner, and ask Jesus Christ to be your Savior and Lord?"

"Oh, yes, if there's a chance for me, I would," she said as her voice broke.

She bowed her head ready to pray when the telephone rang. It was the front office. "We need you at the desk immediately," her boss said.

"I'll be there in two minutes," she said. She wasn't going to let this opportunity go by. She prayed, "Dear heavenly Father, I know I have sinned against you. I've gone my own independent way. Thank you for sending your Son to die on the cross for my sins. I now receive Jesus Christ as my Savior and Lord. I want you to take charge of my life. Thank you for making me a member of your family. In Jesus' name I pray . . . *Amen.*"

When she raised her head, I noticed tears in her eyes but her face was radiant. What a special moment that was. I gave her a hug. After all, we were now sisters in the Lord.

We headed for the front office. Patricia went directly to my husband and said, "I want you to know I just invited Jesus Christ into my life. I'm now a member of his family."

Reflection

If Patricia had not meant business with the Lord, she could have used that telephone call from the front office as an excuse to leave. But she proved that God's offer of salvation came first, regardless of the cost.

In a vague way Patricia knew that Jesus died on the cross for the sins of mankind, but since she had apparently been told that her sin was unforgivable, she felt she didn't have a chance with God.

I judged her mannerisms at the beginning. I didn't see her aching heart. God says that's what we do as humans. ". . . Man looks at the outward appearance, but the LORD looks at the heart" (1 Sam. 16:7). I'm glad God softened my heart toward her and helped me to see her great need. I'm also glad that God allowed me to be the instrument to lead her to Christ.

It was eight months before I saw Patricia again. One of the first things she told me was, "God has met my needs in ways I never dreamed possible. It's unbelievable."

"We have a great God, don't we?" I responded.

"Besides my other problems, I've also been divorced," she said. "How does God view divorce?"

"God hates divorce. It was his plan from the beginning that families stay together. Divorce creates a lot of problems. It divides families, fosters hatred, hurts children, and robs us of peace. Jesus came to bring peace, and he wants us to live in peace. Matthew 19:8 says that in the law of Moses, God permitted divorce because of the hardness of their hearts. We have to live with our mistakes but divorce is not the unforgivable sin," I said.

She needed to tell me her story. "I was very young when I married. My parents didn't approve. Perhaps they could see things I wasn't aware of. I didn't listen to them. I know I broke their hearts. I went ahead and married. I have so many regrets.

"My former husband is much older than I am and is from another country. Everything was great at the beginning, but then after a while he began to stay away, days at a time. I was left confused and hurt. He finally left me for other women. I was devastated. And I was already hurting because my priest told me I would go straight to hell when I die. I'm so glad God has forgiven my sin and I'm in his family. Since I accepted Christ as my Savior, he has met all of my needs. God has provided. I'm ever so grateful."

"Just think of the blessing your little girl has been in your life," I said.

"She's incredible. She's only nine years old and every semester she has received an award for her Bible memorization. I'm so proud of her. She's taught me a lot. Do you know that she would come home from school and ask, 'Mom, have you accepted Christ yet?' I had to say no because I figured it wouldn't do me any good."

"I'm glad I had a part in leading you to Christ, but your daughter sowed the seed and got you into the Scriptures. Let me tell you how Jesus prayed once. 'I praise you, Father, Lord of heaven and earth, because you have hidden these things from the wise and learned, and revealed them to little children. Yes, Father, for this was your good pleasure' (Matt. 11:25–26). God uses everyone who is available to him, even little children."

23

Facing Surgery Alone

f I could get out of the car and walk straight into the operating room, it wouldn't be so bad. I couldn't convince my doctor that it was a good idea. It's the waiting around that gets to me. So, like an obedient child, I went through the proper procedures.

My husband parked the car and met me in the admitting room. I tried to relax, but all I could think of was my pending operation.

The woman sitting across the room from me seemed to be in a worse condition than I. Her nervousness was more obvious than mine. At least I thought so.

"I guess this isn't your favorite place either," I commented. We laughed, and I think it helped both of us.

"Are you waiting for your husband?" I asked.

"No, I don't expect to see him anymore."

I was puzzled. It must have shown on my face because she then said, "I'm to have a cancer operation. My husband can't handle it, so he said he'd drop me off at the hospital, and that would be the end of it for us."

I was flabbergasted. "You mean he's leaving you?" I asked.

She put her head in her hands and began to weep. "That's what he said."

(God certainly knew how to get my attention away from myself!)

"Would you like me to come and see you after we get settled in our rooms?"

"That would mean a lot to me," she said. "Maybe we could talk and I won't feel quite so alone."

I began to count my blessings and asked God to show me how to help this forsaken woman.

I soon discovered that my new friend, Betty, had a room just a few doors from mine. I believe that it was the Lord's provision. It made it so convenient for me to visit her.

After the nurses and interns had taken their blood samples and asked the proper questions, I walked down the hall to her room.

"I wondered if you would really come," she said. "Since your husband is with you, I didn't know. I thought you might have changed your mind. He seems so nice. You are so lucky," she said wistfully.

"Yes, God has blessed me with a good husband, and I certainly am thankful."

We chatted for a while about our operations—both of us anxious to have them over. Then she told me about her little boy. A neighbor was keeping him for a few days.

"He's too young to visit me here in the hospital, but if things go well, I will at least have him to go home to. He's a great comfort to me." She didn't complain, just stated the facts about her situation. It was hard for her to talk about her husband, so I didn't probe.

"Do you have a church family at all?" I asked. "What I really mean is do you attend church anyplace?"

"No, I haven't attended church in years. My husband didn't care to go, so I stayed home with him. I did try to please him. I just didn't do a good job." She then turned to look at me and said, "I'm so glad you came. I really don't expect to have any visitors while I'm here. It's not fun being alone."

"I've put my trust in Jesus Christ," I said, "because he promised to never leave us nor forsake us. If you will put your trust in him and receive him as your Savior, he'll stay close by. You will never be alone. By the way, I brought a book along I'd like you to have. I think you'll enjoy reading it, and I believe it will help you.

"If you will allow me, I'd like to share my family with you. I have three children, and they plan to visit me. My oldest daughter, Karen, will be returning to Wheaton College soon but you'll get to meet her. Tim will be starting at Michigan State, and Greta is still in high school. In a few days, if you're feeling up to it, my husband will check on you to see if you would like some company. I know you'll love them, and I'm sure they'll love you too," I said.

The next few days were just plain rotten for me. I felt miserable. I did my share of moaning and groaning and waited for the nurse to get me some pain pills. But the pain soon passed. My operation was major but not earth shattering. I began to feel better and wondered how my new friend was. I discovered that she had had a rough time but the doctors felt they had gotten all the cancer. The future looked brighter for her.

When the children heard that Betty's husband had left her they were sad.

"How could he leave his wife when she needed him so desperately?" my daughter Karen asked. "How can a husband be so cruel? I know Daddy would never do that."

"Not everyone is blessed with a Christian husband and father," I replied. "Knowing Jesus Christ makes all the difference in the world."

The children were so used to the kindness of their father that they found this situation incredible.

They took some of the flowers I had received from my friends and brought them to her. She couldn't get over their loving ways. I was proud of them.

My hospital stay lasted about ten days, and I spent the next few weeks recuperating. Then it was time to outfit the children for school. Because of the busyness of life, I lost track of my new friend.

At Christmastime, two years later, I received a card. I couldn't decipher the name of the sender. And because there was no return address on the envelope, I had no idea where it came from. The following Christmas I received another card. It was again difficult to read the name. This time I called the telephone operator and told her my dilemma. "Would you be willing to help me decipher a name?" We tried several combinations, and finally she said, "Let me try this number." I couldn't believe a telephone operator would be so patient. She must have been sent by the Lord. When the phone rang and the woman answered, I told her my name and that I had received a Christmas card two years in a row. "I'm embarrassed to say that I don't recognize the name."

"Don't you remember me? You led me to Christ in the hospital through the book you gave me that explained how I could be in God's family. I accepted Christ as my Savior, and my son and I now attend church regularly. We even help at the church. We take care of the flower beds around the church. We love it."

Amazing, I thought. "I would love to see you. Would you be able to come and have lunch at my home? I want you to meet some of my Christian friends. I want them to share in the goodness of God. I didn't feel that I had done a good job in sharing the gospel with you, but God overruled and used the book I gave you."

"It was the love you and your family showed me that made me want what you had. I have discovered for myself that it's Jesus Christ who makes the difference."

She came for lunch. It was exciting to see my Christian friends seated around the dining-room table getting acquainted with this new member of the family of God. It was a great day of rejoicing.

"You told me something important that has stayed with me. It has been a great comfort. You said that God would never leave me nor forsake me. I have found it to be so true. I now have wonderful security in him."

Reflection

Going to the hospital and having surgery is never fun—but God can even use an unpleasant experience to bring glory to his name. I gave her a book to read. I had no idea how effective it would be—but God used it.

I'm glad I responded to the nudge God gave me to minister to someone who had a greater need than my own.

Being an effective witness takes time and experience. If we give God what we have, he multiplies it and brings blessing out of the small things in life—like the little boy with the loaves and the fishes. It has been said before, "Little is much when God is in it." Let's give God what we have and see what he will do with it.

24

When a Salesman Intrudes

*E*verything seemed to go well that morning. The feeling of always being behind was fast fading away. I was finally catching up on my household chores. I had finished the laundry and even polished some company silver. *I'm on top of things this morning*, I thought.

I had just settled down to do some writing when the telephone rang. Since my husband wasn't home, I felt compelled to answer it. It might be an important call.

"Hello," the intruder said. "Are you Mrs. Pickard?"

"Yes, that's my name."

"How are you feeling today?"

"Just fine, thank you."

"Haven't we been having beautiful weather lately? And isn't it a beautiful day?"

I felt an attack of impatience coming on. It seemed as though my friends and I had been bombarded with solicitors calling anytime of day and night. I knew this was another such call. I wanted to hang up. A battle was going on, inside me. One part of me said, "Be polite, Nellie; he's only doing his job." The other part said, "Why doesn't he get a job that doesn't bother people?"

The better part of me finally won out, so I said as politely as was humanly possible, "I really don't have much time to chat this morning. I'm working on a manuscript. I would appreciate it if you would tell me the purpose of your call."

"I'm offering you a wonderful opportunity. We can give you a complete food service, guaranteeing you the best nutrition available anywhere. We bring everything right to the house."

"Thank you, but we won't need it," I answered.

"But nutritionally, it's the best."

"Thank you so much. My sister is a nutritionist, and she gives me all the help I need." I didn't add, "when she can get me to listen to her advice."

"Before you hang up," he said, "would you mind telling me what you're writing about?"

"Strange you should ask. That is something I always have time to talk about. I write about people with whom I have shared God's requirements to be in his family, the Bible being my authority."

"Now I find that very interesting," he said. "I just recently accepted Jesus as my Savior. You are the third person this week that has mentioned something about God. In fact, a man said to me just yesterday, 'Something good is going to happen to you today.' And it did."

"What happened?" I asked.

"I won the lottery."

I was totally unprepared for that answer. "Did you say you have accepted Jesus Christ as your Savior?" I asked.

"Yes, I have."

"Then what in the world are you doing playing the lottery?"

There was dead silence, then he said sheepishly, "I think I need a little help along that line."

"I think you do, too. Now that you've won some money are your plans to spend more and more money on the lottery, hoping to win the big one?"

"Yeah, I guess that's what I was hoping for," he answered.

"Don't you realize that all your energy, time, and thoughts are going to be consumed with winning more and more money? Now that you have accepted Christ as your Savior, don't you think you should be spending time reading the Bible? If you do that, then you will get to know God better. That is more exciting than anything money can buy. Don't you agree?"

"I see what you mean. I was pretty excited about my winnings. I guess God meant for me to talk to you today. Strange that your phone number was on my list of calls for today."

"Let me give you a good suggestion. Start reading the Gospel of John. Read a little each day, and think about what you've read during the day. It will change your entire outlook on life. It will add sparkle to your life. After all, the Bible is God's letter to us. If we seek him first he will add the things we need in life."

"Thanks again," he said before he hung up.

I put the phone back on the hook. Then I stood in the middle of the room and laughed at myself and thought, *I can't believe what just happened.* Then I prayed, "Thank you, Lord, for helping me overcome my frustration at the salesman on the telephone. I could have muffed it but you turned my weakness into a blessing. You are great and deserve all my praise. Help me never to forget that I'm your ambassador."

Reflection

I'm grateful for the restraining force of the Holy Spirit. I almost gave in to my human impulses to hang up the phone on the troublesome caller. What caused me to change my mind? It was the gentle nudge of the Spirit of God within me. He reminded me that I had made a commitment to be available to God. I needed that. I so easily forget.

I almost missed an opportunity to encourage a brother in Christ. I knew only two things about the caller. He had just accepted Jesus Christ as his Savior and he had won the lottery a few days previously. These two things are opposed to each other. They are two different mind-sets. The first one longs to know God better. The second yearns to fulfill the fleshly desire for more and more things. As it says in Matthew 6:33–34:

> But seek first his kingdom and his righteousness, and all these things will be given to you as well. Therefore do not worry about tomorrow, for tomorrow will worry about itself. Each day has enough trouble of its own.

Becoming a believer in Jesus Christ is just the first step. Maturing in the Christian life takes one step after another. There is much a new believer doesn't know. This man needs to

be discipled. He needs to get into the Word on a daily basis, so
that he will know what the will of God is for his life. Then he
will be able to distinguish between the devil's wiles and God's
best for his life.

Since the caller was a man, I did not want to go beyond what
I felt was proper. I prayed for him. I prayed that God would send
someone alongside him to encourage him in the faith and in
the study of God's Word.

I often put a P.S. on my letters, and I think this episode needs
a P.S.

I thought I had finished this chapter but decided to add
something that just happened.

I went to pick up a few needed items at the store. While waiting to pay my bill, I noticed the woman in front of me hesitate,
then she picked up one of those trashy newspapers available
at the counter. She turned around and gave me a strange smile.
It was as though she was apologizing, or that she had been
caught in the act of doing something wrong. *Interesting,* I
thought.

The headlines said, "Lucy was in contact with the dead
before she died."

"You don't believe that do you?" I asked.

"Naw, I didn't buy this paper for myself. It's for my mom.
What else is there for a sixty-seven-year-old woman to do? She
gets a big kick out of it."

"Sixty-seven! Mmm, that *is* old," I said as I chuckled to
myself. "I would think she'd enjoy reading the Bible. That's
where you find out about life after death."

"Uh, my mother reads the Bible, and I do, too."

"I'm surprised to hear that. The things you read in that paper
and the things you read in the Bible are opposed to each other.
The Bible says in Deuteronomy 18 that trying to consult the
dead is a detestable thing in God's sight."

Because the young lady in front of me didn't seem to object
to my talking (in fact she appeared to agree), I continued.
"Reading the Bible and reading those sensational newspapers
are a part of two opposite lifestyles. They just don't go together.
Then I said with a smile and in a teasing voice, "How about

telling your mom about our conversation? And don't forget to remind her of Deuteronomy 18."

"I'm going to do that," she said. "Have a good day, and it was nice chatting with you."

Romans 16:19 says: ". . . be wise about what is good, and innocent about what is evil." Philippians 4:8 says, "Finally, brothers, whatever is true, whatever is noble, whatever is right, whatever is pure, whatever is lovely, whatever is admirable—if anything is excellent or praiseworthy—think about such things." And as Paul continues, "Put these things into practice" (see v. 9).

In one day I talked to two people with the same problem. Both were toying with the devil's tools. Not knowing them personally I had no idea in which stage of growth they were. It did make me realize how important it is for Christians to be discipled and to be encouraged not only to read God's Word but also to obey it.

I continually pray that God will help me to love what he loves and hate what he hates. I want to be his faithful servant.

25

A Spouse's Unfaithfulness

"I hope Caroline shows up in class today," Joanne said. "I've called and invited her several times. Even though she says our Bible study is exactly what she needs, I sense a reluctance on her part to make a commitment to come. I'm not sure what her problem is."

"Do you think she's shy? Maybe she doesn't like coming by herself," I suggested.

"I'm not sure. I've offered to pick her up, but she doesn't want me to go out of my way. I think I'll call one of our mutual friends and invite her to our class. They live near each other. Maybe that will give her an incentive to come."

Joanne was a real asset in our Bible class. She brought several unbelievers during the course of the year. She would introduce me to her friends and leave. I often laughed to myself. I wonder if Joanne is thinking, *Now I've done my part by inviting my friends. Here, it's up to you to lead them to Christ.*

As time went on, I realized how beautifully the body of Christ worked together. Everyone did his/her part.

Joanne didn't give up on Caroline and was finally rewarded by seeing her friend come to class.

I sensed Caroline's initial insecurity but the women were so loving and friendly, that it wasn't long before she felt a part of the group.

During our discussion time one day, Caroline said, "I had wanted to come to this Bible study for a long time but I have a problem: I'm fearful of leaving the house. I don't like to be in a car alone either. I wasn't sure if I'd be able to handle being in a group, but my desire and need to study the Bible helped me to overcome my fear. I finally got the courage to come and I'm glad I'm here. I do need your prayers though."

I was surprised and pleased that she was so honest and open with the class. She was becoming more outgoing, and I was glad she was willing to take part in class prayer requests. Caroline wanted help and wasn't afraid to ask. I found her to be a most delightful person. *There's hope for her*, I thought.

She confided in me later that her problem was called *agoraphobia* (a dreadful fear of being alone in open or public places). Even though Caroline was tense at first, little by little she began to relax.

From the start I could see this new member of the class eating up the Scriptures. I wanted to talk to her about her personal relationship with Jesus Christ but didn't want to rush her. I wanted her to feel secure in the group first.

I had made a point of including the plan of salvation in our lesson. I felt when I did approach her about her relationship to Jesus Christ she would have had time to think it through and make a decision.

Since this was a neighborhood Bible study the women attending were from various backgrounds and denominations. We decided from the beginning that we would not pick at the differences in our churches' beliefs but our authority would be the Scriptures.

"Feel free to ask questions," I said, "but the answers will come from the Bible. After all it is the Word of God."

Everyone agreed but, once in a while someone would say, "But our church believes. . . ."

"Let's see what the Bible has to say about it," I replied. "After all that's God's Word, and we did agree from the start that it would be our authority."

The women who were knowledgeable in the Scripture would help by looking up the answers in their concordances. The ones who weren't familiar with the Bible soon learned where to find the answers.

I recently met a woman who had been in our class several years ago. She confided in me that she used to be confused about some of the traditions in her church. "I've learned where to find my answers. I go directly to the source of truth now. I really enjoy studying the Bible."

I was delighted. That's what Bible studies are all about—to teach the women where to go for their source of truth.

One day someone brought some religious material from Unity. It was a daily reading booklet.

"This has a lot of good things in it," the woman said. "I need to know if it's according to the Bible. What do you know about it, Nellie?"

"I do know that Unity does not believe Jesus is God," I said. "We have just been studying the Book of John and we have seen convincing proof that Jesus is indeed God in the flesh."

"Let's look at a couple of verses in the first chapter of John," I suggested. "The answer is in the very first verse. 'In the beginning was the Word, and the Word was with God, and the Word was God.' It goes on to say, 'He was with God in the beginning. Through him all things were made; without him nothing was made that has been made.' Let's skip down to the fourteenth verse. 'The Word became flesh and lived for a while among us. We have seen his glory, the glory of the one and only Son, who came from the Father, full of grace and truth.'

"If we had no other evidence in the Bible but the Book of John," I said, "we have enough proof that Jesus is God in the flesh. Anything contrary to God's Word is a false religion. I would not continue reading that booklet."

"Are you sure they don't believe Jesus is God?" she asked. "They don't say anything about that in their literature. Everything in this booklet sounds so right. It makes me feel good."

"We live by faith in Jesus Christ, not by our feelings," I said.

"I tell you what I'll do. I'll call Unity and ask them, and then I'll tell you exactly what they say."

The next week I came with my answer. "I called Unity Temple. I asked the woman who answered the phone, 'Does Unity believe Jesus is God in the flesh?'

"The woman hemmed and hawed. She had a hard time answering. Finally she said, 'I don't know what to say but we believe God is within you. We don't worship anything outside ourselves.'"

"'Do you believe we are born sinners?' I asked.

"'No, we believe we are born perfect,' she said.

"'Then why did Jesus Christ have to die on the cross?' I asked.

"'You are taking isolated verses out of the Bible,' was her answer.

"'I perceive that you don't know the Scriptures at all,' I said. Our Bible class is studying the Book of John in the New Testament. It is full of evidences of God's love for us by sending his Son, Jesus Christ, to die in our place and for our sins.'

"The woman insisted that she believed the Bible. I very kindly suggested she start reading in the Book of John."

The class accepted my report and decided they wanted to be better Bible students.

After we had finished our lesson, Caroline shyly asked, "Could you come to my home and have lunch with me next week? I have a lot of questions that have been piling up in my mind. I don't feel free to ask them in class. I hope you can come."

I had been waiting for this opportunity. I didn't have to ask to talk to her. She asked me. *A perfect situation*, I thought. I sensed she was ready to apply the truth she had been hearing.

"I would love to come for lunch," I said.

Caroline was excited as she greeted me at the door. I had no sooner entered when she said, "My husband left instructions for me to bake something special for you. He said to be sure the house was in spick-and-span condition when you come. 'After all, it is your Bible teacher.'

"It's interesting," she went on, "my husband was very fussy about the house being in good order. It was very important to him because my Bible teacher was coming. But his life is anything *but* orderly."

There was a quiver in Caroline's voice as she said, "I've discovered that my husband has been unfaithful. I don't know what to do."

"Are you sure about that?" I asked.

"Oh, yes. It's one of the neighbor women," she replied. "They jog together every morning and then end up at her house. I've known about it for some time. My friend Jane says I should throw him out of the house, but I love him and he's my children's father. What do you think?"

"Have you confronted your husband or the woman about it?" I asked.

"No, I'm not sure how to do that," she answered.

"Before we try to solve your problem," I said, "let's pray about it. But before we pray, I need to ask you if you have ever asked Jesus Christ into your life to be your Savior and Lord."

"Actually that's why I invited you to come over today," she said. "You probably don't know it but my religious background is Christian Science. From what I learned in class it isn't very different from Unity. I know they don't believe Jesus is God in the flesh. Also we have been taught that we don't sin because we're born perfect. I never did believe that. I see the evidences of sin all around me. What my husband is doing is sin. I know I sin and my children sin. Now that I'm reading the Bible, I know that being born perfect isn't true. We're all sinners. Because of that I need Jesus Christ in my life. I need to be forgiven of my sin. I do want him as my Savior. Will you tell me how I can do that?"

Talk about picking ripe fruit—Caroline was ready. She understood what it was all about.

"All you have to do is to ask him. Jesus said '. . . whoever comes to me I will never drive away'" (John 6:37).

"You mean I should bow my head and pray?"

"That's the way you talk to God," I said. "I'll help you. It isn't so much the words you say that are important. It's the attitude of your heart that God sees."

Caroline prayed and invited Jesus Christ into her life to be her Savior and Lord.

"Caroline, you can now talk to your Father in heaven and tell him all your needs. You can ask him for wisdom concerning your husband. He's promised in Philippians 4:19 to meet all your needs according to his riches in glory. There is another verse you should hang on to. It's Hebrews 4:16. 'Let us then approach the throne of grace with confidence, so that we may receive mercy and find grace to help us in our time of need.'"

We then thanked God for his mercy and grace and for making Caroline his very own child. We thanked him for the security we have in him because he said: "Never will I leave you; never will I forsake you" (Heb. 13:5).

"Could you stay and have a cup of coffee and another brownie before you leave?" Caroline asked.

I had tasted her brownies earlier. "They're the best I've ever eaten. I can't resist. I'd love to stay."

As we began sipping our coffee, she asked, "Do you have any idea what I should do about my husband's unfaithfulness?"

"Let's stop and pray and ask God for his wisdom. He has promised that if anyone lacks wisdom we should ask him and he will give it to us [see James 1:5]. Now that you have put your trust in him, you have every right to ask him for help. In fact, he wants you to ask him."

We both prayed concerning the problem.

"I've waited long enough," she decided. "I think this woman has a hold on my husband. Perhaps I should write her a letter and tell her I know what's going on. She has a husband and family too. I wonder if she's willing to lose them."

"What will you tell her?" I asked.

"I don't know but I'd like you to read the letter before I send it. I do want to be wise about it."

I prayed much for Caroline the following week, knowing she had a difficult task before her.

One day she called and asked if I'd stop over. She had finished the letter and wanted to read it to me.

The letter came right to the point. She told the woman that she knew what was going on between her and her husband.

"I can't handle it any longer," she wrote. "You are welcome to my husband but you can't have it both ways. Make up your mind immediately, or I will be compelled to go to your husband and tell him what has been going on."

"Are you prepared for the consequences?" I asked.

"I have a feeling neither one of them are willing to give up their families. As I told her in the letter, they can't have it both ways."

Caroline mailed the letter, and then she gave her husband a copy. She told me later that he panicked. "Oh, you shouldn't have sent that letter," he said. "What if someone gets a hold of it?"

Caroline replied, "You should have thought of that before you got involved." She told me later, "It's amazing how calm I was. I just stated the facts."

"I am so sorry," he said. "It never should have happened. I really don't love her. It's you I love. I will talk to her right away."

Within a few days the problem was resolved. The woman involved also panicked. She was concerned about losing her family, too. They agreed to stop their foolishness immediately.

"I have forgiven my husband," Caroline said, "but he is having a hard time forgiving himself. I know he loves me and I know he loves the children. I want to be a good wife to him. I'm trying to get him to come to church with me. He needs help with the guilt he's carrying around. He needs to know that not only have I forgiven him, but God is willing to forgive him, too. I know this will take place when he invites Jesus Christ into his life."

Reflection

From Caroline we can all learn a lesson of forgiveness. I've noticed there is no bitterness in her heart. Her desire is to grow in the Lord and go on with her life. She is praying that her husband and two boys come to know Jesus Christ as their personal Savior.

"As you look back on your life," I asked Caroline one day, "what do you think triggered your agoraphobia?"

"My mother had a severe case," she replied. "I remember going shopping with her one day. As we were walking next to a wall, her breathing became heavy, and she collapsed. I thought my mother was going to die. I was able to get her home to bed. She had me call the Christian Science practitioner. She came and talked to her and calmed her down for the time being. My mother became worse, however, and it seemed to have an effect on me. I began to panic every time we went out together. My mother would accept dinner engagements, then at the last minute she would freeze.

"Caroline, you have to go in my place," she'd say. "I'm just not up to it."

"I felt so awkward," Caroline said. "I'd always have to make some kind of excuse. I don't know why her friends didn't give up on her.

"My mother developed cancer but denied being ill. 'I'm not sick. I'm made in the image of God and I'm perfect,' she'd say.

"The practitioner had convinced my mother that it was so.

"I stayed and took care of my mother until she died. I had a lot of bitterness and resentment for a long time. But now I'm free. The Lord has delivered me from that burden too.

"I was also able to resolve a long-standing conflict I had with my cousin. She had hurt me badly. I was angry and wrote her a scathing letter. My mother died last year, and as I thought about life, I realized that at its best it's short. There isn't time for quarrels and bad feelings. I wrote another letter telling my cousin I was sorry for my part and that I loved her.

"Just today she and her husband stopped over to pick up her mother who had spent a few days with me. It was the first time I had seen her in a very long time. I greeted her at the door with a hug. Once again I told her I loved her. When she left, I hugged her again and told her I loved her. Her only response was, 'Well, I'm not dead yet.'

"It really doesn't matter to me what other people's responses are," she said. "I just want to be sure my heart's attitude is right before the Lord. It was a relief to be able to tell someone I loved them and not worry about the response."

We who have been raised in Christian homes have a lot to be thankful for. How easy it is to take for granted the goodness of the Lord.

26

Not My Turn

I patiently waited my turn to order the Danish pastry I had been eyeing at the bakery. I didn't see anyone ahead of me so I said to the clerk, "I have number thirteen."

"I don't know what happened to number twelve," the clerk said, as he looked around. "I don't see anyone else, so I guess you're next, lady." He took my number.

As I was giving him my order, a man walked up and said, "Wait a minute! My number is twelve."

"I'd better wait on him first," the clerk said apologetically.

"I'm terribly sorry," I said. "I didn't mean to get ahead of you. It was my fault."

"No, it was my fault," the man insisted. "I was standing here talking to my friend. I really wasn't paying attention."

"It was my fault," his friend added. "I shouldn't have been talking to him."

Then with a smile and half laughing, the clerk said, "Actually it was my fault. I didn't call his number!"

By that time we all had a good laugh, and no one was offended.

"I think it's great that all of us were willing to take the blame," I said. "That's rather unusual these days. Most people would say, 'It's not my fault' or 'you're to blame.' When it comes right down to it, all of us are guilty.

"It's just like God's requirement to get to heaven," I continued.

"Yeah, what's that?" one of the men asked.

"We have to admit we're sinners, that we're wrong, and can't measure up to God's perfect standard," I replied.

"Tell it to him again," his friend said. "That's exactly what I told him last Sunday. He's got to confess he's a sinner." They looked at me to verify it.

"That's absolutely correct," I answered. "You have to confess to God that you're a sinner."

"Okay, I confess. Now what?"

"You've gotten a good start, but you have to receive Jesus Christ as your Savior. He's the only one who can save you from your sin."

The man seemed interested, and it appeared that he wanted to talk further, but his friend said, "Take your baked goods, and we'll talk about it on the way home. Thanks for setting my friend straight," he said to me good-naturedly.

The clerk smiled and said, "That was an interesting conversation."

"We've had a lot of fun but what was said was gospel truth," I said.

"It will give me something to think about," the clerk replied.

Number fourteen was waiting to give her order. I took my package and left.

I was conscious of the fact that even in fun, we can say a word for the Lord.

I have also discovered I can witness when people are fearful about things they can't control—like the woman I met at the grocery store.

"What do you think about the strange weather we've been experiencing lately?"

I turned to see to whom the woman was speaking. My back was turned to her, so it surprised me when I realized she was speaking to me.

"You mean the drought we had last summer and now the rains?" I asked.

"Yes—and also the hurricanes. What do you make of it?"

This stranger actually expected me to give my opinion, so I said, "I think God is trying to get our attention."

"What do you mean?" she asked.

"Have you noticed that when things go well in our lives, we don't pay much attention to God? But when we're in trouble, the first thing we say is 'Lord, help me.' Then if he doesn't come to our rescue we become angry with God and blame him for our problems."

"You're probably right. I haven't thought about it that way before."

"According to the Bible," I went on, "God created us to have fellowship with him. He really loves us. He doesn't want us to use him like a Santa Claus. He wants us to be his friends. Sometimes he has to hit us over the head to get our attention."

"You've given me a lot of food for thought, and you just might be right."

I then had to give my attention to the cashier as she checked out my groceries.

There is never much time to talk at the checkout counter, but I had a chance to answer a question that troubled a customer. Perhaps the seed will be germinated by someone else. I don't always have the opportunity to share the gospel when involved in conversation, but God can use the little that is said. We can trust him with the rest.

I pray that this woman will think about what was said and that she will have other questions about God.

I rarely go shopping or leave the house for any reason that I don't find an opportunity to say something for the Lord. I don't plan to do this. It just comes up in the course of things.

Last week, while trying on a sweater, I met a woman. We were comparing our finds and commenting on them. I noticed that she was wearing a cross. It was about an inch and a half long. She also had on some gold chains. After commenting on our purchases, I said, "That's a beautiful cross you're wearing. Tell me, what does it mean to you?"

"It means I'm Presbyterian."

"Oh. What I mean is, what does the cross mean to you personally?"

"It means I follow Jesus when it comes to the Golden Rule."

"I had hoped you would say it represents the fact that Jesus Christ died on the cross for your sins, and that you have accepted him as your personal Savior."

"No, I don't believe that. I just believe in his teaching. You know— the Golden Rule."

I smiled and said, "I love reading the Bible daily. It has so much more to it than the Golden Rule. It has the answer to life—eternal life."

That's all I could say. I hope it caused her to think. I prayed that night that God would give her a hunger to know his Word and find eternal life in his Son.

Reflection

As I reflect back on these experiences, I am aware that much sowing and watering of the seed has to be done before there can be any reaping. Whatever God has called us to do on a particular day, he requires faithfulness. It is so exciting to think God would allow us to have a part in bringing someone to himself.

In the case of the man at the bakery, I learned that God can use a bit of humor to get a truth across. In fact I've found that a little light-heartedness goes a long way. It can often be turned into a serious discussion. It appeared that the two men were planning just that as they traveled home from the bakery.

As I was driving home, I was reminded of Jesus who could find an illustration in the ordinary things of life. He said, "I am the bread of life. He who comes to me will never go hungry, and he who believes in me will never be thirsty" (John 6:35).

Every time we buy or eat bread, we are reminded of the "Bread of Life," Jesus Christ. When we turn on the light in a dark room, we are reminded of the Light of the World. How awful it would be to live in complete darkness! When we go swimming or boating, we are reminded that as human beings we can't walk on water or command the storm to be still. But Jesus did. These illustrations can be openers to talk to someone about the Lord.

We can take the little we have and know and share it with people who are confused about the events happening in this world. We then trust God to use it.

In the case of the woman with the gold cross, I have many fine Presbyterian friends who have accepted Jesus Christ as their personal Savior. Just because a person says she belongs to a certain denomination is no guarantee that she is a believer. We shouldn't automatically take for granted that she has accepted Jesus Christ as her personal Savior. We just can't lump people together. Salvation is a personal matter, not a group event.

27

Lunch in the Lounge

The bartender, a young woman in her early twenties, listened attentively as I gave my testimony. She put her elbows on the counter and with her head in her hands, she seemed to concentrate on what I was saying.

What was I, a committed Christian, speaking to other committed believers, doing in a place that served drinks? Let me tell you the rest of the story.

My husband was asked to drive a busload of "Seasoned Saints" from our church, many of whom were role models to me as I grew up. They had faithfully served the Lord as Sunday school teachers, youth sponsors, and church board and committee members.

John Orme, our associate pastor, asked me to come along and give a brief message. "I will be delighted," I said. I never dreamed I'd ever be able to minister to those special friends, many of whom had lost their mates and needed Christian fellowship. *What a privilege,* I thought.

We arrived at a quaint little inn overlooking the St. Claire River at exactly noon. Pastor Orme had made arrangements previously for us to use one of the small, private dining rooms. "Stay here on the bus until I double-check on the location of our room," he said.

He looked disappointed when he returned. "I'm sorry. They have switched rooms. We will have to use the lounge. They did promise, however, not to serve drinks while we are there." He explained this to the satisfaction of the seniors. (Later, contrary to that promise, a few people were allowed in and were quietly served alcohol, but they were not intrusive and left quickly.)

It was not at all what we had planned, but most of us focused our attention on the beautiful view of the river rather than on the inconvenience.

Remember the bartender? She stayed there, quietly observing us. No one else seemed to pay any attention to her but she intrigued me. She was very attractive, and I appreciated her poise and lack of resentment at our being there. She knew we wouldn't be ordering drinks from the bar!

I sat in a corner, sizing up the situation and wondering how I would handle it, when my friend Ruth Long, who was sitting at the next table, whispered loudly, "Nellie, how are you going to handle this one? Maybe you should change your message," she said with a twinkle in her eye.

"I've been sitting here seriously thinking about that."

Then I thought, *This room was given to us. I'm the speaker so why not take advantage of the situation?*

I began to pray, "Lord, I'm prepared to speak to the senior citizens today but the bartender has needs too. Please give me a message for both."

After our dessert, the pastor introduced me as their speaker. I noticed the bartender was listening.

As I walked to the middle of the room, I didn't know exactly what I was going to say, but I *did* know God was in control.

Where I stood, I was separated from my audience by a railing and was unable to see the young woman leaning on the bar behind me.

"As I look around the room," I said, "I want to thank all of you who have been an encouragement to me. Your influence has helped make me the kind of person I am today."

What do I say now? Give your testimony. The thought flashed through my mind.

What I said next was not planned. I began, "Many of you may not know that as a young teenager I sometimes skipped church and spent my collection money at the corner drugstore. I didn't do it all the time, just once in a while, when I thought I wouldn't get caught. Oh, I read the Bible and even memorized Scripture verses but reading the Bible in those days was like reading my history book. I believed it, but it didn't affect my life.

"One day when I began to listen, not only with my head but with my heart, I began to realize the great sacrifice Jesus Christ made for me when he died on the cross for my sins. By dying in my place, he chose to be my substitute. He who knew no sin became sin for me. I was overwhelmed. I didn't deserve it, and I couldn't work for it. All I could do was to accept what Jesus Christ did for me on the cross as a gift. I received him as my Savior. He took all my guilt on himself, and I went scot-free. And because of his forgiveness, I have peace. And to think, when I die I will go to heaven and be with him. That is tremendous security.

"After years of sharing my experience, I have seen God work in other lives besides my own.

"I gave a series of Bible studies at a Lutheran church a few years ago. We were studying the Book of Galatians. I noticed a woman sitting in the audience, arms folded, and looking at me as though to say, 'Now what do you think you can teach me?' It made me feel a bit uneasy but I went on to explain that as Paul was addressing the people in Galatia, he said, 'Grace and peace to you . . .' (1:3).

"You can't have God's peace in your life until you've experienced his grace.

"At the close of the session the woman with the folded arms came up to me and said, 'I guess I don't have God's grace because I certainly don't have his peace. Could you help me?'

"I explained to the woman that until we confess we are sinners before a holy God and accept Jesus Christ as our Savior, we will not have peace.

"'Oh, I know I'm a sinner and I would love to be forgiven and experience his peace.'

"Yes, she accepted Jesus Christ as her Savior.

"I had mistaken her folded arms and the stern expression on her face as belligerence. Later she told me, 'I was desperate for help.' It is so easy to judge people by outward appearances, isn't it?"

The senior citizens were delighted to hear about what God had been doing in my life. They were glad the message was shared with the young woman at the bar. Perhaps that's why they clapped when I finished speaking.

As we prepared to leave several of the seniors came to me and said, "I'm so glad you shared your testimony with us today. The bartender was listening so earnestly."

I decided to go back into the lounge after the group left. I walked up to the young woman serving at the bar and said, "We had a lovely time today. The view of the river is so beautiful. It has been a very pleasant day for the seniors." Then I noticed she was wearing a cross. "Your cross is beautiful. What does it mean to you?"

She smiled and hesitatingly said, "It—umm . . . well, it means . . . a lot."

I was conscious of all my friends waiting for me on the bus, so I briefly stated what the cross meant to me. "When I see a cross, I am reminded that Jesus Christ died for me: that he took on himself the guilt and penalty of my sin. I've accepted Christ as my Savior and now I have peace. I don't have to worry about the future. It's all in God's hands.

"I would like to give you a booklet. It explains the basics of the Bible. Would you like to take it home and read it? Then see if it makes sense to you?"

"Is it Christian?" she asked.

"Oh, yes."

"Then I'll take it. You see I am getting married in two weeks. My fiancé and I have been going to the priest for instructions."

"If you want a good marriage, I suggest that you and your new husband read a portion of the Bible together each day. My husband and I do that. If you obey what the Bible says, I'll guarantee you'll have a good marriage."

"Oh, thank you," she said. "We do so much want to have a good marriage. I get frightened when I hear about so many divorces. I'm really going to work on my marriage."

Reflection

We don't always know the situations where we will be placed. We do know that God is sovereign and never makes a mistake. None of us would choose to have our lunch in a lounge, but there was no other choice. Yes, the inn had let us down, but

Pastor Orme graciously accepted the inconvenience. That in turn put the senior citizens at ease.

I am reminded that Jesus ate with the publicans and sinners. He showed them love.

We, too, as a body of believers must follow Jesus' example and show love to those who are without.

We teased Pastor Orme later and told him, "You really didn't need to apologize for the room we were given. It gave us an opportunity to share the gospel with a stranger, a most unlikely person—a beautiful bartender."

The Trinity Question

I was driving down a well-traveled road in our area when my attention was drawn to an object in the middle of the street. My curiosity caused me to stop the car.

I parked at the side of the road and picked up what looked like a textbook. Then I discovered it was a Jewish prayer book. On the fly leaf was printed: PRESENTED TO SARAH ROTH FROM RABBI ABRAHAM 1967. There was no address in the book.

When I got home, I called the nearby Jewish temple and told them my story. "Is Rabbi Abraham still at your temple?" I asked. "And do you have a Sarah Roth on your records?"

"The rabbi is no longer with us," she said. "Let me look in the files to see if the young woman's name is listed."

When the secretary returned she said, "I'm sorry, we have no such name on our records. I suggest you bring the prayer book to us."

"What will you do with the book?" I asked.

"We will put it in the Lost and Found."

"I don't think that's such a good idea. After all, if she isn't a member of your synagogue, she won't be looking for her book there," I answered.

"It belongs here. You should really bring it to us."

"I will first try to find the rightful owner. If I can't find her, then I'll bring it to you."

I prayed: "Heavenly Father, I don't believe it was an accident that I found the Jewish prayer book. Please help me to find the rightful owner. Show me how I can be of help."

I looked in the phone book to see if I could find her name.

There were twenty-five people by that name in the directory. *The only thing to do is to start calling*, I thought.

"I am looking for a Sarah Roth. Am I calling the right number?" I asked.

"No, there is no one by that name living here."

"Do you know anyone by that name?" I questioned.

I was getting a bit discouraged but decided I would call all twenty-five names if I had to.

Finally, by the tenth phone call, the woman answering said, "Sarah is my daughter. Her name is no longer Roth since she is now married. Her name is Rosenthal now. She is not at home. May I give her a message?"

"I found a prayer book in the middle of Thirteen Mile Road with your daughter's name in it."

"Oh, thank you," she said. "You have no idea how badly my daughter felt when she realized she had lost it. The prayer book never meant so much to her until she couldn't find it."

"If you give me your address, I'll bring it to her," I said.

"Sarah is taking flying lessons right now. I'll call the airport and leave a message. She will be ever so grateful. I'm sure she'll want to meet you. I'll tell her to stop by your house on the way home. It will probably be around three-thirty."

I was sitting in the family room preparing the lesson for my Bible-study class when she arrived.

I invited the young woman to come in. She was tall and slim, probably in her thirties. She had a gracious charm about her that was immediately noticeable.

"I can't tell you how much I appreciate your finding my prayer book," she said. "It is something I treasure. We were on the way to the temple to celebrate Yom Kippur when I lost it. My hands were full, so I put the book on the roof of my car and forgot about it. When I got to the temple I remembered but, of course, it was gone."

"I'm glad I was able to locate you," I said. "I lost my Bible once. I was in a hurry to go shopping, and it must have fallen out of the car as I opened the door to get out. A Jewish family found it and called my church. I had left a bulletin in it with the address of my church.

"I thought of that incident when I found your prayer book. I asked God to help me find you. He answered my prayer."

"That was thoughtful," she said.

"It's interesting that you should arrive just now. I was preparing my lesson for our next Bible-study class," I said. "I was reading a verse in the New Testament. It says in Mark 12:10 that the stone the builders rejected, this became the chief cornerstone. It's the same in the Old Testament. See, the exact words are in Psalm 118:22."

Before I could say another word Sarah said, "I know who it is speaking about. Jesus Christ, right? He's the head of your faith."

I couldn't help wondering. *If I had asked my Bible class before they had studied the lesson, would they have known to whom the cornerstone referred?*

I commented on her insight.

"My father once told me I had great understanding about spiritual things and he encouraged me to be open-minded."

"That's incredible," I said. "That means you and I can discuss the Bible without feeling intimidated. We can agree or disagree with each other without getting angry, right?"

"Absolutely," was her response. "I would like to repay you for finding my book and taking the trouble to call me."

"I couldn't possibly accept anything," I said. "I am so happy I found you and now I have met a very special person. I don't want a reward."

"Would you let me take you out to lunch?" she asked. "I have a lot of questions I would like to ask you about your faith."

"I would like that very much. I would like to get to know you better, too," I answered.

She picked me up the following Thursday, and we went to a nearby health-food restaurant.

"No wonder you look so great," I teased. "Eating this kind of food would keep anyone in shape."

She laughed.

"Tell me something about yourself," I said. "Do you have children?"

"Yes, I have two boys and a girl. I'm a practicing attorney, a writer, and I enjoy flying."

"My, you have quite a full life," I responded.

"I also do some volunteer work. I read to the fourth graders once a week. I enjoy that too."

After we ordered our lunch, Sarah started to ask questions pertaining to my faith. Her questions were legitimate, and I could well understand why she was puzzled about such things as the Trinity.

"Nellie, can you explain why you have three Gods and we only have one?"

"We don't have three Gods. We have one God, but three manifestations of God: the Father, the Son and the Holy Spirit. They are one, and yet they each have a special function," I said.

"The Trinity is a mystery. It can't be explained but we know it is so. The Bible speaks of each one being fully God.

"The Bible also says that Jesus is God in the flesh. Jesus came to show us what the Father is like. We can know God through Jesus Christ.

"Perhaps I can explain it somewhat in human terms. We have water, ice, and steam. They each have three different functions and yet they are one. Also an egg has three parts, the shell, the white, and the yolk, and yet an egg is one and closely related.

"When I asked Jesus Christ to come into my life, it wasn't a man that came to dwell within me; it was. . . ." Before I could finish she said, "It was the Holy Spirit. Am I right?"

Once again I was amazed at her ability to understand. She was polite and listened as I shared with her my belief that Jesus Christ was the promised Messiah.

"Our form of Judaism doesn't believe that Messiah is a person," she explained, "but a final state of being. You might say an age of utopia."

As we drove home, we discussed the Bible.

"If we want to know God, who he is, and what he's like we need to read and study the Scriptures," I said.

"I don't agree with that at all. I don't think we need to read the Bible to know God."

We had agreed not to argue but to explore each others' beliefs, so we let that statement go for a while.

"Do you believe in the Signs of the Zodiac?" she asked.

"No, I don't. It is one of the things God speaks against. You'll find that in the Old Testament, the eighteenth chapter of Deuteronomy to be exact."

"Well, don't you want to know what my sister told me?"

"What did your sister tell you?" I asked.

"She told me that my spiritual understanding may not necessarily come from my family but from someone else. Maybe you are the one to help me."

"I don't know anything about your family," I said, "but I will be happy to share my knowledge of the Scriptures anytime."

As we continued driving, Sarah said, "I do enjoy reading to the fourth graders. Right now I'm reading them a story by a Russian author. I told the teacher that I would like to take some time to tell them about the man who wrote the story. It would give them an understanding of the background of the story. The teacher doesn't want me to take the time. She doesn't feel it is necessary to tell them about the author. I totally disagree."

Sarah seemed a little put out. I was glad to see her a little fired up about it.

"What do you think?" she asked. "Do you agree that I should tell the children about the author? Don't you think that would help them understand the story better?" she asked.

"Absolutely," I answered. "That's exactly what I mean about getting to know God. The only way we can get to know him is by reading his Word, the Bible."

"I get the point," she said. "Tell me which Bible to get, and where do I start reading?"

What a delightful person, I thought. It was refreshing to see a person with her abilities not puffed up with pride. She was actually open to learn.

"Would you like to visit our church to see what it's like?" I asked.

"I would love to," she answered.

The following Sunday, she came to our home. The three of us, Sarah, my husband, and I went to church together. This was a new experience for her. She took it all in.

"I had such a warm feeling while sitting in church," she said. "When the speaker was giving the sermon, I felt like I was sitting by a cozy fire listening to a story. I just loved it."

After the service, I introduced her to many of my friends. She had a hard time understanding why my friend Elise, who is a completed

Jew (one who has recognized Jesus Christ as the Messiah), would become a member of our church. Sarah was very open about it.

"Why would you leave the synagogue?" she asked. "That really puzzles me."

My friend Elise said, "I have to be honest with you. It was too secular. It didn't meet my need. My experience was like that of Paul in the Bible. It was as though I was blind, then my eyes were opened and I could see. It has changed my entire life."

Each time Sarah and I met for lunch, we discussed the Bible. I loved being with her.

The next time Sarah came to church with us, she turned to me during the singing of the hymn "He Lives" and said, "I won't be able to sing this song. You understand don't you?"

"Of course I understand. I don't expect you to sing songs about Jesus and I really wouldn't want you to. Only people who have received Christ as Savior and believe in him should sing that song. You can listen and observe. You'll understand better what makes me tick."

I appreciated her honesty.

A few weeks later, Sarah called and said, "My children keep asking me what God is like. Can you help me with that?"

"I believe I can. God has many names. Each one denotes his character, which will help your children know in a small way what God is like. For instance, Moses asked God at his experience with the burning bush, 'Suppose I go back to the Israelites and say to them, "The God of your fathers has sent me to you," and they ask me, "What is his name?" Then what shall I tell them?' God told Moses to tell the Israelites 'I AM has sent me . . . the God of Abraham, the God of Isaac and the God of Jacob . . .' (Exod. 3:13–15).

"Remember when God asked Abraham to sacrifice his son? God provided a ram in place of Isaac. It was a test and Abraham passed.

"You see, sacrificing their firstborn was a pagan custom. Their offering was to false gods. Would Abraham be willing to do anything less for the true and living God? Was God first in Abraham's life?

"Abraham had faith that his God would provide. He believed the promise God had made to him that he would have a son and his descendants would be like the stars in the sky (Gen. 15).

"God was called Jehovah-Jirah, meaning God will provide.

"God has many names. It is a very interesting study. I'll type up a list of names and references. You'll enjoy going over them with your children."

"I'd really appreciate that!" Sarah seemed excited.

"If I'm not loading you down too much and you're interested, I'd like to give you a list of events that were prophesied in the Old Testament and fulfilled in the New Testament. They were predicted hundreds of years before they came to pass."

"That sounds interesting. I'd like to see your material."

"Did you know that Jesus' birth, death, and resurrection were talked about in the Psalms and in Isaiah? You might want to check it out."

One day, Sarah called. She was very excited. "I have something interesting to tell you. I was doing some volunteer work for the opera, and one of the women in the group started to tell me some things about the Bible. I was interested but told her I'd have to check it out with my Bible teacher."

"What is your teacher's name?" the woman asked.

"I told her that my teacher's name is Nellie Pickard."

"I know her. She's a friend of mine," the woman answered.

"I was so excited," Sarah said, "I just had to call you and tell you about it."

We continued to have lunch from time to time. Each time we discussed biblical truths. We had a wonderful time together.

As time went on Sarah's workload became heavier. Her family needed her, and she wanted to continue flying so there wasn't much time for us to get together.

We, in the meantime, moved into a townhouse and began to spend five or six months in Florida.

My speaking schedule was heavy and I worked hard on my book *What Do You Say When* . . . There seemed to be many demands on our time.

Before we left for Florida that winter, I called her and told her I had written a book.

"We are on our way to church right now. May I stop by and give you a copy? I know you may not agree with my writing but I'd like your opinion anyway."

"I'm so proud of you, Nellie," she said. "I would love a copy of your book."

We dropped it off and continued on to the evening service.

I really didn't know how she would receive the stories of one person after another receiving Christ. It was important for me to know.

I didn't hear from her while we were in Florida. When we got home in April, I called her and asked if she would be available for lunch.

"We can discuss my book. I'm eager to know what you think about it," I said. We had lunch the following week.

Sarah had been in court that morning so I waited in her office for her to arrive.

I was a bit tense as I tried to concentrate on a magazine article I was reading. *I hope I didn't make a mistake by letting her read my book*, I thought. *Maybe she'll think I was presumptuous by giving it to her, knowing she didn't believe in Jesus Christ.*

As these thoughts were going through my mind, Sarah walked in.

We looked at each other, and then Sarah opened her arms and we both hugged.

"Nellie, I loved your book," were her first words.

I was greatly relieved.

During lunch we discussed my book.

"Nellie, you and I are more alike than you realize," she said. "You try to help people find God, and you are doing a good work. I too, try to help people. I work with abused children and alcoholic parents. It's so sad to see these hurting children. I try to do everything possible to help them. I really work hard for them.

"I can relate to so many things you say in your book. Remember when you told how you and your husband had agreed that you wouldn't spend more than $25.00 on any item without consulting each other? You said money was tight in those early years. Then you said that you saw something you really wanted and it was beyond the agreed amount. You bought it anyway. Then you felt badly."

"Yes, I remember."

"You confessed that to Jesus. Now I would do the same thing. But I would confess it to God."

Yes, Sarah and I are alike in many ways. The big difference is, Jesus Christ is Lord of my life. God the Father sent his Son to die on the cross for my sins and the Spirit of God lives in me, teaching me, convicting, convincing, and guiding me in all truth. He also is my comforter.

On the way out of the restaurant Sarah said, "Nellie, I love Jesus. I think he is a wonderful person."

Of course I wish she knew him as her Savior but that is something beyond my control. Only the Spirit of God can convince her of that. I will leave her in his hands.

"Don't let it be such a long time before we get together again," she said.

Reflection

Knowing Sarah has been a delightful experience. I called her the other day and read this chapter to her. I wanted to know if it would offend her if *our* story were published.

"I think it's beautiful. I would love to have it as a chapter in your book."

Sarah is not her real name. That is the name she has taken temporarily so my readers could eavesdrop on our friendship. She is truly a generous person.

We plan to see each other soon. Only God knows our future. It's wise to trust him in all things.

A Reluctant
Chairperson

orcas was an exceptional leader, full of life and always ready and willing to do anything that would further the cause of Christ. She was the chairperson for our Bible-study group. Everyone seemed to love her, and I enjoyed working with her too.

Perhaps that's the reason I was somewhat puzzled when her usual exuberance about an experiment I had suggested wasn't there. She even seemed reluctant to be a part of it. The rest of the class appeared interested.

"This idea is not original with me," I said. "My friend Carol tried it in one of her classes and felt it was most profitable. You don't have to participate in this project if you don't care to, but I think it will end up being a blessing to all of us.

"This is what you're to do: Write a letter to each of your children, and tell them all the good things you've tucked away in your heart—things you have told your friends because you were so proud of them—things you neglected to tell them for one reason or another. You are not to say anything negative. You mention only the positive. In about two weeks, we'll share the experiences."

The following week one of the women came up to me before class started. With a big smile on her face she said, "I wrote my letters and I feel real good about it. I hope my children do."

The time finally came for the women to share their experiences. Several were eager to tell their story.

One woman said, "I wrote to my daughter in Chicago and told her the qualities in her that I appreciated. A few days later, a letter came back in return. As I opened the envelope and unfolded the paper, it had one word written on it: '*Wow.*' I understood what it meant. I think it was a giant step of growth in our relationship. I'm glad I participated."

Another woman got up and said, "I haven't spoken to my father for eight years. I wrote him a letter asking his forgiveness for my attitude. He immediately called me and, he not only forgave me but confessed he hadn't been the father he should have been. I plan to see him soon," she said, as she choked down the tears.

To clear the air I told them that I too had written to my children. I told them about the letter I had written to my son and the strange response I had received. He was in law school at the time. I told him how pleased I was with him, for the choices he had made in life, for the hard worker he was, and the lovely girl he had married. My greatest joy, I told him, was that he trusted Christ as his Savior.

My son's response was unexpected. He called on the phone one day, and without announcing who he was said, "When's the next one coming?"

"The next *what?*" I asked.

"The next letter telling me all my faults."

"There is no next letter." We were both laughing as I hung up.

I told the class that I, too, was glad I had written to my children—that it was long overdue.

According to the results thus far, I thought this had been a worthwhile project.

"Would anyone else like to share their experience?" I asked.

Dorcas hesitated at first, then she said, "To be truthful, I really did not want to take part in this assignment, but since I'm the chairperson of this group I felt it wouldn't look right if I didn't cooperate. You see, it was easy to write to two of my boys. The youngest hadn't yet reached the rebellious stage and the oldest had seen the error of his ways. He had settled down nicely. But Steve—he was right in the middle of teenage rebellion. He's been such a problem lately. As I sat down to write, I thought, *What can I say to him?* I couldn't think of a thing. I began to cry; then I began to pray. 'Lord, isn't there one good thing about Steve?' Then I remembered—Steve was a great help to me when Gramma came to live with us. She wasn't too easy to get along with but Steve had a way with her, and she loved him. *I could tell him how much I appreciated that,* I thought. Then something else came to my mind. *He really does keep his room neat, and that means a lot to me.* Before I knew it many other things came to my mind that I appreciated about him. Then I thanked the Lord for bringing these things to my attention.

She told us that she was tempted to tell him a few of his faults but remembered that was not allowed in this assignment.

"I finished the letter and put it on his pillow, and the next day I found a note on my pillow. It said, 'I don't know what to say, Mom, but thanks.'"

That act of love changed their relationship.

Steve went off to college. Three months later he called his mom. "I'd like to come home next week and bring a friend. I want him to see how our family loves each other." That weekend Steve led his friend to Christ.

I was so pleased at the results of this experiment that I tried it again. I had been invited to hold a series of Bible studies at a church on the east side of our city. It was supposed to be a women's group but several men attended. They were deacons checking me out. You see it was a different denomination from mine. Of course they had to check out my theology. They discovered everything was fine, and some asked if they could continue to attend. They even did their weekly assignments.

One deacon said, "I must confess, I have been pretty hard on my son. He's a doctor and makes hospital rounds every Sunday morning. I have been getting after him for not attending church. I shouldn't have been so hard on him. It really didn't do any good because he didn't pay any attention to me. I decided I would write him a letter just as you asked. You see it finally dawned on me that on Sunday mornings he was ministering to people. He was doing God's work. I told him, 'I'm proud of you son. I've been so wrong in nagging you about church attendance. Will you forgive me?'"

Not only did he forgive his dad but arranged his schedule so that he was able to attend church services with his family.

One of the sweetest stories that came out of this experiment was when one of the others sent her five-year-old son a letter. She told him how special he was and that she loved him very much. He didn't know how to read, so he asked his sister to read the letter to him.

When he got ready for bed that night, he sidled up to his mom and said, "Could that little boy you love so much have a cookie before he goes to bed?"

"Of course I gave him a cookie. This was an exception, wasn't it?"

Reflection

It's amazing isn't it? When we do what's right and ask God by his Spirit to lead us, the results are unbelievable. It ought to teach us a lesson.

How easy it is to get irritated at the disagreeable incidents in life, whether they are caused by things or people. We try to work these out in our own way and fail.

If only we could learn to commit our ways "unto the Lord." Most of us have to learn the hard way. Eight years is a long time to be silent with a loved one. Dorcas cried and struggled and then called on the Lord. He is always there when we call on him. He says so in Psalm 50:15:

> and call upon me in the day of trouble;
> I will deliver you, and you will honor me.

Dorcas did just that and was rewarded.

My own son discovered that I was really proud of him.

The doctor was not a child to be ordered around but he responded to love.

The little five-year-old responded to love. It must have been easier to obey his mom after that.

Christians are to be known by their love. Learning a truth brings the greatest blessing when we act on it.

30

Getting Back in Line

I stepped out of line just for a moment. I wanted to check the price of the two-pound box of chocolates at the next counter. The price was horrendous. As I started to get back in line, a woman stepped in front of me.

I said, "Oops, that's what I get for stepping out of line. I shouldn't have looked temptation in the face. Can you believe a two-pound box of candy costs twelve dollars and seventy-five cents? And they call this a *discount* store? Back in the good old days that same box of candy cost five dollars and ninety-five cents!"

We both laughed and shook our heads in disbelief. Then the woman said, "Come on, get in line. You didn't lose your place. I saved it for you."

How kind, I thought.

The woman looked at my purchases. "*Fisherman's Friend.* I'm curious. What is that?"

"They are throat lozenges. I bought them for my pastor. That is, he used to be my pastor but now he's the president of Moody Bible Institute. When we met him in Florida last month, he had to speak four times in one day. And, believe me, it took a toll on his throat.

"I had some of these lozenges with me and gave him some. It helped him immediately. I promised I would get some for him as soon as I got back to Michigan. This store is the only place I know of that carries them."

155

"They're really good, huh? Have you tried them yourself?" she asked.

"I do quite a bit of speaking and use them all the time. It keeps me from coughing."

"Tell me, what do you speak about?" (I had hoped she'd ask.)

"I tell people about Jesus Christ, and how they can have their sins forgiven. I tell them what the Bible says and God's requirements to be in his family."

"That's the most exciting thing I've heard in a long time," she said. "I know about Moody Bible Institute. We used to live in Chicago. My son just recently went to some function there.

"Let me show you something," she said as she opened her purse, took out a notebook, turned the pages until she came to the one she was looking for. "Look at this," she smiled.

I read: Romans 3:23; Romans 6:23; Romans 5:8; John 1:12, and several other Bible verses.

With her face aglow, she said, "I'm memorizing these verses so I can be better prepared to witness.

"To think this all happened because I let you get in front of me. Isn't the Lord good?" she said.

God gives us so many goodies along the way when we take the opportunities that come before us. It makes life exciting and gives us a real purpose for living. My friend Virginia had been conversing with the woman in front of her at the grocery store. They both spotted the tabloids on the shelf next to the cash register. My friend said, "Those papers are just a bunch of lies. I don't believe a word they say."

"You've probably right, but what is truth anyway?" the woman asked.

"Why, Jesus Christ is truth. He said, 'I am the way, the truth and the life. No one comes to the Father but by me.'"

The woman didn't say a word. She turned and finished her business and went on her way.

I was proud of Virginia. She knew what truth was and wasn't afraid to speak up. The answer may have fallen on deaf ears or—perhaps it gave the woman something to think about.

I walked over to the office center with my husband to pick up the *Wall Street Journal* one morning. As we were walking down the hall,

I overheard two women behind me talking rather loudly. They were probably secretaries. One of the girls kept saying, "Oh, my God."

After repeating this three or four times, I just had to turn around and say something.

"Did you say, 'Oh, my God'?" I asked. She looked puzzled and then said, "Yeah."

As kindly as possible I said, "God is holy. His name should not be taken in vain. It hurts me to hear you use his name in that manner."

Immediately her friend spoke up. She seemed relieved that I had addressed the issue. "I know what you're talking about. I'm Catholic, and my sister is a nun. I know we shouldn't take God's name in vain."

"Because I'm a believer in Jesus Christ," I said, "I want to honor his name."

"I'm Jewish," the offender said.

"Then you really should know God's laws, right?"

"I suppose so, but I don't."

She smiled and walked away.

Reflection

What would you have said if someone asked you if you had ever used the lozenges you were buying? In my prewitnessing days, I probably would said, "Yes, I've tried them and they work."

Now I took it as an opportunity. I threw out my bait. I told her I found them helpful when I had to speak. She nibbled at the bait.

"What do you speak about?" she asked.

That question opened up a conversation that ended in blessing for both of us.

In the case of Virginia, what would you have said? Would you have had courage to quote a Scripture verse if someone asked you, "What is truth?"

Spiritually it puts us on the spot. We have to make instant decisions as to whether we will take the opportunity standing before us, begging to be taken.

What about the girl who took God's name in vain?

I don't know why I felt compelled to speak up that day. Perhaps it was because the young woman was defaming the name of my best friend. It always cuts me to the core when I hear someone take God's name in vain. I spoke the truth in love. I pray that our conversation will stay in her memory and cause her to think about God, his holiness, power, and beauty.

Second Timothy 4:2–5 says:

Preach the Word; be prepared in season and out of season; correct, rebuke and encourage—with great patience and careful instruction. For the time will come when men will not put up with sound doctrine. Instead, to suit their own desires, they will gather around them a great number of teachers to say what their itching ears want to hear. They will turn their ears away from the truth and turn aside to myths. But you, keep your head in all situations, endure hardship, do the work of an evangelist, discharge all the duties of your ministry.

Paul wrote this to Timothy. We can learn from these verses that we should take every opportunity to speak up for our Lord. Let people know that we are on his side.

31

Witnessing in Nursing Homes

an you tell this nurse how she can be sure she will go to heaven when she dies, R. E.?"

Robert Ernest Thompson, better known as R. E., had served the Lord in China for many years. He then established Missionary Internship, an organization which trains young men and women for the mission field. We often called him "Our Missionary Statesman."

I sat under Rev. Thompson's ministry many times. He preached the gospel clearly and with fervor. I had often said to him, "R. E., you have been such a blessing in my life. You've taught me many things about the Christian life. I want to thank you."

"Well, now, you'd better be careful or I'll get a swelled head," he'd say in his beautiful Irish brogue. But now there was a problem. He was suffering from Alzheimer's disease and had to be taken to a nursing home. It was sad to see him in that condition. Even though he had been in our home many times, he now did not recognize me.

Now his body had been afflicted with this dread disease which effects the memory long before the patients are physically disabled.

One day, while visiting the nursing home, I asked him, "Can you explain to this nurse what it means to be 'born again'?"

I knew he was familiar with this term. I'd heard him use it often.

He turned to me and in a very clear, precise voice said, "Now the first thing you have to do is to confess to God that you're a sinner. Then you need to receive Jesus Christ as your personal Savior. You can't save yourself, you know."

"Is that all you do?" I asked.

"No." He hesitated a moment and went on, "Then after you've done that, tell him you want to be his child, and want to live for him. That's about it."

His nurse was amazed, and so was I. It was proof that though his flesh and his mind were weak, the Spirit was strong. I left that nursing home uplifted. A sick man with Alzheimer's disease had ministered to me that day.

My husband's parents were in the same nursing home. My father-in-law had had a stroke. It affected his speech so he couldn't talk. We would sometimes sing hymns when we visited him. He sang right along with us as clearly as though he hadn't been affected by the stroke. We often read or quoted Scripture. He had memorized great portions of the Bible and would repeat or mouth the words along with us. He always carried a small New Testament with him. He would show it to us from time to time, indicating to us that it was very important to him. We could not carry on a normal conversation with him but his eyes would light up when we talked about his Savior.

It was hard to see this man, who at one time had lived a very productive life, now needing help in almost everything he did. Once I told his nurse, a perfect stranger to him, "Would you believe that for years my father-in-law was the superintendent of our Sunday school and also chairman of the Christian Businessmen's Committee in our area?"

She shook her head and said, "Strange what happens to people, isn't it?"

"Have you ever heard him sing hymns and quote Scripture?"

"Yes, I have and that's an amazement to me," she said.

"He's forgotten most of the things that ever happened to him in life," I said, "but he never forgets Jesus Christ. To me that's remarkable."

My friend Sam was dying of Lou Gehrig's disease (ALS). He too was in that same nursing home. His mind was sharp as it was not affected by his illness. We visited him often and had long talks. But as time went on his speech became more and more slurred. We strained to understand him. He then began to use a pad and pencil in order to communicate with us.

Sam was a completed Jew, a most remarkable man. He had accepted Christ while mowing his lawn one day. His manager at work, Harry Johnson, had shared the Scriptures with him on several occasions. One day it hit him hard. *Jesus Christ is the Messiah. I know he is,* were his thoughts.

When he announced to his family that he had become a believer in Jesus Christ, he was immediately rejected. He was not allowed to eat with the family and had to live in the basement of his home—but he was expected to pay the bills.

I don't know what caused his illness but he could not continue to live in the basement any longer. He moved to Florida but continued to support the family financially.

Sam never complained. He continued to pray for his family, that they too would come to know Jesus Christ as their Savior. He asked all of his friends to join him. It wasn't easy for him to leave his family as he cared for them deeply.

Even though we knew he was ill, none of his friends suspected he had Lou Gehrig's disease. A year later he was forced to go to a nursing home. He just couldn't take care of himself any longer.

We visited this special man often. We wanted to encourage him.

"Sam," I said, "we'll be going up north shortly but expect to come back in a few months. We'll see you then."

Sam shook his head and pointed his finger upward. With a smile he tried to say, "Heaven, heaven."

I knew what he meant. He knew it wouldn't be long before he would be with his Savior. He was looking forward to that time.

Sam was greatly loved because of his stand for Jesus Christ.

People visited him daily and prayed with him. The nurses commented on his many friends.

One day as I visited him, I noticed his new roommate. I introduced myself and he told me his name was Mr. Peartree. "I'm here on a temporary basis. I have my own apartment and expect to return after they finish with my tests."

"Do you have a family in the area?" I asked.

"No, I'm sorry to say, I don't have a family in the area, so I never have visitors. My wife died a year ago and my son lives in Massachusetts. I'm really all alone."

"Don't you have a church home here?" I asked.

"No, I haven't gone to church for quite a while. I do notice that Sam has lots of visitors from his church. It must be nice. They always pray with him. No one ever prays with me."

"That can be easily remedied," I said. "I visit here quite often and I promise I will stop and see you and pray with you."

I told him about Sam and how his family had rejected him when he had accepted Jesus Christ as his Savior.

"Being a Jewish Christian isn't always easy," I remarked. "Sam had to make a choice between Jesus Christ and his family. He's looking forward to being with his Savior.

"I wish the two of you could talk more; but even though Sam has a keen mind, his speech is slurred and it is difficult for people to understand him. You can talk to him though, and he will communicate somehow."

Then I said, "Tell me something about yourself. Have you always lived in Florida?"

"No, actually I'm from Atlanta. The mailmen always got a kick out of delivering my mail—my name being Peartree, and I lived on Peachtree Street in Atlanta."

"I bet you've had a lot of fun with your name."

"Yeah, some people think I'm joking when I tell them my name, especially when I tell them the name of my street, but tell me more about Sam."

"Sam is very special," I said. "He has taught his friends a lot about loyalty when it comes to his love for the Savior. Jesus Christ means more to him than anything else in the world. He still loves his family and we, along with him, are praying that his wife and children will come to know the Lord, too."

"That's a sad story."

"Yes, in one way, but happy because Sam knows when he dies he will go to heaven and be with God. Tell me, do you believe the Bible when it says that everyone has sinned?"

"Yes, I know that. I've been confessing my sins on a regular basis," he said.

"Have you ever received Jesus Christ as your Savior?" I asked.

"Can't say I've ever done that. Maybe I don't have the complete picture."

"The Bible tells us in the first chapter of John that Jesus Christ was God in the flesh. He came to earth so that we might better understand what God the Father is like. He was without sin and yet he took our sins on himself. Just think, God loved us so much that he was willing to send his only Son to die in our place (John 3:16). If we believe and receive Jesus, we can have everlasting life. Kind of overwhelming isn't it?"

I then shared with him my little booklet that showed him that he too could be in the family of God.

"Look, in Revelation 3:20 Jesus is talking. 'Here I am! I stand at the door and knock. If anyone hears my voice and opens the door, I will come in and eat with him, and he with me.' Jesus is saying that if you will open your heart and invite him into your life, he will be with you and have fellowship with you.

"Mr. Peartree, would you like to receive Jesus Christ as your personal Savior?"

"Yes, I think I'm ready to do that. I've been close many times but I've never taken that step. I would appreciate it very much if you would pray with me."

We bowed our heads and he prayed after me, "Dear Father, I admit that I am a sinner. I believe that the Lord Jesus Christ died for me. I receive him now as my Savior. Thank you for forgiving my sin and for accepting me into your family. In Jesus' name I pray, *Amen.*"

"Mr. Peartree, you are now a brand-new member of the family of God. I want to welcome you into the family."

We shared the good news with Sam, and there was great happiness in that room. Sam's friends stopped to talk and pray with Mr. Peartree, and he was no longer alone. He had a new family, the family of God.

The tests came back shortly after that, and it was discovered that Mr. Peartree had inoperable cancer. He never did have the opportunity to go back to his apartment. Three weeks after his new membership into God's family, God took him home to be with him. He went to a far better home than the apartment he had left.

I have another dear friend I visit in a nursing home in Michigan. Her name is Audie and she is ninety-three years old. Just a few years ago Audie helped with the senior citizens' group at our church. She helped make arrangements for small trips, luncheons, and other interesting adventures. She seemed to have the gift of help and encouragement. She loved to crochet, and I was the recipient of many beautiful pot holders which she would make us as love gifts. To me, she was a very special lady.

The time came when Audie had to be taken to a nursing home. Her memory had failed, and it appeared that life was over for her. At first many of her friends visited her. They would sign her guest book and write some encouraging words alongside their names.

As time went on, she wasn't able to read. She couldn't comprehend or understand what she was reading. I would visit her and she didn't know my name. Most of the time she couldn't remember five minutes previously. For some it didn't seem worthwhile to even visit her.

"After all, she doesn't recognize anyone," some of her friends said. "She can't remember from one minute to the next what has been going on. I can't see that it makes any difference to her if we visit her or not."

So the visits have become fewer and fewer. I heard someone say, "I don't understand why God doesn't take her home."

I have reflected on that statement many times. Yes, the Lord could take her home. She's done her work on earth. I believe she was left here for *our* sake. God is keeping her here so we can learn something about ministering to others, about patience and love.

I have been more observant lately. I notice that even though she doesn't know my name, she knows I'm a friend and gives me a big smile, and says, "What brings you here today?"

I love to tell her, "I came to see you, of course. I couldn't think of a better thing to do."

She recognizes love and responds.

Audie has taught me much about human needs. I noticed that Ola, her daughter, put the words of hymns on her bulletin board. They sing every time she visits her. I decided I would do the same. She loves to sing and she knows these hymns by memory.

I visited her recently and decided I'd ask her some questions concerning her faith. I remembered R. E. Thompson's remarkable answers and I am convinced that the Spirit is stronger than the flesh.

"Audie," I asked, "if someone in this place should say to you, 'I would like to go to heaven when I die. How do I get there?' what would you tell them?"

At first she said, "I don't know." Then she gave me a strange look and said, "Well, I'm not sure, except you've *got* to know the Lord."

"Is there anything a person has to confess?" I asked.

"Well, you've got to confess the Lord Jesus."

"Yes, but how about the bad things in us?"

"Oh sure, you have to confess your sin."

Once again I was impressed with the work of the Holy Spirit in a person who doesn't have much physical life left. I prayed with Audie and left. I was walking on air. My friend Audie in the nursing home had ministered to me that day in a way she will never realize.

My heart was moved and warmed as I observed my friend Ola care for her mother. She spoke gently and lovingly as she made sure her sweater was put on properly. I listened as they sang together. It was a beautiful sight. Audie can't keep on tune any more, but she knows the words. They are as much a part of her as breathing.

One day she said to me, "Hymns are all I know. I don't know the other songs."

"You don't need the other songs. You know the best songs," I told her.

"Can you quote any Bible verses?" I asked.

"I'm not sure."

"Let's try John 3:16," I started: "'For God so loved the world . . .'" Audie took over. "'He gave his one and only Son, that whoever believes in him shall not perish but have eternal life.'"

"That is just wonderful," I remarked.

"Well, I guess if he loves us, he'll take care of us," she said.

We quoted a few more verses, sang "Jesus Loves Me," and she remarked, "That's a good song for children isn't it?"

"It certainly is and I think it's good for all of us to know he truly loves us."

On the way out I stopped and talked to the nurse about Audie's singing and quoting Bible verses.

"Oh, I know all about that," the nurse said. "That's how we get her back to normal when she gets disoriented. It's what we call 'reality orientation.'"

That made my day. My heart was rejoicing. As I was about to leave the building, I stopped at the front desk. I was so excited I just had to share this good news.

"Tell me," I said to the aide on duty, "do you know any portion of Scripture?"

"No, I'm afraid not."

"Well, then Audie is better off than you are—right?"

The aide thought that was funny and started to laugh.

"It really isn't funny. You ought to start reading and memorizing the Scriptures so that when you get old you'll have something on which to fall back."

"You're probably right. You might have something there."

I turned to leave when the aide said in a more serious vein, "It truly is a miracle, isn't it?"

"Yes, it is. I've learned that the spirit is stronger than the flesh. What we store up in our hearts, pertaining to godliness, will benefit us all the days of our lives."

Reflection

My attitude has completely changed about visiting nursing homes. I used to go to give of myself and I guess that is still true to a point—but I receive so much more than I ever give.

God has given me a special privilege—the privilege of having shared in the lives of a few people in their twilight years.

Can a person be a witness in a nursing home? . . . You bet!

Both Jesus and Buddha?

I opened the door, and the young man standing on my porch greeted me with a broad smile.

"I'm Loo Kim," he said. "My mother sent me to see you. She wants you to talk to me."

I invited this tall, handsome Korean teenager to come in. I figured he was about seventeen years old and close to six feet tall. As most Orientals, he had jet-black hair.

I had never seen him before but I was expecting him. I liked him instantly.

Loo's mother was in my Bible class. She had been a Christian for about a year. She was concerned for her teenage son.

"He is a very rebellious young man. I have been sending him to some very wise men for counseling but he refuses to go anymore."

"They don't help me," he said.

"Well, then, you *must* go to see my American Bible-study teacher. You need some wise counsel, and maybe she can help you," his mother said.

To my surprise, Loo was willing to come to my home. There was no formal introduction. His mother just dropped him off at the street, and he came to the door by himself.

"I give you a lot of credit for coming to see me," I said. "I'm not so sure my son would be willing to talk to a woman he had never met before."

"I really don't mind," he answered.

I have watched many times with great interest the respect the Orientals have for their elders. I admire it. We, as Americans, can learn much from them.

We sat down and talked about generalities for a while. Then he said, "I had thought about becoming a doctor, but I've looked into it and I think it's going to take too much of my time. I intend to enjoy life and have some fun."

"You're about ready to graduate from high school. What are your intentions? Will you go to college?" I asked.

"Oh, yes, my grades are very good. I have no problems with my studies. I plan to go to the University of Michigan, but I want to take some courses that leave me a lot of free time," he responded.

"What about God in your life?" I asked. "Have you ever accepted Jesus Christ as your Savior?"

"No, I haven't. We were all Buddhists in our family, but my mother has become a Christian. She's told me all about Christianity and would like me to become a believer in Jesus Christ, too."

"What is keeping you from becoming a believer?" I asked.

"Well, if heaven would open up and I would see God, I would believe."

"That will never happen, Loo," I said. "The Bible says, 'The righteous will live by faith'" (Rom. 1:17).

"How does a person get faith?" he asked.

"The Bible says in Romans 10:17, 'Faith comes from hearing the message, and the message is heard through the word of Christ.' In other words you learn about God and Jesus Christ, who is God in the flesh, by reading his Word. The Bible is God's Word," I said. "Would you be willing to read the Book of John and then in a couple of weeks come back, and we'll discuss what you've read?"

"I would be happy to do that."

I was delighted with his response.

Exactly two weeks later, Loo called and wanted to come over. When he arrived, he announced that he had not only read the Book of John but also Matthew and Luke.

"It was fascinating," he said.

I was encouraged with his interest. He seemed eager to learn.

"Do you know that Jesus Christ came to earth for the very purpose of dying on the cross for our sins? That he actually was our substitute? We deserved to die but he took our place? Let me read to you what the Bible says in John 3:16. 'For God so loved the world that he gave his one and only Son, that whoever believes in him shall not perish but have eternal life.'

"To be in the family of God, you have to receive Jesus Christ as your personal Savior. The Bible says that in John 1:12: 'Yet to all who received him, to all who believed in his name, he gave the right to become the children of God.'"

"You have given me a lot to think about," he said. "I'd like to talk again."

We had many talks before he left for the University of Michigan. Each time I felt he got a little closer to understanding what Christianity was all about.

One day I said, "Loo, do you understand what it means to be a Christian?"

"Yes, I feel that I do."

"Would you like to receive Jesus Christ as your personal Savior?"

"Yes, I would," was his answer.

I helped him pray. He confessed that he was a sinner, and said he would like to receive Jesus Christ as his God.

Of course I was delighted. Loo came to church with me the week before he left for college. I introduced him to some of the young people. He seemed happy to get acquainted with other Christians.

The disappointment came a short time later when he announced to his mother that even though he had become a Christian, he was still a Buddhist. He had just added Jesus Christ to his list of gods.

His mother was greatly disappointed, and I was devastated. I had never had an experience like that!

I discovered that I had a lot to learn. The Oriental culture is different from ours. It is natural for them to have many gods.

I will be better prepared the next time, I thought.

The next time came a few months ago when I was in Florida. I had been asked to counsel a Chinese woman. She had responded to the pastor's invitation to receive Jesus Christ as her Savior.

After our introductions, I asked, "Ghigi, what is your religious background?"

"I'm a Buddhist, but I want to receive Jesus as my God."

"If you receive Jesus as your God," I said, "he has to be your only God. You cannot have Buddha as your God any longer. Are you willing to do that?"

She hesitated briefly and then said, "Yes, I am."

"Do you have any idols in your home?" I asked.

"Yes, I do. I have three."

"You will have to get rid of them. You cannot have Jesus Christ and your idols too," I said.

"I see that my Christian friend has much joy and happiness. I do not have that. She says that Jesus makes the difference."

"Yes, Jesus Christ does make a difference in a person's life. You see there is much joy when we realize that he died on the cross for our sins. He took the penalty we deserved, and we are free. He takes our guilt, and we have peace. I call that God's loving exchange. That is why the real Christian has joy in his heart."

I told her the story of Loo, and said, "You see now why you cannot have two gods? The Bible says, 'Thou shalt have no other gods before me.'"

"Yes, I want Jesus as my only God."

She bowed her head, confessed she had sinned against God and received Jesus Christ as her personal Savior and Lord.

I was glad her friend was with her. She would disciple her and help her to understand the Scriptures better.

I met my Chinese friend a week later at a restaurant. My husband suggested that I ask her if she got rid of her idols.

I approached her and asked, "Ghigi, have you gotten rid of your idols yet?"

"Yes, I destroyed the idols I had in my house. But I had a gold necklace that had an idol on it. It was very expensive. I gave it to my friend. She is a Buddhist. I didn't want to waste the money."

"Are you going to tell your friend about Jesus Christ?" I asked.

"Yes, I already have."

"What will she do with the necklace when she accepts Jesus Christ as *her* Savior?"

"Oh, I hadn't thought about that," she exclaimed. We all laughed. She got the point. She was just a beginner. She will learn.

Reflection

The Eastern religions are not the only ones who do not believe Jesus is God in the flesh. Many religions in America have good things about them, but unless they believe that Jesus Christ is God they are a cult and a false religion. We need to be on guard that we are not deceived. We need to know the Word of God so we can help these deluded people.

The Bible is our only source of truth. The person we witness to must know we are not presenting our own ideas or opinions but the teachings of the Scriptures. The Bible is the only place we can learn anything about God or Jesus Christ.

Another young friend of mine was invited to a study group. It was called "The Making of Miracles." He wasn't sure what they were studying but he brought his Bible.

As they began discussing miracles, my friend brought out his Bible and referred to a particular Scripture verse. In disgust one member of the group ordered, "Put that book away. We don't believe that stuff."

My friend couldn't stay for the rest of the meeting. "I would be compromising my stand for the Lord," he said.

We all need to take a stand for the Lord Jesus. We need to let people know that our first allegiance is to our Savior, the Lord Jesus Christ and that we can have "no other gods before him."

33

The Subtlety of Evil Influences

My husband and I stopped at a rest area on Interstate 96 one day. A woman about thirty-five years old came in, singing something about the greatest love. Her four-year-old daughter came happily bouncing along beside her.

"What's the name of the song you're singing?" I asked.

"It's called 'No Greater Love.'"

"I know something about *that* love," I said. "You're singing about God's love, right?"

"Oh, no, I'm singing about self-love."

I was really surprised. "But the greatest love is God's love."

"Oh, no, you can't love anyone until you first love yourself," she said.

Mmm, I thought, *this is the world's answer to the poor self-image problem. They've got the cart before the horse.*

"I'm afraid I can't agree with you," I said. "You see, when you understand God's love and the price he paid to forgive your sin by sending Jesus Christ to die in your place, only then can you love yourself. You must be worth a lot to God since he was willing to send his Son to die on the cross for you. The greatest love beyond question has to be God's love."

"Well . . ." she said thoughtfully, "I've never thought about it that way before."

Her little girl began tugging at her mother's dress, and they were on their way.

I wanted to give the woman something to think about and I pray someone else will water the seed that was sown. She needs to be a good role model for her daughter. Only the truth of God can accomplish that.

Before the evening news came on, I listened to a commercial.

"You all know happiness is lots of money in the bank, food on the table, and of course the right kind of tires on your car. That all adds up to security in life," the TV announcer proclaimed.

Daily we get bombarded with lies from the media. We are told what kind of cars to buy, slacks to wear, cereals to eat, cosmetics to use, and so forth. Generally it is not based on the merit of the product but by the sexy young men or women who are used to enhance it. (So the advertisers think.)

Most of us try to ignore these ads, and some feel the commercials are perfectly harmless. In a subtle way, however, they have their influence. The advertisers have our eyes and ears. All they need to do is to pressure us and tempt us to loosen our purse strings.

I began to wonder, *Am I easily influenced?*

That evening, my next-door neighbor, Sheila, and I walked over to our vegetable garden.

"It looks like you got yourself some new tennis shoes," I said.

"No, they're not new; I just washed them."

"I'm wearing the same brand. What a difference," I said. "I was thinking about getting some new ones. Maybe I should try washing mine first."

I was pleasantly surprised when after applying a little soap and water, and of course a brush, my shoes looked as new as Sheila's.

I showed my newly scrubbed shoes to my husband.

"Wow, what a difference a little cleaning makes," he remarked.

A few days later, I noticed my husband's shoes out on the porch drying. He too had been influenced.

I became more acutely aware that there are good and bad influences in life. I was discussing this with my friend Ola one day.

"It's interesting, you should mention that," she said. "I've been thinking about the same thing lately."

"My little three-year-old granddaughter," she said, "was sitting in the backseat of our car when I heard her cry out, 'Oh, oh, oh, my!'"

"What's the matter, Audie?" she asked.

"My nail polish doesn't match the color of my outfit," she said in a very distressed tone of voice.

From a three-year-old, that was funny. Where did she get the idea? From her mother, of course.

I had watched my *own* three-year-old granddaughter, Annie, do an imitation of her mom. She was staying with me for a few days. She seemed so proud of her new purse. I noticed she would take out a tube of chapstick and apply it to her lips and then smear it on her cheeks. She put it back in her purse only to take it out again and repeat the process over and over again.

Finally I asked, "Annie, what are you doing?"

"I'm putting capstick on my yips and my keeks, Gramma."

"You mean your lips and your cheeks, don't you?"

"Yes, Gramma," she said impatiently. "I'm putting it on my yips and my keeks."

She wanted to be a grown-up like her mom.

Children learn to imitate early in life. It's rather scary when we think about it.

I began to realize what an awesome responsibility we, as mothers and grandmothers, have toward our children.

I think the first time I became keenly aware of how my behavior affected my children was when I heard my oldest daughter, Karen, scolding her doll.

"Now, you just behave yourself. If you don't, I'll put you right to bed." She shook her little finger at the doll as she was speaking. "And if you're not good, there won't be any treats today either."

Dear me, that sounds just like me, I thought. It made me realize the responsibility I had in raising my children. What I said, and how I said it, would be imitated by my children. How else do they learn?

Being a grandmother is different. We don't need to do much scolding or disciplining. We can leave that to the parents. Romans 5:3–4 says, "We also rejoice in our sufferings [tribulations], because we know that suffering produces perseverance [patience]; perseverance, character; and character, hope." We experienced tribulation with our children to prepare us to be more patient as grandparents. We tease about being able to love them and leave them. Grandchildren are wonderful, and we do have a responsibility to be good role models.

I watched my four-year-old granddaughter leave her seat and walk down the aisle toward the platform of the church. She hesitated, and then walked up the steps to the podium and stood right next to me. I was speaking at the mother-and-daughter banquet of her parents' church. I had to make a choice quickly. Should I send her back to her seat and tell her she did not belong on the platform? What should I do? With an automatic impulse I put my arm around her shoulder and kept on talking. She stood quietly beside me until I had finished. Then she looked up at me and said, "Gramma, I just wanted to be with you."

I will never forget that experience. (I'm glad I didn't send her back to her seat!)

Annie's twelve years old now and is still willing to listen to what I have to say. We're great friends. I was amazed and pleasantly surprised when her mother told me she was interested in reading her grandmother's writings on evangelism. She's old enough to understand what it's all about, and has accepted Jesus Christ as her Savior. She is growing as a Christian.

Annie is the oldest of three girls. Her two sisters look to her for leadership.

Each of the girls has her own bedroom. One night Ruthie, her ten-year-old sister, had a nightmare and woke up crying. Annie got out of bed to see what was troubling her.

"What's wrong, Ruthie?" she asked.

"I had a terrible dream about the program I saw on television today. It was about saying no to drugs. They showed the needle drug addicts use and the terrible things that happen when people take drugs. I've been thinking about it all day, and it's really scary. That's what I was dreaming about."

As Ruthie continued to cry, Annie said, "Let's pray about it. God will help you. Then it will be okay." As Annie was praying, their mother came up the stairs and waited quietly until they were finished. Then Annie said, "Maybe God allowed you to watch the program so you could see what happens to people who take drugs. Then you won't be tempted when someone comes along and offers them to you."

Annie may only be twelve years old but she knew how to help her sister. She didn't say, "Oh, it's only a dream. It really didn't happen." She went to the God of all comfort. She had confidence he would help.

Because someone was a good influence in Annie's life, she in turn was able to be a good role model to her sister. It doesn't matter if we are young or old—we influence the behavior of those we are around. Whether it be for good or bad, Just think, at any age we can be God's tool for helping others. What a privilege!

The world is screaming its lies at us every day. "Look, and taste, it's good," it says. "Then you'll discover what you're missing." It's no different today than it was for Eve in the Garden. She took a look, lusted, and then tasted. Then it was too late. As Christians we need to be discerning, lest we get trapped in Satan's clutches.

We also need to be in constant prayer for our loved ones. We need to pray not only for our children, grandchildren, and our friends, but for those we have opportunity to influence for the Lord.

Reflection

As I look back I realize there is a certain chain of influence. We influence our children and our children influence their friends. Annie may be young but she influenced her sister to pray and talk to God when a problem arose. We can encourage children to do this. I remember the first time I apologized to my son. "I'm sorry, Tim. I was unfair. I was unduly hard on you. Will you forgive me?"

"Aw, it's okay, Mom," he said.

I discovered after that, it was much easier for him to admit his faults to me.

I often say, "I wish I had done things differently. If only I knew then what I know now I'd have been a better mother. God didn't make us mothers in our old age. He gave us children when we were young, when we had the energy and capacity to take care of them. Yes, we make mistakes but we can learn from them. We can learn to forgive and to love as the Father forgives and loves us, and be a positive influence on others.

34

Things Don't Satisfy

J met Kelly one Sunday morning in the counseling room at the church. She had responded to the pastor's invitation to be available to God for witnessing. She gave me her name, and I told her my name was Nellie Pickard.

Kelly had a surprised look on her face. She hesitated a moment, then said, "Nellie Pickard? Are you the author of the book *What Do You Say When* . . . the book on witnessing?"

"Yes, I am," I answered.

Kelly started to laugh. "You won't believe it but that book is one of the reasons I came forward this morning."

"Tell me about it," I said.

"I'm a rather new Christian," she said. "I loved reading your book. It really challenged me, but I felt I could never witness effectively to anyone because I don't know the Bible like you do. You seem to witness so easily and naturally."

"God doesn't expect you to witness like I do. No two people ever have the same testimony. But if you are willing, he'll bring people to you who need to hear what God has done in your life. You needn't be fearful. God's in control, you know."

"I can hardly believe it," she said, as she reached over and gave me a hug. "To think God put us together this morning is incredible. Thank you for writing the book."

"I wrote the book hoping God would use it to motivate Christians to witness," I said. "You have no idea how you have encouraged me this morning. Isn't God good to allow us to see some of the fruits of our labor?

"You said my book was one of the reasons you responded to the invitation this morning. What did the pastor say that caused you to come forward?" I asked.

"When he said, 'Lost opportunities can never be retrieved,' I couldn't help but think that someone went out of their way to speak to me about Christ. When he said, 'God wants you to take the opportunities he gives you to share the gospel with others,' I felt that was meant for me. Between the book I read and the sermon this morning, I decided to take another step of faith. I made a commitment to be a witness for the Lord," she said.

"Tell me, Kelly," I said, "how did you become a Christian?"

She smiled, "I was a very unhappy person. I could have just about anything money could buy. One day I looked at my beautiful house, my car and my lovely wardrobe. *What's wrong with me?* I asked myself. *Why am I so unhappy?* I sat down, and for the first time in my life I prayed seriously to the Lord: 'Dear Lord, help me out of my misery. Something is very wrong in my life. Please send someone to show me the way.'

"I meant every word of my prayer," she said. "I wanted to know the truth and God answered. About an hour later, a neighbor came to my door, and invited me to a Bible study. 'I can't believe you're here,' I said. 'I just prayed and asked God to help me out of my misery. Here you are in answer to my prayer.'

"My neighbor introduced me to Jesus Christ, the way, the truth and the life. I received him that day as my personal Savior. I now know what the abundant life is all about. It certainly isn't in things but in Christ."

There was an air of excitement about Kelly as she said, "I really do want to be a witness for Jesus Christ. I want to be available to him."

"Perhaps you can get involved in the 'Evangelism Explosion' group. They call every Monday night on the people that have visited the church. It will be a wonderful way to learn to share the gospel with a stranger. You observe someone else share at first, and then when you are ready, you get a chance to share. The training is excellent," I said.

We prayed together and then we both left. She left happy about her new commitment to Christ. I went home rejoicing because of the opportunity I had to encourage a new believer in Christ.

Reflection

Christians need Christians! As the body of Christ, each one of us can contribute to the needs of another believer. In the case of Kelly, God met her need when she called on him for help. He provided a Christian neighbor. The neighbor showed her that it was normal for her to feel dissatisfied. *Things* can never satisfy the longing of the soul. Only Jesus Christ can meet that need.

After growing in the Christian life for a while, God provided a challenge for Kelly. She understood that the gift of salvation was not something for her to keep only for herself. It was to be shared. Her problem was one of timidity. "I don't know the Bible very well. I'm afraid I won't do a good job," she said.

The longer we live the Christian life, the more we realize that God is in control. He brings people into our lives that he wants us to minister to. Some need to accept Jesus Christ as Savior. Others may need discipling. Some may just need encouragement to live for the Lord. All of us can share what Jesus Christ has done for us. We don't need to be theologians to do this.

We have learned from Kelly's story that God met her need when she was ready, when her heart was prepared to receive Jesus as her Savior.

When she had walked with him for a while, the Spirit of God nudged her to be his witness. She struggled with that for a while and yet in God's mercy he brought the right circumstances about to encourage her.

There is nothing like the Christian life. It is never boring and it seems as though God has surprises for us every day.

For the Christian, witnessing is not an option. It's a command of the Lord. What he has asked us to do, he will give us the power to follow through. And with it comes joy. It really puts the sparkle into life. Step out in faith and try it!

35

A Stranger's Invitation

hile in church, my husband drew my attention to three people sitting across the aisle. "Have you ever seen them before?" he asked.

"No, I haven't. Let's try to talk to them after the meeting."

Paul and I try to be friendly to visitors. We want them to feel welcome.

Torrey Johnson was speaking on "The Glory of Israel's Future." My eyes kept wandering to the people across the aisle. They kept looking at each other in a strange way. They seemed uncomfortable.

"I wonder if they're Jewish," I whispered to Paul.

"Could be," he answered.

As soon as the "amen" was pronounced in the closing prayer, the three people rushed for the door. They had a distance to go since they had been sitting about halfway down in the auditorium that had a seating capacity of two thousand. I quickly went after them. When I caught up to the younger woman, I tapped her on the shoulder.

"Are you a visitor?" I asked.

"Yes, I am," she answered.

"Did you enjoy the service?"

"Well, I've never heard anything like it and I don't agree with the message," she said.

"I understand," I said. "You're Jewish, right?"

"Yes, I am. My parents and I decided to visit here tonight. We didn't realize it was a church since it looks like a community center from the outside. We saw an ad in the paper which said there was to be a lecture on the 'Future of Israel.' Of course, the speaker is not correct in his assumptions."

"Interesting you should say you are Jewish. I love the Old Testament. In fact I taught the Book of Genesis in a Bible study. I find it fascinating to see how God dealt with his people."

Just then her father came up, waved his arm, and said, "Come on, let's get going." He seemed to be in a hurry.

"Oh, please, don't go." I said, "We're just getting acquainted. Tell me, where do you live?"

"We live in Florida in the winter," he replied, "but our home is in New York."

"Do you ever get to Detroit?" I asked.

"Once in a while."

I don't know what made me say it, but I heard it come out of my mouth. "If you ever get to Detroit," I asked, "would you come and have dinner with us?"

"Well, now, aren't you nice!" he exclaimed. "We want *you* to come to *our house* next Friday, six o'clock prompt."

I was overwhelmed. I hardly knew what to say. Refusing was out of the question. After all I had issued the invitation first.

"We'd be delighted to come," I said.

The woman introduced herself as Janice, and said, "This is my father, David Cohen."

Before we had a chance to introduce ourselves her mother came to join us.

"This is Mr. and Mrs. . . .?" She laughed, then turned to her mother and said, "Dad's invited these people for dinner next Friday, and we don't even know their names."

Her mother looked surprised but responded, "How lovely. We'll certainly look forward to your visit."

"Our name is Pickard, Paul and Nellie. I didn't get your mother's name."

"Mom's name is Rachel," Janice said, as we shook hands.

"My husband is a rabbi," Janice said with a twinkle in her eyes. "He'll set you straight." Even though she was teasing, I felt she meant it.

"That will be exciting," I said as I gulped. "I've never met a rabbi before. I'd love to talk to him and pick his brain."

On the way home I turned to Paul and said, "*Wow,* I wonder where this will lead us!"

"I think it will be very interesting," he said.

During the following week both Paul and I prayed much for the coming event. We asked God for wisdom and that he would love these dear people through us.

Friday evening came and I must admit I was a bit nervous. We arrived promptly at 6:00 P.M. Janice came to the door and graciously invited us in. We were introduced to three other couples. They seemed friendly and made us feel at home.

The men then departed to the closed-in porch on the opposite side of the house. The women stayed in the living room.

It wasn't long before the women started to talk about their disappointment in a certain TV personality. "She used to be one of my favorite talk-show hosts, but lately her language is so smutty I can't stand listening to her," one of the women said. "I'm thinking of writing her a letter and telling her I thought she was above the smut and dirt of the media. I'd like her to know I'm disappointed in her."

Mmm, I thought, *these women have high standards. I like that.*

Janice leaned over and whispered, "Let's go out on the porch and see what the men are doing." She seated me right next to her husband.

"Aaron," Janice said, "Nellie says she wants to 'pick your brain.'"

The rabbi looked interested. "What would you like to know?" he asked.

"I am interested in knowing how you conduct your services. Do you preach a sermon like our minister does? As a rabbi what is your procedure?"

"We usually have a discussion. I may ask a question like, 'Do you believe the Bible is true, and is it relevant in our lives today?'"

"That sounds interesting," I said. "I believe the Bible is true, and it certainly is relevant in our lives today. Humans are still as rebellious as they were in Bible times.

"How would you handle the story of Cain and Abel?" I asked.

"We would discuss rebellion and how it affects us."

"What about the fact that Cain didn't bring the proper sacrifice? It was supposed to be a blood sacrifice."

I had not been aware until then that all the men in the room were listening. By the expression on their faces it was apparent that they were keenly interested in what was going on.

"What makes you so interested in the Jews?" a man named Isidore asked. He seemed rather belligerent.

At that point, my husband spoke up. "I'm glad you asked. On the way over here tonight, Nellie and I were talking about the fact that the Oracles of God were given to the Jews. Also, almost every book in the New Testament was written by a Jew. We owe them a great debt."

"Oh, well now, I never thought about that," Isidore said. "But we don't believe in those bloody sacrifices."

"Then you don't know your Bible very well," I teased.

"She's right," the rabbi told the group. Then he turned to me and with a smile said, "We usually don't let Isidore speak, but since you're here, he's taking advantage." Everyone laughed.

We all chatted for a while. Everyone seemed to be in a good mood. Then Mrs. Cohen came in the room and handed each man, including my husband, a yarmulke (a little black skull cap the Jews wear to show reverence to God).

Paul's hair gets quite curly in the Florida weather. When he put the yarmulke on I thought, *My husband would make a very handsome Jew.*

We were all invited to a beautifully set table. The food had been prepared ahead of time. Since Friday night is the beginning of the Sabbath, no cooking is allowed.

The attention was focused on us. We were different. We were outsiders. It was understandable. Since I was the one who had been asking the rabbi questions, others were eager to get in on the conversation.

Rachel, the rabbi's mother-in-law asked, "Tell us about your children. Do they believe as you do?"

Before I could reply, Isidore (the man who didn't believe in a bloody sacrifice) interrupted and said, "If you're born into a Jewish family, you'll always be a Jew. If you're born into a Christian family, you'll always be a Christian."

"Not necessarily so," I said.

"Well, then how does a person become a Christian?" he asked.

"If I tell you, I have to mention Jesus Christ, and I don't want to offend you."

"You may mention Jesus Christ as long as we ask you. But not if you initiate it," Janice said.

"Well, then, I'll tell you how a person becomes a Christian. Someone may be born into a Christian home but they are not born a Christian. Everyone is born a sinner. God's standards are perfect. No one can reach them.

"God provided a way that we could be accepted by him. Each individual must confess he or she is a sinner in the sight of a holy God. That is not enough, however; each must receive Jesus Christ as his or her personal Savior. Jesus Christ is our perfect sacrifice. He was without spot or blemish and willingly bore the penalty of our sins on the cross.

"The Bible also says if you confess with your mouth that 'Jesus is Lord' and believe in your heart that God raised him from the dead you will be saved (Rom. 10:9).

"I have done that and Paul has too. It doesn't mean we never sin again. We are human and we have learned to hate sin because of what it cost our Savior, Jesus Christ. When we sin in word or deed and become aware of it, we confess it to God and he forgives us.

"I was born into a Christian home and was taught all of this. For many years I took all my teaching for granted. I didn't appreciate what Jesus Christ had done for me. It didn't affect my life. I had head knowledge but now I've made a personal commitment to Jesus Christ. He is my Savior and Lord. It's changed my life. I'm a new person. I now want to live for him and please him.

"My children experienced the same thing. They weren't sure what Mom and Dad taught them was what they wanted. They did a little experimenting on their own but found out that Jesus Christ was the only answer to life.

"Not only has my life been changed but I have seen the change in many other lives as well," I added.

The rabbi turned to me and said, "If what you believe changes people's lives for the better, then what you believe is valid."

"I was born in England," Rachel said. "As a young person the kids in the neighborhood called me a 'Jesus killer.' It made me feel awful. They wouldn't play with me."

"It was our sins that sent him to the cross. He was willing to die on the cross for our sins. You need to know not all people who call themselves Christians are true believers. You see, God said, 'I will bless those who bless you [referring to the Jews], and whoever curses you I will curse . . .'" (Gen. 12:3).

"Well, we asked you to tell us about Christianity and you did. Thank you." Rachel said.

It seemed as though the air was cleared. The questions everyone had, seemed to be answered for the time being.

We spent a pleasant evening but then it was getting late and people began to leave.

"Before I leave, Aaron, I want to ask you who you think Isaiah is writing about in the fifty-third chapter."

"I'm not familiar with that Scripture but I'll look it up and tell you the next time we see you."

As we were walking out the door, one woman who had recently returned from Hungary came up to me and whispered, "My grandmother told me about Jesus and taught me to pray."

"I'm so glad," I said. There was no opportunity to talk further.

Mr. and Mrs. Cohen walked us to the car and talked to us for a long time. "We will be leaving for New York next week but when we come back next year, we must get together," Rachel said.

"The next time, you must come to our home," I urged.

By the time we finally left it was 1:30 A.M. We generally retire around 11:00 P.M. On the way home, Paul and I talked about the freedom we were given to share the gospel. "To think they would ask us to tell them about our faith," I said. "To me, that's amazing."

It was early morning before I could settle down to sleep. The stimulus of the previous evening kept me awake. We had had a good time. We thanked God for the beautiful experiences he is pleased to give us.

One of the first things I thought of when we returned to Florida the following year was, *I must call my new Jewish friends and invite them over.* I was anxious to know if Rabbi Aaron had read the fifty-third chapter of Isaiah and what his conclusions were.

When Rachel answered the phone, I asked if all four of them could come over the following Thursday evening for dinner.

"I'm not sure about Aaron and Janice, but my husband and I would be delighted. Tell us what time you want us and we'll be there."

"I need to know if there is anything you should not eat. I'll be careful to serve the proper food," I said.

"Why don't you just serve dessert this time; then there won't be a problem."

I was disappointed when Aaron, the rabbi, and Janice didn't come. They had previous engagements. Paul and David sat at the dining room table and talked while Rachel and I sat on the sofa. She told me about the trips they had taken abroad and the beautiful things they had brought home with them. Every once in a while she would put her hand on my knee and say, "Nellie, I just love you." She must have done that six times during the evening.

In my heart I said, "Thank you, Lord."

When they started to leave, I expressed my disappointment at not seeing the rabbi and Janice.

"Aaron's going to be chairing a discussion next Saturday at the clubhouse. Maybe you would find it interesting to attend," Rachel said.

I looked at Paul. He nodded so I said, "We'd love to come."

They gave us directions and the time of the meeting.

I could hardly wait for the time to come. When we arrived, there were about a hundred people in the audience.

The rabbi talked about three wise men, the wise men being Pharaoh, his cupbearer, and Joseph. Pharaoh was wise because he told the cupbearer about his dream (Gen. 41). The cupbearer was wise because he admitted, "This day I remember my shortcomings," and Joseph was wise because he had the smarts.

The rabbi promised that the lecture would end on an upbeat note.

"When I'm finished, we'll have a discussion.

"I can trust a man who remembers his shortcomings," he said, "but I can't trust President————[one of our former presidents] because he didn't remember *his* shortcomings."

As the lecture continued statements were made about Joseph and his intelligence. Then the talk went to the problems in the Near East.

One man raised his hand. "I thought this lecture was going to be upbeat. Frankly I'm scared to death about the happenings in the world. The city I live in hates Jews. I don't like to tell anyone I'm Jewish. As far as I'm concerned, they're all going to be extinguished." Then the man sat down.

I impulsively raised my hand. My heart went out to this group. I will never forget the fear on the faces of the people in that audience. Then I remembered. I was a Christian in a Jewish meeting. I felt I had no right to speak. I quickly put my hand down. Rachel noticed, and to my surprise, took my arm and lifted it—high.

"Nellie's got something to say," she declared.

"Oh, please, I shouldn't have raised my hand. I'm just a visitor. I have no right. Please forgive me."

"If you've got something to say, say it," Rachel offered.

"Nellie, would you like to contribute something?" the rabbi asked.

I quickly turned to my husband. He didn't look at me. I'm sure if he'd found a hole in the floor he would have crawled into it.

Then I realized he would be praying. *He knows how quickly I react,* I thought.

I stood up and explained, "Don't you realize the very fact Jews are alive today is one of the greatest miracles of all time? Remember that God took Abraham and showed him the heavens? He said, 'I will surely bless you and make your descendants as numerous as the stars in the sky and as the sand on the seashore . . .' (Gen. 22:17; see also Gen. 15:5).

"Although President————didn't remember his shortcomings, King David remembered *his.* He confessed his sin and God called him 'a man after his own heart . . .'" (1 Sam. 13:14).

I trembled as I sat down. I was surprised when the people clapped. They seemed delighted that a Christian could remind them of the blessings God had bestowed on the Jews. It calmed their fears.

After the lecture a crowd of people gathered around. One man said, "Thank you for your encouragement. We needed that reminder."

I was both amazed and grateful to God.

David Cohen then announced, "We want you to come to dinner with us. We won't take *no* for an answer."

"We'd love to," I said, "but we are expecting guests from Michigan tomorrow, and I need to do some grocery shopping on the way home tonight," I said.

"There's plenty of time for that," David said. "It's Hanukkah, and we want you to celebrate with us. Come now, let's get going," he insisted.

It was no use arguing with David, so we went.

When we arrived at their home, the rabbi opened his arms and said, "You sure helped me out today. Thanks a lot."

"I disagree with one thing you said in your lecture," Paul said. "Joseph wasn't wise because he had the smarts. He said God revealed the meaning of the dream to him."

"You're right, Paul, it does say that God revealed it to him. I shouldn't have said that. Thanks for bringing it to my attention."

We looked up the verse later and the exact wording says when Pharaoh sent for Joseph, he said to him, "I had a dream, and no one can interpret it. But I have heard it said of you that when you hear a dream you can interpret it."

"I cannot do it," Joseph replied to Pharaoh, "but God will give Pharaoh the answer he desires" (Gen. 41:15–16).

It was a privilege to celebrate this special holiday with our Jewish friends. Rabbi explained to us that Hanukkah, which means *dedication,* is called "The Jewish Feast of Lights." It lasts eight days. At sundown on each day a new candle is lit. By the end of the celebration, eight candles stand together.

The feast started about 165 B.C. by Judas Maccabaeus to honor the rededicating of the Jewish temple in Jerusalem. Three years before, a Syrian conqueror had used the temple for idol worship.

This particular evening marked the seventh day of celebration. It was interesting to hear the rabbi pray before the meal. He addressed God as *Adonai* (Lord). The Jew does not address God as we do. The name God is too overwhelming to be expressed or described in words. Too awesome or sacred to be spoken.

He thanked Adonai for his abundant provision and goodness to them. I missed not hearing the prayer end in Jesus' name. *Oh, if only these dear people knew that the veil in the temple has been lifted,* I thought.

After we finished eating there was a knock at the door. A couple we had met earlier at the discussion group came in. Rachel introduced me saying, "Nellie knows the Bible better than any Yiddish woman I know. I mean it, better than *any* Yiddish woman I know. I just love her."

I couldn't believe the love that was shown to us. God had given us a love for each other. I was moved emotionally.

About a month later we were invited to David's eightieth birthday party. The following Sunday after the evening service we went out with the Zondervans, Pat and Mary. I told them about our Jewish friends and the birthday party we were going to attend.

When we got home Pat called and asked, "Will you be up at eight o'clock in the morning? I've got something to give you."

"Yes, we're up before eight."

I wondered what he was up to. Many times in the past he had given us a book or two. When I opened the door the next morning, there stood Pat with a large picture book of Israel. It was in color and had beautiful, breathtaking pictures of the land.

"I want you to give this to your Jewish friend for his birthday," he said.

"You overwhelm me," I said. "What else can I say? I know Mr. Cohen will love it. Thank you. This is what the body of Christ is all about. One fills in where the other one lacks. We didn't know what to get him. This is absolutely perfect."

As we suspected, David loved the gift. It was the second edition of this book. The first book had pictures of Israel but no Scripture was included. Between the time of the first and second edition, both the author and photographer had become Christians and had inserted Scripture verses on each page. It was an exciting gift to give.

When all the gifts had been opened, I went over to the rabbi. I wanted to tell him about my dad.

"My father died since the last time I saw you," I told him. "It was beautiful. He died praising the Lord."

"That's remarkable," he observed. "I don't know any people like you. Your faith is beautiful."

As we were talking, Janice came over and handed us a plate.

"Help yourselves to the goodies on the table. There's plenty of food to eat," she said.

I filled my plate and went to look for a place to sit on the porch. Paul sat on the opposite side of the room. There were forty people in attendance. We didn't know any of the guests.

I'm sure it was obvious that Paul and I weren't Jewish. One of the women seated near me asked, "How do you know the Cohens? Where did you meet them?"

"They came to a meeting at our church, thinking it was a community center. The speaker was talking about Israel's future, but they didn't agree with the message."

She chuckled. "That's a riot. By the way, my name's Betty, and I'm glad you came to the party.

"Rachel tells me you are doing some writing. What do you write about?" she continued.

"People, and their relationship to God."

"Sounds interesting."

She then noticed her empty plate and said to her husband, "Will you please take my plate into the kitchen? Bring me some coffee while you're at it."

Her husband graciously took the plate, and as he left, Betty's friend said, "After twenty-five years, it's time our husbands start waiting on us, don't you think?"

"I couldn't agree more," Betty answered.

I couldn't help it. I had to say something.

"Oh," I said, kiddingly, "who's been bringing home the bacon for the past twenty-five years?"

For a moment there was dead silence. Then they started to laugh. I thought they'd never stop. I finally caught on. Bacon—Jewish? The two don't mix.

I apologized profusely. "I've never used that phrase before—ever. I don't know what made me say it."

"We think it's hilarious. I want you to write that in your book, and I want my name in it. Do you promise?"

"Yes, Betty." (I've kept my promise!)

Sometime after the party, we invited our Jewish friends to our home for dinner. We asked for instruction concerning food.

"Don't serve us any meat or any butter. Fish, fruit, and dessert will be fine."

We had a good time. Our guests all have such a good sense of humor that the evening was without any tension.

After dinner, we got comfortable in the living room. At times everyone would talk at once. It gave me an opportunity to talk to the rabbi.

"Have you had a chance to read the fifty-third chapter of Isaiah?" I asked.

"No, I haven't. Bring me a Bible, and I'll read it right now."

I brought him my Bible and opened it to the text.

After he had finished reading it, I asked, "Who do you think Isaiah is talking about?"

"I think Isaiah is talking about himself," he answered.

"Would you think it strange if I thought Isaiah was talking about Jesus Christ?"

"No, I wouldn't think it was strange. Do you know you are the only one I can talk to about these things?"

Paul kept the rest of the group busy, so we could keep on talking.

It wasn't long before David stood up. "It's time to go. Come on, everybody." As usual, he began waving his arms.

"Go ahead. I'll meet you in the parking lot," the rabbi said.

"We all have to leave together." No one argued with David and so they left.

When we got back to Michigan, we received an invitation to a wedding in their city. When we arrived, we called the Cohens and told them we'd like to see them if it was convenient.

"You must come to dinner," Janice said.

Arrangements were made and we arrived at six o'clock on Saturday evening. Dinner was ready, and we sat down at a beautifully decorated table. When the rabbi gave thanks for the meal, I recognized quotes from Isaiah. He also used some of the names of God. I commented on it when he had finished.

He beamed as he said, "That was from Isaiah, the sixth chapter. I've been reading that book lately."

We sat at the dining room table until 10:30 P.M. discussing our faith and God's dealings with the Jews.

"I don't understand why the Jews are called God's chosen people," Janice said. "What were they chosen for?"

"Many Jewish people have asked me that question. The Jew was chosen to carry the Messiah seed and to tell the Gentiles what God is like."

"How can we do that? We don't understand it ourselves."

"Maybe we Christians can help the Jews to know more about God's plan."

The evening ended on that note. There were many hugs and "I love yous" as we left.

Reflection

We still see our Jewish friends from time to time. It is hard to discuss the Bible with those who are not familiar with Scripture. Even the rabbi knew only the first five books of the Old Testament. He now has started to read other portions. I believe he is searching.

I wrote this chapter to show my readers that witnessing is not just sharing the gospel and then having people sign on the dotted line. We are called to be witnesses. Only God can give the increase.

36

Desperate for Answers

J've got to ask you some questions before class starts," Dawn pleaded. I had just been introduced to her at our Neighborhood Bible Study. I noticed the woman seemed distraught.

"I won't be able to sit through the session unless I get some answers. I'm desperate. Noreen said you'd be able to help me and invited me to come today. Could we go in another room so we can talk privately?"

I left my coffee cup and roll on a nearby table. Noreen, our hostess, led us to her husband's office.

"When I told you I was desperate, I meant it," Dawn said. "I've got to know how I can get to heaven. What is my part and what is God's part? Who is the Lord and how do I know what truth is?" The words came pouring out of her mouth like a sudden rush of water from a spring. She didn't stop.

"Wait a minute," I said, "One thing at a time."

"It's just that I've gone everywhere for help and I'm about ready to give up. It seems useless. No one seems to know the truth about God."

"There is only one place to find the truth about God and Jesus Christ," I said. "The Bible is the Word of God. It's the only reliable source of truth I know. No one knows anything about God or Jesus Christ apart from the Scriptures."

"Well, then, how can I get to heaven?" she asked.

"First of all I need to ask if you agree with God when he says in Romans 3:23 that 'all have sinned and fall short of the glory of God.'

193

Do you recognize that you, Dawn, have fallen short of God's standards and can't make the grade on your own?"

"I know I'm not good enough," she replied. "Every week I go to confession because I know I have sinned. I try to keep a clean slate but I just can't make it from one week to the next. Fact is, I go to confession on Saturday at 4:00 P.M. and then to Mass on Sunday at 9:00 A.M. I sleep eight hours a night so that doesn't give much time to sin. I thought I might make it to heaven if I died on Sunday right after Mass. I would have fifty-two chances in a year. I just can't take the strain anymore. I feel so empty and hollow on the inside. There's got to be a better way." She put her head in her hands.

"Oh, Dawn," I replied, "there is a better way. Jesus said in John 14:6: 'I am the way, the truth and the life. No one comes to the Father except through me.' You see, Jesus is the way. Let me give you a couple of other verses. Romans 5:6 says, 'Just at the right time, when we were still powerless, Christ died for the ungodly.' The eighth verse says, 'But God demonstrates his own love for us in this: While we were still sinners, Christ died for us.'"

"That's his part," she said. "Now what's my part?"

"Now listen to this. John 1:12 says, 'Yet to all who received him [Jesus], to those who believed in his name, he gave the right to become the children of God.'"

"Don't I have to do some sort of penance?" she asked.

"Jesus Christ took your penalty. He paid the price for our salvation. We can't work for it. Look, see what it says in Ephesians 2:8–9. 'For it is by grace you have been saved, through faith—and this not from yourselves, it is the gift of God—not by works, so that no one can boast.' The Scripture goes on to say in the tenth verse: 'For we are God's workmanship, created in Christ Jesus to do good works, which God prepared in advance for us to do.'

"You see, we don't work for our salvation. Jesus Christ is our salvation. But after we have been welcomed into the family of God by accepting Jesus Christ as our Savior, then we show our love for him by doing what pleases him. He shows us his will through his Word, the Bible. It comes supernaturally then, because we have his Spirit living in us.

"If you did penance that means that would be paying the penalty for your sins. That's really an insult to the Savior. He paid the supreme penalty. He gave his life. Now he wants to give you a gift, the gift of salvation and eternal life. Would you like to receive his gift?"

"Oh, yes, with all of my heart."

"Then why don't you tell him that right now?"

There was a strong emotional response as Dawn prayed: "Oh, God, I confess I have sinned over and over again. The horrible part is that I've continually offended Jesus Christ. I'm truly sorry. I want to live for you. Thank you for offering me forgiveness and making a way for me to be accepted by you. I, here and now, receive Jesus Christ as my Savior and Lord. In his name I pray, *Amen.*"

Dawn looked at me and said, "Thank you for helping me today. What a relief. I've been living in torment. I can't believe it's so simple. Now I don't need to strive any longer. I can come to these Bible studies and learn more about Jesus."

The women in the other room were patiently waiting for us to return and start the study. I shared with them what had happened. They were excited as they expressed their joy about Dawn's decision to follow Christ. Some of the women knew why Dawn and I had a private conversation and had been praying for us.

Dawn loved the Bible studies and was growing in love and knowledge of the Scriptures. She was eating it up.

I was surprised when she announced one day, "I've decided I'm not going to go to church anymore. I've been to all kinds of churches, and each one confuses me more than the previous one. I'm only going to come to this Bible study. It's really all I need."

"Why don't you come to my church?" I asked. "I know you'll love our pastor. You say you love the Bible study. I guarantee you'll love his preaching even more."

"I don't know." She hesitated then she said, "I'm really satisfied just coming to the Bible study. I work on my lesson each week and I'm really getting a lot out of it."

"What about your children? What kind of teaching are they getting?" I asked.

"I know you're right. I must see to it that they get good teaching." She then turned and looked directly into my eyes and said, "You think we'll like it, huh?" She gave me a skeptical look.

"It won't hurt you to try," I answered. "How about next Sunday?"

"I suppose you won't let me come back to the Bible class if I don't come," she said.

"Of course I will. That has nothing to do with it. You don't have to come. I just think it will meet a need in your life and that of your children," I said.

"Okay, I'll see what the children say. I've got a couple in high school. I hope I can persuade them."

Dawn's husband was gone a great deal of the time. His business kept him away most of the week. He chose not to attend the service. The following Sunday Dawn and her children came to church. As I arrived, I noticed them sitting at the front of the church. They were actually sitting in the second row. *My, they're brave to sit this close to the speaker their very first visit,* I thought.

Before I could ask her how she enjoyed the service she walked over to me and said, "I know this is where I belong. This is it for me. I've never heard such a wonderful sermon before—ever," she declared.

"Joe Stowell is truly a man of God," I replied. "You'll learn a lot sitting under his ministry."

Dawn's children weren't as happy about the service as their mother, but she told them they must attend church with her.

It wasn't long before Peter, her oldest son, became acquainted with some of the young people at the church. He joined in their activities and soon became a part of it.

Peter recently told me that the first two Sundays at church he hated it. "It just wasn't for me," he said. "I really didn't listen to the sermon. My mind kept wandering. I was confused. I had so many problems, I just wanted to get away from everything. I thought if I could just start life over again maybe I could make it. I was attending Cranbrook Academy [a private boys' school]. Anyone should be grateful to be able to attend there, but I wasn't happy.

"One of the young people from the church invited me to a retreat. I decided to go, and there, under the ministry of Dawson McAllister, my eyes were opened. I made a conscious choice to follow Jesus Christ.

"It took a year though, before I realized that every Christian has a responsibility to share the Good News of the gospel. It was made clear to me at another retreat I attended.

"Joe Stowell, our pastor, was speaking. His message hit hard. 'Are you satisfied with being just another Christian in a pew?' he asked. 'Or do you want to go all the way with the Lord? Do you really want to live for him?'

"I said to myself, *I'm either going all the way or not at all.* That is when I told the Lord, 'I'm not going to play at being a Christian. I'm ready to take that responsibility. I want to be a witness for you.'"

I was delighted to hear Peter's story. I couldn't help but think, *If Dawn hadn't taken her family to church that first Sunday morning Peter might not be telling me this wonderful story.*

"Have you had many opportunities to witness for the Lord?" I asked Peter.

"After my commitment to be a witness for Jesus Christ," he said, "I had an opportunity to go to New York City with some young people from the church to do street evangelism. There I had many openings to witness. I talked to the rich, the poor, and to people from other countries. There are so many needy people in New York. Many people responded to the gospel message. It was a wonderful experience.

"I had the mistaken idea that it was mostly the poor people that we should try to reach for Christ," he went on. "The rich didn't seem to have any needs. I soon discovered that the rich had just as many problems—different perhaps—but problems nevertheless. It's just that they didn't show their hurts on the outside. I got close to a few and found once they were willing to talk, they too were hurting. They were people needing the peace and forgiveness only Jesus Christ can give.

"I had been home only two days," Peter said, "when I was asked if I'd like to go to Guatemala with a team of young people from the church. I didn't have much time to get ready but I jumped at the chance. There we helped missionaries. We painted and repaired whatever needed fixing. We did whatever we could to ease the load of the missionaries. I gained a lot of insight as to the work of missionaries. Our Spanish was marginal but we had a chance to pass out tracts. We tried to communicate the love of Christ by our attitude toward them."

"What have you been doing since you graduated from high school?" I asked.

"I've had a desire for a long time to climb Mount McKinley. A couple of years ago the opportunity came. I had the privilege of going with a group. One of the team members was a Christian. Between the two of us we witnessed to every member of the team.

"Now I have a chance to go to Kenya and to climb Mount Kilimanjaro," Peter went on. "I'm going with the National Outdoor Leadership School. We will be learning camping skills and survival training. There will be sixteen people in our group. Everything that happens is dependent on the cooperation of each individual member."

"How long will you be gone?" I asked.

"We'll be gone three months. It will also include a safari and time spent with some tribespeople hunting and fishing."

"It sounds exciting," I said. "Do you know any of the other team members?"

"No, I don't know anyone. I am praying though, that God will send another Christian on the trip. I want to be a witness for the Lord while I'm there. It would be nice to have another believer along whose mind-set is the same as mine. Then we could work together."

"I'll be eager to hear about your trip when you return," I declared. "I'll pray with you that God will make this a profitable trip, and that you'll have many witnessing opportunities."

"Someone said, 'There are risks when you follow the Lord.' But I don't believe that." Peter added, "There is no safer place to be than walking in obedience with the Lord. When you're in step with God, it's a matter of faith."

Reflection

As I look back I ask myself, *Is this the same young man that visited our church and hated it?* It shows what happens when the Spirit of God is allowed to take over in a person's life.

Recently someone asked Peter, "Are you doing full-time Christian work?"

I loved his answer. He replied, "Is there any other kind?"

To think this young man has only been a Christian for four years is amazing. The maturity he has is truly a miracle of God. It's refreshing to see a young man only twenty-one years of age so enthusiastic about following the Lord and doing his will.

As I was reviewing this story with Dawn, she related to me that the only reason she visited our church was to get me off her back.

I laughed and said, "I thought I was being an encourager."

"I know now, however, that God was in it. The results are the proof," she declared.

As Dawn was reflecting back on God's workings in her life, she recalled the many times he had nudged her to follow him. "I kept putting him off. I remember once when I was late for a tennis match, I grabbed a sweater and started to run. I tripped and fell from the top of the stairs to the bottom. I knew I was hurt and I sensed God's presence. I remember saying, 'Not now God, I'm too busy.'

"I was able to get up and call an ambulance. I will never forget the trip to the hospital. A woman came along with the paramedics and all she said to me was, 'Young lady, you need to trust the Lord.'

"As I was carried out of the ambulance, I turned to the woman and asked, 'May I see you again?'"

"'No, you'll probably never see me again. Just remember what I said.'"

"I have often wondered," Dawn mused, "if God sent that woman to warn me. You see, Nellie, even though I was desperate that day at Bible study, I really wasn't ready to receive Christ until then. I know there were other times when I ignored God's promptings. I'm glad he didn't give up on me."

"God's mercy and grace is something we cannot understand. We know we don't deserve it," I said. "We just accept it with gratefulness of heart. It is something I never want to take for granted."

"Let me tell you what happened recently," Dawn went on. "I was thinking about the goodness of the Lord, and all he had done for me. Then I pictured myself leaving the church. I was wearing a new white robe. My old clothes were all in a heap on the ground. I was new. All the hollow emptiness within me was gone. It was all behind me.

"As I sat in church the following Sunday, I said to the Lord, 'I must really love you to be sitting in such an ugly church.'"

I was flabbergasted. "Dawn," I protested, "I think we have a beautiful church."

"Being a decorator, I've always dreamed of worshiping in a cathedral-type church," she said. "I love the magnificent church structure, the majestic beauty, and the stained-glass windows. I also love the stone carvings on the buildings."

"But we don't worship a *building*," I explained. "The building isn't the church. Do you know that many of the cathedrals of old symbolized the power of the church and the pride and wealth of the town in which it was built? That isn't what Christianity is all about."

"Oh, yes, I see that now," Dawn said. "The beauty is not in the building but in the people who worship there. They are the true church since they are the body of Christ.

"I must admit," she went on, "I loved all the trappings, the pomp and the ceremony. But now I've shed my dirty clothes and put on a white robe. I'm free! I'm clean! and I'm living for the Lord."

One of the most effective ways of reaching people for Christ is through informal neighborhood Bible studies—all who can, should get involved.

Christians can bring their neighbors who may be churchgoers but haven't the slightest idea how to be in the family of God. Many people feel that because they are regular church attenders they automatically are a candidate for heaven. The disappointment comes when the emptiness of ritualistic services does not meet the needs of their hearts. We must point them to the Savior.

A woman in our Bible class confided in me one day, "I have gone to church all of my life and I don't know anything about the Bible. How is it that you know so much? Have you gone to school to learn these things?"

"No," I answered. "I've read the Scriptures since I was a little girl. We have had excellent Bible teaching both at our church and in my home. My Sunday school teachers encouraged everyone in the class to memorize verses from the Bible. It's been a continual learning process. It's the best education I've ever had."

I'm a Hypocrite

I saw the young teenage girl head for the front of the auditorium. The speaker at the Bible conference had invited those who wanted to receive Christ as Savior to come forward.

"Counseling will be available at the close of the service," he explained.

She did not walk over to him but stood off at the side by herself. She was sobbing and seemed devastated.

The speaker nodded for me to go and speak to her. I approached her gently.

"Would you like to talk?" I asked.

"I need desperately to talk to someone. I am absolutely miserable."

"What prompted you to come forward?" I asked.

"I'm confused," she said. "I don't think I've ever really accepted Christ as my Savior. I think I've just been playing around at being a Christian. You see, I've always attended a Christian school. I know all the right words, but I know my heart isn't right before God."

"Is that why you came forward—to make things right with God?" I asked.

"I can't stand living another day with the guilt of being a fraud. I've just been playacting. I realize for the first time that I, Mindy, am a hypocrite and I hate it. Please help me to make things right with God. I want to live a good Christian life."

"If you mean what you say you'll have no problem. The Bible tells us in Luke 19:10 that Jesus came to seek and to save the lost."

"That's me," she wept. "I'm lost."

"Mindy, do you know why Jesus Christ died on the cross?"

"Yes. He died on the cross for my sins. You see I know all that but until now I really wasn't interested. I wanted to have fun with my friends, but I'm not having fun because my insides aren't right."

"Do you know how to pray?" I asked.

"Yes," she seemed a little embarrassed. "I don't deserve God's forgiveness."

"None of us do," I replied. "It's only by his grace that we are saved. Grace means unmerited favor. We don't deserve salvation but because of his love he is willing to forgive us and even make us a member of his family—his royal family.

"First John 1:9 says: 'If we confess our sins, he is faithful and just and will forgive our sins and purify us from all unrighteousness.' Then in John 1:12 it says: 'Yet to all who received him, to those who believed in his name, he gave the right to become the children of God.'

"Are you ready to take that step of faith?" I asked.

"I really want to," she replied.

Mindy prayed and confessed her lack of dependence and trust in Jesus Christ. "I do trust you now and want to be in your family. Right now I receive Christ as my Savior. Please help me to live for you and be a good influence in the lives of my friends. Help me to tell them what I did today. In Jesus' name I pray, *Amen.*"

The lights in the auditorium dimmed. They were preparing to show a missionary film. Mindy and I left after deciding we would meet the following day.

I saw Mindy after breakfast.

"I looked for you after the film last night," she said. "I wanted so much to talk to you further. Can we go some place now?"

We found a corner in the lodge and sat down to chat.

"I'm so glad I made a decision to follow Christ last night. I feel so different. I feel so free, like a load has been lifted. It's like I'm a new person."

"You are a new person, a new person in Jesus Christ," I said. "This is just the beginning though. You took a step of faith last night. The Christian life is one step after another. To grow in Christ you need to begin reading your Bible on a daily basis. God's Word is nourishing. It's like food for your soul. It will make you a healthy Christian if you obey what it says."

"Do you have any Christian friends?" I asked. "I mean the kind that take their faith in Christ seriously."

"Yes, but most of them have been faking it like me. You see I always wanted to be popular. I know how to get attention. If I'm loud and act like a smart aleck people seem to like me and want to be around me. The problem is I don't like myself. I don't want to be that kind of a person.

"No one knows the hurt I have on the inside. I've kept it all to myself. My friends would be surprised if they knew how I really felt.

"My mother and father are divorced. My father abused her. I saw him hurt her. I'm glad she doesn't have to live with him any longer."

"Did your father ever abuse you?" I asked.

"Yes, and he still does," she said. "You see, I have to go and visit him regularly. I would run away if it wasn't for my younger sister and brother. If I don't go he will hurt them. I have to stand in their way."

"What do you mean by that?" I asked.

"My father has a violent temper. He hits and slaps us at the least little thing. Once when we were visiting him, he got mad at my little brother. He doubled up his fist and started toward him. I put my hand up to stop him, and he took my three fingers, bent them backward and broke them. It was absolutely awful. I hated him for that. Once he almost choked me to death."

"Does your mother know about this?" I asked.

"Yes, and she went to the judge to see if he could be denied visiting rights."

"Did the judge do anything for you?"

"No, he said my father still had the right to see his children. My mother cries when we visit him. She hasn't given up though; she's trying to get us help.

"Right now my biggest problem is the hatred and resentment I feel for my father. What can I do about it?"

"There are no easy answers," I replied. "I do know that hate and resentment eat away like a cancer and destroy our insides and are not the answer God would give. The Bible says in Luke 6:28 to do good to those who mistreat you. That's a hard saying. A thought just came to me. Jesus took our hate and replaced it with his love. Do you think you could replace your hate for your dad with pity? The turmoil you are experiencing will disappear. If your father sees your changed attitude, it might soften him. The time may come when you can tell him what Jesus Christ has done for you. In the meantime pray for your dad. He must be a very unhappy man."

"Do you think my father will ever change?" she asked.

"I don't know. It says in Matthew 19:26 '. . . with God all things are possible.' Take one step at a time. I will be praying with you. Even if it doesn't change him it will change you. You'll be a better person because you have forgiven your dad."

"What if Mom can get a restraining order—should I still see him?" she asked.

"My advice would be to accept the order if it comes through. That would be for your own safety and that of your brother and sister. If you are obliged to spend time with him, pray for God's guidance, wisdom, behavior, and protection."

"I'm so glad I came this weekend. My grandparents invited me. In fact my whole family was here last Friday. I was the only one who chose to stay. I'm glad I did. I feel for the first time I have some direction in life."

"You'll be returning to school next week. You are attending one of the finest Christian schools in the country. Why don't you have a talk with your counselor? I'm sure you'll find her to be a good friend."

"Yes, I think I'll be comfortable with that. My new goal in life is to live for Christ."

Reflection

Attending a Christian school gives the student an opportunity to be exposed to spiritual matters. But it is no guarantee that he or she will embrace the teaching it affords. The good part is students are constantly being reminded what the Word of God says. The Spirit of God then has something to activate. Mindy was miserable because having been taught in the Word, she knew what the Christian behavior should be. On the outside she felt she measured up, but her heart betrayed her. "I feel awful," she said.

I recently visited my daughter Karen in Boston. It was her birthday. I told her she needn't make any rich desserts for us since I had just recently discovered my cholesterol level was a bit elevated. We began to discuss the no-cholesterol foods on the market. My seven-year-old granddaughter, Elizabeth, was listening intently.

"Mom, may I go to the store with Grandpa?" she asked. "It's your birthday you know."

Karen smiled and said, "Don't be gone too long."

When she returned, her friend Lindsay was waiting for her.

"I feel so good on the inside," Elizabeth excitedly said to her friend. "I just bought my mother a birthday present with my own money. It was something she needed badly. I want my grandmother to see it before I wrap it."

I went upstairs with her and she took the present out of the bag. It was a package of no-cholesterol muffins. She was so proud. I didn't have the heart to tell her I was the one, not her mother, that had the cholesterol problem. She felt so good on the inside because she wanted to please her mother and she knew that was right.

Admitting to being a hypocrite wasn't easy for Mindy. But living with that burden was eating away her insides. Only the cleansing blood of Jesus Christ could wipe away the guilt and misery of her young life. When she confessed her sin and received Jesus Christ as her Savior she was transformed; she was a new person. She felt good on the inside. Her new goal was to please the Lord.

38

I'm an Atheist

hile at poolside one of my neighbors, a professional near retirement age, said to me recently, "I haven't seen you at the tennis courts this year. I saw you a lot last season but I don't think I've seen you at all this year. Aren't you playing anymore?"

"I still play but I've been rather busy lately."

"What have you been doing with yourself?" he asked.

"I've been busy speaking and doing some writing," I replied.

He seemed curious and asked, "What kind of speaking do you do?"

"I speak about God's dealings in people's lives. My speaking is all Bible based; that is, the Bible is my authority. It's very exciting."

"I don't believe in the Bible," he said. "I don't even believe in God. I believe in scientific facts. God just doesn't fit in to my way of thinking."

"I would think the very fact that you are a scientist would be proof enough. Why, doing research every day would leave no doubt that God exists," I said.

"Well, if there is a God, why doesn't he do something about the starving people around the world? People like the animists who don't know about God?" He sounded annoyed.

"Now wait a minute. There isn't anyone that has an excuse. The Bible says in Romans, chapter one, that what has been known about God has been made plain. For since the creation of the world God's invisible qualities—his eternal power and his divine nature—have

been clearly seen, being understood by what has been made. Therefore men are without excuse. Actually men suppressed the truth
about God. They didn't want to believe. They chose to rebel against
God."

"What if they didn't know any better?"

"God will hold them responsible for the light they have been given.
As I said, creation is evidence there is a God."

"Well, I think God should take care of the starving people in the
world," he continued.

"Here you are, a mere man telling God how he should run his universe. It reminds me of the verse (Isa. 45:9): 'Does the clay say to the
potter, "What are you making?"'"

He didn't get the point, but continued making accusations about
God. He was not angry. I believe he was trying in a friendly way to
trap me. After all he was a scientist, and who was I?

What he didn't know was the power of God. I didn't feel a bit
intimidated.

"The animists don't know about God," he said, "so I don't think
it's fair. And another thing, why have the Jews suffered so much? I
just don't understand it."

"I believe God is trying to get their attention. He wants the Jews
to turn to him in repentance. The Bible says so in 2 Chronicles 7:14:
'If my people, who are called by my name, will humble themselves
and pray and seek my face and turn from their wicked ways, then
will I hear from heaven and will forgive their sin and will heal their
land.'

"By the way," I said, "are you Jewish?"

"Yes, I am."

"You have been talking about people who haven't had a chance
to hear about God. *You* don't have that excuse, do you? I believe you
just refuse to believe.

"God says you have a choice," I said. "He says in Joshua 24:15:
'. . . choose for yourselves this day whom you will serve. . . .' You see
the problem is that man has chosen to go his own way. The Bible
says in Romans 1:20–21 that man is without excuse.

"You have been talking about the people who haven't had a
chance to hear about God," I said. "The Jews have had many chances.
Just think of the privilege God afforded them by giving them his Ora-

cles. They were indeed a blessed people, and yet so many refuse to believe and don't give thanks to their Creator. That's hard for me to comprehend.

"One of my greatest disappointments in talking to Jewish people is they don't know their Scriptures, the Old Testament. I would love to discuss it with them but they are ignorant of it. They are knowledgeable about so many things, even outstanding. I would go as far as to say they are brilliant except for the most important thing in life—God. The Jews have a marvelous heritage. I would think they'd want to know more about it."

"I just don't believe there is a God who created the universe. It's just not possible," he declared.

"Your watch," I said, "that just came into existence by itself? There isn't such a thing as a watchmaker, right? I suppose it stands to reason that because my mind can't conceive of making a watch, it just couldn't happen. But you're wearing it, and it works."

My neighbor had no answers. He stood up to leave. Then he surprised me by saying, "My wife and I will be going to Russia, Poland, and other parts of Europe. We'll be back in about six weeks. When I get back I would like to talk to you further. I am very interested in what you have been saying. Maybe I'm really not an atheist—maybe I'm an agnostic."

"There might be hope for you yet," I teased. "An atheist refuses to believe in God. An agnostic just doesn't know. A smart man like you should look into it."

We had a stimulating discussion without being angry. He was an intelligent man, but his reasoning about God was faulty. I am praying that God will give him a hunger to know his Word, and that he will want to know God.

Reflection

We may not have all the answers. The Spirit of God leads us. Remember the words of Jesus: "But the Counselor, the Holy Spirit, whom the Father will send in my name, will teach you all things and will remind you of everything I have said to you" (John 14:26).

We can only remember what we have read and studied. The Bible says to "Always be prepared to give an answer to everyone who asks you to give the reason for the hope that you have. But do this with gentleness and respect" (1 Peter 3:15).

Think about it. Be prepared and take a step of faith.

There is a price to pay when you're available to God for witnessing, however. You might get so excited about sharing the gospel while doing your grocery shopping that you forget to take your groceries home! That happened to me the other day. Of course it was the first time it ever happened but that's the cost of enjoying God's work to the fullest.

39

The Newcomers

[Jesus said:] "A new command I give you: Love one another. As I have loved you, so you must love one another. By this all men will know that you are my disciples, if you love one another."

John 13:34–35

y name's Mary Martin," the voice on the phone said. "I'm not sure you remember me. You autographed my book when I attended the 'Walk through the Bible' at your church. At the time, I told you that my children attend your Christian school but I'm a member of a Presbyterian church."

"It's been some time ago, but I think I do remember talking to you," I answered.

"I have a new friend who is attending our church," Mary said. "She's from New York and doesn't know many people in this area. She seems drawn to the people in our congregation, yet I don't believe she understands the Scriptures and God's way of salvation. After reading your book, I thought you might be of help to her. Would you be willing to have lunch with us?"

"Sure! I'm tied up until after the holidays but I'm available after the first of the year." So we arranged a meeting for January 8 at Mary's house.

Mary lived about five miles from my home. The garage door was open when I arrived, making it convenient to enter through the back door and so avoid the heavy drifts of snow.

"Welcome to my home," Mary said as she ushered me into the kitchen. "Nellie, meet Jennifer." I turned to see a young woman bent over as she tried to put on her boots.

"I'm sorry," she said. "I meant to have these on before you arrived. I've been in my stocking feet all morning."

"Jennifer's been here all morning helping me," Mary explained. "In fact, she made the lunch. She's a good cook."

I peeked over at the counter and noticed three plates, on each of which was chicken salad in a hollowed-out tomato, with carrot and raisin salad alongside.

Jennifer finally got her boots on and stood up. She looked to be in her early thirties and was quite pretty. *Different, but cute,* I remember thinking. Under her eyebrows was deep pink eye shadow. Below that was blue shadow and lots of mascara on her lashes. She wore one dangling earring. A large cross hung around her neck, and her blouse was unbuttoned to the waist. I pretended not to notice. It was as if she were trying to make a statement, perhaps testing her new friends to see if they would accept her as she was.

"Come here, so I can give my new friend a hug," I said. Jennifer hugged me back real hard. The ice was broken.

I asked Jennifer how she liked Michigan.

"I hate it," she said. "We hadn't lived here long when someone shot bullet holes through the window of our home. When we called the police they told us they'd been having trouble with kids shooting at houses as they drove by."

"That certainly wasn't a very good reception to our fair state. I hope you meet some nicer people," I said sympathetically.

"Oh, I have," she said. "The people at church are great. I've never experienced such love anywhere."

"Do you have children?" I asked.

"No, I don't. I'm a nurse and I worked in a children's psychiatric ward when I lived in New York. I loved the children but I'm not sure I want any of my own."

At that point Jennifer excused herself. "I need a cigarette," she explained as she put on a beautiful fur coat and went outside. *A person of contrasts,* I thought.

When she returned I asked, "As a nurse, do you agree that smoking contributes to the incidence of cancer?" (It concerned me that her voice sounded husky.)

"Absolutely! But I like to smoke," she said nonchalantly.

"Well Jennifer, the Bible says, 'A man reaps what he sows' (Gal. 6:7). If you develop cancer from your smoking, you won't blame God, will you?"

"No, I'll take the blame. It will be my own fault. But I've got endometriosis and I didn't do anything to deserve *that*. If God loves me, why did he let this happen?"

"God created everything perfect in the beginning," I said, "but man's sin brought consequences. Sickness and death are some of the troubles we now face as a result of our disobedience."

Mary put the food on the table and invited us to sit down.

"Nellie, before we give thanks for the food," said our hostess, "I want you to know I've told Jennifer all about you. She'd like to discuss some of her viewpoints concerning God, the Bible, and life in general. I told her I thought you'd be willing to listen and maybe answer some of her questions."

Jennifer was outgoing and had no problem expressing herself. "When I came here from New York," she said, "I didn't know a soul. My husband and I were lonesome. I left the church I was raised in because I was disillusioned, but when we arrived in this area, I looked in the newspapers to find a church. I had visited a Presbyterian church in New Jersey and liked it, so I decided I'd try one here. I called one near our home and was surprised when the minister answered. He was very cordial and we chatted for about twenty minutes. He told me the time of the service and my husband and I attended the next Sunday. When I arrived, though I knew immediately that I was not like those people, their friendliness amazed me."

At this point Mary laughed and said, "Well, I'll admit your appearance was—well, different."

"I suppose you're right. But one of the women came over after the service and introduced herself. 'I'm Sandy,' she said. 'I see you're new. I'd like to take you out to lunch next week.' I looked at her and thought, *We're not one bit alike. No way is she going to like me. I'd better tell her a few things about myself.* So I said, 'Well, you need to know that I smoke, I drink, I curse, and I like sex.' Sandy didn't even blink before she asked what day was convenient for me.

"She's been my friend ever since. I can't get over the love these people show me. It amazes me that they don't judge me at all. And I love them, too. I don't agree with everything they say or teach, but they don't mind if I ask questions, even when I say, 'Prove it!'

"One night the fellow in charge prayed for me," Jennifer went on. "He actually asked God to bless me for making them look up the answers to the questions I asked. No one has ever asked God to bless me. It was incredible. But they talk about submission to God at that church, and I'm never going to submit to anyone," she said firmly. "My husband and I are liberated. We don't believe in submission." She waited for me to respond.

I began by telling her that my first book—*What Do You Say When . . .* —was dedicated to Paul, my husband. Then I said, "His life verse is Ephesians 5:25: 'Husbands, love your wives, just as Christ loved the church and gave himself up for her.' Do you think I'd have any problem submitting to someone who loved me that much?

"That same chapter tells us that partners in a marriage are to submit *to each other* for their mutual benefit. It's not talking about lording it over each other. A corporation has a president. A shop or store has a manager. Someone has to be in charge or else there would be chaos. I've committed my life to Jesus Christ." I explained. "It's the best decision I've ever made. I've never regretted it. In submitting to him, I'm safe and free to do what is right—because I know God loves me."

Jennifer changed that subject and commented, "I don't think God is fair. I don't see why he doesn't let Buddhists, Muslims, and people of other faiths into heaven. If he were really a God of love, he'd do that."

"Sounds like you want to make the rules, Jennifer. Maybe you'd like to be God," I said with a smile.

"Of course not, but it still doesn't seem fair," she answered.

My answer was: "Jesus said, 'I am the way and the truth and the life. No one comes to the Father except through me' [John 14:6]. If you could get to heaven any other way, his death on the cross would have been a total waste. There would have been no need for him to die.

"Do you realize," I went on, "that Jesus, who was sinless, actually paid the penalty for our sins? He opted to be our substitute. *We* deserved to die on the cross, but because of God's great love for us, he was willing to take our place."

"What happens to people who don't believe in Christ?" Jennifer asked.

I said, "The Bible tells us they will be cast into outer darkness. God says, 'You shall have no other gods before me' [Exod. 20:3]."

I looked at my watch and realized it was getting late. "I'm going to have to leave, Jennifer. But, before I go, would you like to read a booklet that gives the basics of the Bible? It's helped a lot of people understand God's requirements for salvation."

The booklet I planned to give Jennifer was *The Four Spiritual Laws*, which is distributed by Campus Crusade for Christ. I like to use it because it forces people to face their spiritual condition. The booklet begins with "God loves you and has a wonderful plan for your life."

We went into the den and sat down. I began reading aloud about God's love in sending his Son to die for our sins. I explained to Jennifer that the only way we can approach our holy God is through Jesus Christ. "That's why it's so important that we admit or confess that we're sinners and accept him as our Savior. In fact, the greatest sin you can commit is not murder, but rejecting Jesus Christ. Jennifer, where do you think Jesus is in relation to you right now?"

"I think he's in my life—a little." She seemed hesitant.

"Jesus can't be in your life 'a little.' He's either in or he's not. You remind me of a woman in my Bible class," I said. "She claimed Jesus was out on the porch. She hadn't invited him inside. I told her that wasn't very polite. She wouldn't keep a friend standing at her closed front door. She'd invite that friend into her home.

"This is what Jesus says in Revelation 3:20: 'Here I am! I stand at the door and knock. If anyone hears my voice and opens the door, I will come in and eat with him, and he with me.' He's knocking at *your* door, Jennifer. What are you going to do about it?"

She started to cry. "I want to invite him in. I want him to be my Savior."

After praying through her tears, Jennifer asked Jesus to be Lord of her life.

"You know, Jennifer, an hour ago you said, 'I'm *never* going to submit to anyone. I'm a liberated woman.' Now you belong to the family of God. You belong to the King of kings. You're special in his sight. Would you like to thank him? I'll pray first."

When I finished praying, she began, "Hi, Lord, this is me, you know, Jennifer."

My heart melted as she thanked the Lord for all that had happened that day and ended with: "I believe that with Jesus I'm going to make it. In fact, I won't give up, because I *know* I can make it," she repeated.

"When I see you again," she said to me, "I would like to tell you why I was so adamant about not submitting to anyone. I really want to tell you about myself."

As I left, I reminded Jennifer that she was a child of the King, which made her special.

I've talked to Jennifer a few times since that day. On one occasion she told me that when the news of the war with Iraq was announced, she was greatly disturbed and frightened. She kept her ears glued to the television set all day. When evening came she said to her husband, "I can't listen another minute. Please give me the book."

"What book?" he asked.

"You know, *the* book—the good book—the Bible," Jennifer said. "I don't know what part I'll read, but God will show me," she had insisted.

Later she commented to me:

I turned to the Psalms and read the first ten chapters. It was so exciting. It tells what's going to happen to the nations that turn against the Lord. But if we trust God, he will bless us. Because he's in control, I don't have anything to be afraid of. I now go to sleep with my Bible next to my pillow. I wake up often in the middle of the night. I used to read a novel at such times, but now I read my Bible and it comforts me.

"I'm anxious for you to meet my husband," Jennifer then added. "Richard is the greatest—so good and kind. You'll just love him."

"We'll plan to get together soon," I promised.

I met Richard sooner than either of us had expected.

Mary called the following Thursday afternoon. "I know it's late to be calling," she said. "But we just learned it's Jennifer's birthday. We've arranged for Richard to bring her to the pizza place. Several families from the church want to surprise her. It would mean a lot to her if you and your husband could come."

"Oh, I'm sorry, but I'm supposed to be at a writers' group meeting."

"It would mean so much to Jennifer if you could come," Mary urged.

"Well, I guess she is my top priority these days," I said. "I'll cancel my engagement."

It was interesting to watch Jennifer's face when she entered the restaurant. She saw many familiar faces, both children and adults. All of them were her friends. She was speechless when they shouted, "Surprise!"

Jennifer cried, laughed, stammered, and stuttered. Then she saw me. "I just can't believe it," she went on and on. I thought she would never settle down.

"Richard, you've got to meet Nellie." Jennifer brought her husband over and introduced us. I also introduced them to Paul.

Richard was tall and pleasant-looking and seemed to have a gentleness about him. I liked him immediately. It was evident that he and Jennifer loved each other very much. He was as pleased as Jennifer when she was presented with a gift certificate to the local Christian bookstore.

"Ours is a Presbyterian church, and you belong to a Baptist church," Jennifer said to me later in the evening. "What's the difference?"

"There are a few differences, but the basics are the same. Your pastor's children and Mary's children attend our Christian school. We all get along quite well," I said.

"I'd like to visit your church with Richard," she replied.

It took about three weeks before our schedules would allow us to get together. Paul and I met the young couple in the foyer of our church. Our sanctuary is large and was a bit overwhelming to them, since the church they were attending was new and rather small. The group met in a school building, but finer people would be hard to find. They are known throughout the community by their love.

At our church, Jennifer and Richard entered right into the singing. When the opening music was finished, we were asked to greet the people near us. I introduced the couple to several people, and later they got a chance to meet Pastor Crowley.

Seven people were baptized that night. I knew that neither Jennifer nor Richard had ever witnessed adult baptism, but they seemed to enjoy the service.

When the service was over, they came home with us for a bite to eat and we had a chance to talk.

"Tell me about baptism. I was baptized as a baby. Does that count?" Jennifer asked.

I said, "Tonight you witnessed believers' baptism. Though it doesn't save a person, it is an outward demonstration of what has happened to that person on the inside. It tells the world that you identify with Jesus' death, burial, and resurrection.

"In many churches, parents bring their babies to be baptized as a dedication to the Lord, promising to raise their children in the nurture and admonition of God. I've heard others say that baptism saved them, but Scripture doesn't teach that. In order to be saved, a person has to confess that he or she has sinned against holy God. Then they must receive Jesus Christ as their personal Savior."

I pointed out that all those who were baptized that night gave their testimony about how they came to Christ. Some told of their rebellion against God at one point in their life. Others told of attending church but never understanding what it meant to have a personal relationship with Jesus Christ.

"Richard," I said, "I don't know you well, but you seem to be such a kind person, and that's how the pastor of the church you're attending described you. But in Romans 3:22–23 the Bible says, 'This righteousness from God comes through faith in Jesus Christ. . . . For all have sinned and fall short of the glory of God.' Where do you stand in the light of those verses?"

"Well, I've not had the struggles Jennifer has had throughout her life. I don't think I've rebelled against God."

"I believe you," I said. "But that doesn't make you right before God. Why don't we go step-by-step through the little booklet I gave Jennifer? That way you can be sure where you stand with the Lord. You don't want to take anything for granted."

Richard seemed to understand that Jesus Christ died on the cross for our sins. But then I asked him, "Where is Christ in relation to you? Is he on the throne of your life or are you pretty much in control of your life?"

He hesitated to ponder that question, but finally answered, "I wish I could say that he was running my life. I think I'm pretty much in control of things, but. . . ." Then he looked at me and said, "I'd like *Jesus* to take control. I really would."

It was a beautiful moment. Jennifer sat on the floor next to Richard's chair. She touched his arm as he prayed and asked Jesus Christ to be Lord of his life. We all rejoiced together. I thanked the Lord for Richard's commitment. Then he prayed again, thanking the Lord for making salvation plain to him. It was clear that for the first time he understood what it was all about.

"Now we're really together," Jennifer said with tears in her eyes.

Reflection

Events such as these allow me to see the power of the Holy Spirit at work. Because there is no greater joy than to be a part of God's work, I am grateful to be God's instrument.

Recently Jennifer told me about the circumstances in her past that made the very idea of submitting to the Lord—or anyone—so painful. "I was a victim of incest," she said. "My father, a psychiatrist, took advantage of me until I was eleven years old. The word *submission* had always brought fear to my heart. But now I know that submitting to Jesus Christ is liberating. It brings real freedom.

"I also want you to know that I no longer hate my father. I have only pity for him. O, yes, I had anger and rage to work through, but I don't hate him anymore. He was a tormented man. He's dead now, I've forgiven him and I wish I could have helped him. My desire now is to help other victims of abuse. Now I know that God can help them get through their pain, just as he helped me."

Can Presbyterians and Baptists work together for the Lord? You bet!

40

Not So Different

Do not be overcome by evil, but overcome evil with good.
Romans 12:21

J knew it! I knew something would happen sooner or later. How dare that woman!" Dorcas said angrily to her husband. She held the curtain aside with one hand and the phone with the other.

"What's wrong, honey?" Bob asked. "What are you so upset about?"

"That Iraqi woman next door took our brand-new snow shovel," she told him. "I knew the minute I laid eyes on those people that I wouldn't be able to trust them. They're so different from us."

"Why, only a few weeks ago you had plans to invite our new neighbors to church," Bob said. "The movers hadn't even unloaded their furniture, yet you could hardly wait to meet them."

"Well—that's before I got a good look. Then I discovered they barely speak English. There are people coming and going all day long, speaking what sounds like gibberish. When I realized that even if I wanted to, we wouldn't be able to communicate with each other, I decided to stay as far away as I could. The incident this morning proves what kind of people they are. Besides, with all my responsibilities and busy life, I don't see why I should be required to be neighborly to people with whom I have nothing in common."

"Aren't you being a bit judgmental? Have you forgotten that all our steps are ordered by the Lord? Seems to me I remember you saying that you were going to pray for them," Bob reminded her.

"Yes, I did, but my problem right now is what to do about our snow shovel. Our own porch and sidewalk need attention."

"Wait until she's finished shoveling. If she doesn't bring our shovel back, go over and tell her you need it. That's simple enough," he replied patiently.

Two hours later, Dorcas picked up the phone and called Betty, her best friend, and told her the story. "That woman didn't bring our shovel back. Bob says I should go to get it before I leave for work. What shall I do?"

"Ring her doorbell," Betty said, "and when she comes to the door, be firm. Let her know you mean business. I'll hang up right now and pray that you will do the right thing."

Dorcas dressed for work, got in her car, and angrily backed it into the neighbors' driveway. (She thought she might need a quick getaway.) When she walked up the steps to the porch, she saw her shovel covered with a piece of plastic. She put one hand on the shovel and the other on the doorbell. Before she could push the button, the door opened and there stood her neighbor.

"I see you borrowed my shovel," Dorcas said coldly. "I'll be taking it back now." She turned and walked toward her car. To her surprise the woman called out in broken English.

"No, no—I bring back later. I just take—bring back later."

"No, I'll take it *now*," Dorcas insisted. She took the shovel home and left for work. Her day was ruined. The thought of that incident infuriated her. Consumed with bitterness and anger, she found it hard to concentrate on her work.

"The nerve of that woman," she told her coworkers. "I can't believe she'd do such a thing. She obviously thinks, *What's theirs is mine.*"

As Dorcas was driving home from work, she thought, *I've got to get rid of this bitter feeling and stop thinking about my neighbor. I should be concentrating on my message for the retreat this weekend.* "Let's see: 'Blessed are the merciful, for they will be shown mercy.' 'Blessed are the merciful,'" she repeated out loud. That verse, Matthew 5:7, was her assigned topic for the mother-and-daughter retreat. *Blessed are the merciful—blessed are the merciful—*those words rang through her mind over and over again until she could think of nothing else. Finally Dorcas said, "Okay, Lord, I hear what you're saying. I'll do it. I'll be merciful."

The Spirit of God impressed on Dorcas's mind and heart that she should buy her neighbors a new snow shovel. She knew she had to be obedient to God's promptings, so she stopped at the hardware store and purchased one. She put a big red bow on the shovel, added a friendly note, and placed it on her neighbors' porch. Suddenly Dorcas was exhilarated and began to feel good about herself. *If I don't practice what I preach,* she thought, *I am a hypocrite. Blessed are the merciful. And I can be merciful—I want to be merciful.* Love replaced the bitterness in her heart.

The next day, as Dorcas went about packing her suitcase for the retreat, she was inexplicably reminded of her rebellious teenage years. *But God in his mercy saved me. In turn, I have to be merciful to my neighbors,* she thought.

Dorcas picked up her luggage, ready to leave, when the doorbell rang. There stood her new neighbor, holding a baked specialty from her own country, hot from the oven and smelling delicious.

"You give shovel me? Tank you much—me all lone—two children—me no shovel—me no car—me no gets K-Marts."

"It's a gift from God," Dorcas said.

"Tank you—My name Nazah. Tank you much," the woman said with a shy smile and turned to leave.

Dorcas closed the door and began to cry. "Thank you, Lord, for not letting me get away with being unneighborly. Now I'm free before you to speak to others."

Because of that incident, Dorcas started having coffee with her neighbor on a regular basis. It has been a time of getting acquainted and learning about each other's ways and customs. Little by little, Dorcas is sharing with Nazah her faith and trust in Jesus Christ.

Nazah allowed her two small children to attend Vacation Bible School that summer. Dorcas experienced immeasurable joy when she heard the tiny six-year-old girl singing as she was riding her bicycle up and down the street: "Jesus loves me, this I know, for the Bible tells me so." It was one of the songs the child had learned during those few weeks!

Dorcas had related this story to me some time ago, and I was eager to hear if there were any new developments. I recently saw her after church and asked, "How are you getting along with your new neighbor?"

"Got a few minutes?" she asked as she smiled broadly. I sat down and listened as she continued her story.

"Even though Nazah is not attending church with us, she allows her children to attend Sunday school. It's a beginning. And I know I've been able to help her feel at home here. Bob and I had decided some time ago to fix up our house and move to a different location. But when Nazah saw our 'For Sale' sign she said, 'I pray God you no move. You move—I move—next door your house.'

"You know, Nellie," Dorcas continued, "it's not easy to live next door to someone from another culture. Our standards and way of life are so different. But God placed Nazah and her children there. He is sovereign, and he makes no mistakes.

"I took Nazah out for lunch last week. She is very appreciative, and I'm gradually getting to know her better. Bob and I are grateful that she trusts us enough to let her children come to Sunday school. I pray that God will give me wisdom as I spend time with her. Perhaps Nazah, too, will soon understand how much God loves her."

I thought I had finished writing this story, but yesterday Dorcas came to me at church and said excitedly, "This morning, on the way to Sunday school, Magdee, Nazah's nine-year-old son, told us he had received Jesus Christ as his Savior."

"How did that come about?" I asked.

"The Spirit of God opened his heart as he read a little booklet Bob had given him. It talked about God's love in sending Jesus Christ to die for our sins. 'I read it over and over,' Magdee said, 'and then I checked it out to see if it was the same as the Bible you gave me. Everything was the same, so I prayed and asked Jesus to come into my heart and be my Savior. I signed my name after the prayer—see!'

"We were so amazed that we questioned him over and over again to see if he understood. Finally he looked at us as if to say, 'Don't you believe me?' Bob turned to him and said, 'We believe you.'

"We knew that Magdee's mother had constantly threatened him with, 'You be good, or God gonna get you.' Then she would shake her finger at him. But when Magdee read about God's love, his heart responded. He needed to know that although God judges, he also forgives and loves us with an everlasting love. I hope Nazah will soon understand that, too."

Reflection

Only God knows the ending of this story, but the apostle Paul has said, "And the peace of God, which transcends all understanding, will guard your hearts and your minds in Christ Jesus" (Phil. 4:7). It is required of a servant to be faithful, but only God can give the increase. Even believers have a tendency to stick up for our rights. We are angry when we discover someone has taken advantage of us. *I'm not going to let my neighbor get away with stealing my shovel,* Dorcas thought, until the Holy Spirit reminded her of the very Scripture she was to talk about at the retreat. Because Dorcas responded to God's promptings to be merciful, she was given a creative alternative.

[Jesus said:] "If someone forces you to go one mile, go with him two miles. Give to the one who asks you, and do not turn away from the one who wants to borrow from you" (Matt. 5:41–42).

"Live in harmony with one another. Do not be proud. . . . If it is possible, as far as it depends on you, live at peace with everyone" (Rom. 12:16, 18).

41

Frustration or Opportunity?

Give thanks in all circumstances, for this is God's will for you in Christ Jesus.

1 Thessalonians 5:18

O h, no! Not again," I groaned to my husband. "We just had the car fixed last week. Here we are at the top of Lewiston Bridge, almost in the good old U.S.A., and the car stops. Just look at the lineup behind us and in front of us. What in the world can we do? We'll never get out of here!"

"Well, Nellie, be thankful we got this far," Paul said. "If our car had stopped on the way up, we'd be stuck here all day. You steer and I'll push the car downhill. Be sure to put on the brakes when you get close to the car in front of you."

You might guess that Paul doesn't get upset easily! He just does what he has to do. As he started to push the car, I sent up an SOS to my heavenly Father. "How are you going to get us out of this one?" I prayed. Then I saw a man get out of his car and come toward us. "Let me help you, pal," he said to my husband. "My wife will drive our car. I'll catch up with her at the bottom of the hill."

"I really appreciate your help," Paul said.

"Are you out of gas?" the man asked.

"No, I've plenty of gas. I don't know what's wrong. I had it in for repairs a couple of days ago. I thought everything was in good running order. But if I get it past customs into the States, I can call AAA and get help."

We paid our toll and looked for a place to park, but the spaces were all taken. Then I heard the stranger call his wife, "Here we are, honey."

"I've been waiting for you," she said. "I saved a place so they can park their car. Be ready to push it in after I back out."

My, such wonderful people, I thought. *What can we do to show our appreciation? I know they won't accept money.*

After I parked the car, I got out and thanked both of them. "You are so kind. You were an answer to my prayer," I said. "I'd like to give you a copy of my book *What Do You Say When* . . . It's about sharing my faith in Jesus Christ. Do you have a church background?" I asked.

"Yes, we belong to the Anglican Church," the man answered.

"I hope my book will encourage you in the faith," I said. "And thank you again for your kindness."

Paul went to call AAA. Though he tried several times, he couldn't get through. "What's the problem?" I asked.

"The lines are busy. It's been a half hour since I made the first call."

We had hoped to get to the Connecticut home of our daughter Greta and her husband, Michael Blanchard, before dark, but now that seemed impossible. Then I thought of God's words in Psalms: "Call upon me in the day of trouble; I will deliver you, and you will honor me" (Ps. 50:15).

"We're in trouble, Lord," I prayed. "We ask you to deliver us. We trust you and want to honor you in all things."

I took a walk while Paul was figuring out our next step. When I heard the beep of a horn, I turned around, and saw him in the driver's seat. "Come on," he said. "The car seems to be okay."

"Thank you, Lord," I breathed. Paul said, "Amen."

We drove all day without any more trouble. Because we had lost so much time at the bridge, we had to drive into the evening hours. At times it seemed as though we were alone in a wilderness, driving up and down hills and around steep curves. *I sure hope we don't get stuck on one of these roads,* I thought. Then I remembered that God had provided help before. Now I must continue to trust him.

With grateful hearts we arrived safe and sound and greeted Greta and Michael with warm hugs. After we unloaded the car, Paul decided to move it to give Michael more room for his vehicle. Our car wouldn't start! But we still went to sleep that night with the sense of God's protection.

We had to have the car fixed twice while in Connecticut. One time, while we were waiting at the repair shop, a tall blonde young man came into the office to pay his bill. Since we both had to wait, we got into a conversation. At one point I said, "I'm curious. I'm wondering why you wear an earring. Would you mind telling me?"

"Oh, that," he said as he touched his ear. "I usually forget I have it on. That's a leftover from my rebellious years when I went to college in California. I'm a responsible person now."

"You mean you've made things right with the people you rebelled against?"

"Well, yeah. It was mostly my parents. But things are all right now," he said pleasantly.

"What about God?" I asked. "Have you made things right with him?"

"I'm not much for religion. When I was a kid, my parents made me go to Unity, but I didn't believe those teachings. I really don't know what the truth is."

"I can understand that," I smiled, "but you ought to start reading the Bible. That's where you'll find truth. By the way, would you be interested in taking this booklet to read? It covers the basics of what the Bible teaches. I've shared it with many people."

"I'd like that. I'm always looking for something to read when I go on business trips and have to wait for a customer. Well, looks like my car is ready. I'm glad we talked. Thanks again for the booklet." He shook my hand and left.

A few minutes later, Paul walked in and said, "I think they've found the trouble. The car should be okay for a while."

A few days later, we went to visit our daughter Karen and her husband, David Green, in Massachusetts. That weekend I was scheduled to speak at a women's retreat in Waldoburo, Maine. Since we arrived at both places without incident, we returned to the Greens and began to relax about the car.

Whenever we visit, Karen usually has a list of things for Paul to fix. (Having a dad who is an engineer comes in handy at times.) "Here's my list," she said. "It doesn't matter which you pick. I'll be grateful for anything you do."

Because we knew the kitchen was important to Karen, we decided to tackle some remodeling there first. All of us would pitch in. Paul did most of the work, but David took a day off from his job and was a big help. It was great to see Paul and our son-in-law working so well together and actually making it seem like fun.

At one point Karen asked, "Mom, do you want to take me to the hardware store? I'd like to pick out some new pulls for the drawers. Dad and David are going to fetch the countertops, so you'll have to drive."

"No problem," I said. "The car seems to be running fine. Let's go."

Driving in the Boston area is treacherous, especially on Route 128. I was so glad to park the car at the store that I heaved a sigh of relief.

We found just the right pulls, which made Karen happy. This would put the finishing touches on the kitchen, so we were both excited as we headed for the car. I turned the key in the ignition, but nothing happened. "Oh, no! Not again"—the same words I had uttered just two weeks before.

"Well," I said, "we know God's in control of our lives. Let's pray." We both prayed for wisdom—and patience.

"Karen, do you know we've had this car fixed five times in the past two weeks? Yet the Lord protected us in every situation. What if the car had stopped on Route 128? I shudder to think about it. I don't know what God wants to teach us, but we'll trust him and thank him."

We called home and Paul and David came to help us. They called a car dealer. Since it was Friday afternoon, we didn't know what kind of service we would get. The dealer said, "I'm sorry we can't help you until Tuesday. We're busy today, we don't work on Saturday and Sunday, and Monday is Columbus Day. You'll have to wait until Tuesday."

On Tuesday I was supposed to be back in Michigan to speak! *Remember*, I told myself, *God's in control. Trust him.*

Paul then called another dealer, who said, "We'll send a mechanic right out. We would rather not tow the car if possible. It may disturb the part that needs fixing. He'll be there in about twenty minutes."

It wasn't long before the young mechanic drove up and parked right next to our car. He made a few tests, checked under the hood, and then said, "Yes, I think I've spotted the problem. I'll make a temporary adjustment so the car will run. Then you follow me." In short order the car was running again. We followed the mechanic to the dealer, who suggested we walk over to the nearby mall and have lunch. "By the time you're through, the car will be just about ready." We were greatly relieved.

We actually relaxed enough to enjoy our lunch. When we went back to pick up our car, five other people were in the dealer's waiting room. One of the men wanted to know what had happened to our car. Paul told him our story, starting from the Lewiston Bridge.

Then I added, "I sure don't enjoy driving on Route 128. I'm glad the car didn't stop in the middle of traffic."

"You could have been killed," the man said dramatically (as if I didn't know!).

"That's right. But if I *had* been killed, I know I would go to be with the Lord."

"How do you know you'd be with the Lord? How do you really know?" the man challenged me.

"First of all," I said, "you need to know that I don't expect to go to heaven because I'm a good person. Heaven is not a reward for any good things I might have done. The Bible says that 'all have sinned and fall short of the glory of God' [Rom. 3:23]. We can never reach God's standards. He demands perfection."

"Sounds like we're in big trouble," he said.

"We would be, if it weren't for Jesus Christ. Only *he* is perfect. He died on the cross for our sins and is the mediator between God and man. If we confess to God that we are sinners and receive Jesus Christ as our Savior, he will accept us. John 3:16 says, 'For God so loved the world that he gave his one and only Son, that whoever believes in him shall not perish but have eternal life.' On the basis of my confession of faith in Jesus Christ, I know I'm going to heaven. I have eternal life. I received that the moment I believed. . . ."

"Say, do you want to hear a good joke?" the man's wife interrupted. She had a wicked gleam in her eye, so I said, "Not really."

"Oh, but this is a good one." She proceeded to tell an off-color story. Her husband touched her gently and said, "Please, don't do that."

She ignored him and continued dominating the conversation. "I want you to know that many times people mistake me for Helen

Hayes. And I'm considered the life of the party. You see, I believe in having fun."

"Please don't talk like that," her husband said quietly. After the rest of the people in the room showed distaste by the expression on their faces, the woman kept quiet for a while.

"I'm a retired newspaper reporter," her husband said. "I've read many books and enjoy reading, but there are two writings I have difficulty understanding: Shakespeare's works and the Bible."

"I don't know much about Shakespeare, but I can tell you why you don't understand the Bible," I replied. "You have to read it with eyes of faith."

"How do you get faith?" he asked.

"The Bible says in Romans 10:17: 'Faith comes from hearing the message, and the message is heard through the word of Christ.' So if you want faith, you have to read the Bible and believe what you read."

"I've scanned it but where should I start?" he wanted to know.

"I suggest you start in the Book of John. It's a good place to get acquainted with Jesus Christ. Perhaps you could read it to your wife as well."

"Yes, we can read it together," he said as he took his wife's hand. She laughed nervously and said, "Yeah, that will be okay."

A woman sitting across the room from us joined in the conversation. "My son used to be very hot-tempered and rebellious. But ever since he's gotten this Christianity bit, he's changed. I can't get over it. Someone hit his car the other day. Once I would have expected him to be madder than a wet hen, but he just took everything calmly. I tell you he's a different person now."

I nodded and said, "Well, that's what happens when a person receives Christ. It's a transformed life."

The woman sitting next to me whispered, "I'm glad you spoke to those people. Just as soon as my car is ready, I'll be on my way to a Bible study class." She showed me her workbook. They were studying Exodus. "This sure has been an interesting experience," she added.

"Pickard, please go to the cashier. Your car's ready," the voice over the loudspeaker broke in.

Reflection

I have reflected much on the events of that day and the two preceding weeks. I can't help thinking that what could have been a series of frustrations turned out to be an ongoing opportunity to witness for the Lord.

Adversity can teach us many lessons. We learn, first of all, that there is pain in frustration but joy in the opportunity it often presents. Most of us must learn the hard way, but believers have a choice. We can complain and grumble about the irksome situations in which we find ourselves. Or we can be "always giving thanks to God the Father for everything, in the name of our Lord Jesus Christ" (Eph. 5:20). Whatever the circumstance, there is always a way to do God's will with joy and thanksgiving.

42

Pain with a Purpose

Some of the Pharisees in the crowd said to Jesus, "Teacher, rebuke your disciples!"

"I tell you," he replied, "if they keep quiet, the stones will cry out."

Luke 19:39–40

Do you realize we've been driving for twelve hours?" I commented to my husband. "I think we'd better stop at the next town. I'm exhausted."

"I'm ready to call it quits, too," Paul said. "I've got a strange pain in my back. It's probably from sitting in the same position for so long."

It had been a beautiful day. We had stopped in Dayton, Ohio, to visit our friend Kenny Wyckoff, something we often did on our way to Florida. Her husband had gone home to be with the Lord a few years ago, so these stopovers were special to us.

"Tifton, Georgia, is just a few miles down the road," Paul said. "It will be a good place to stop."

We found a take-out restaurant and bought some food to eat in our motel room. A few hours later, Paul said, "I'm not sure the pain in my back is from driving. It's getting worse and spreading from my back to my stomach. Maybe a good hot bath will help."

Though he soaked in the tub for about half an hour, it didn't seem to help. I could see Paul was in pain, but he had never been seriously ill, so I didn't think too much about it.

231

We read, watched the news on TV, and tried to relax before we retired for the evening. Around midnight Paul sat up in bed and groaned, "Nellie, something is definitely wrong. This is no ordinary pain. I'd better get to a hospital right away."

I was frightened. Here we were in a motel, hundreds of miles from home and friends. What was I to do?

"Lord, help us," I prayed. Then I called the motel desk and asked for directions to the nearest hospital.

"It's seven miles down the highway with a few turns here and there. Stop at the desk and I'll sketch out a map," said the night clerk.

I was tense as we drove away from the motel. By this time, Paul was writhing in pain, doubled over and moaning. I had never seen him like this. *Is it a heart attack?* I wondered. "Oh, Lord, help us to find the way quickly," I prayed fervently.

We followed the directions carefully and found the hospital without any problem. The "Emergency" sign was in plain view, which was quite a relief.

The attendants could see Paul's condition was serious. "We'll take care of your husband," one of the men said. "You go to the desk and have him registered." When they took Paul through the double doors, a horrible thought ran through my mind: *I wonder if I'll ever see him alive again.*

I went to the desk and gave the registrar the information she requested.

"What is your religious preference?" she asked.

Oh, oh, even they think he's going to die! I thought.

"Don't worry about getting a minister," I said. "My husband has made a commitment to Jesus Christ and so have I. Both of us have received him as our Savior. Paul doesn't need a minister. In fact, if there are any other patients here in the hospital who need spiritual help, I'd be willing to talk to them. If you don't think I can, you need to know that I've written a book about people who don't know how to be in the family of God. I tell them what the Scriptures have to say. That's my authority, since the Bible is God's Word." I nervously rattled on and on. I had not been to an emergency room before, so I didn't realize that everyone who registers is asked about his or her religious preference.

The girl at the desk looked at me and said in a serious voice, "I need your book."

"What do you mean?" I asked.

"I mean I need to read your book so I can know how to be in the family of God. I go to church but it's not been made clear as to what a person must do to be prepared for heaven."

"Oh, I'm sorry, our car is loaded down with suitcases and clothes. I don't think I can get at my books. But I'll sit down and write down God's requirements. I'll tell you exactly what the Bible says."

Other people were waiting in line behind me, so I couldn't take any more of her time. But I found a quiet corner and sat down to write. It had a calming effect on me. This is what I wrote:

> We must first of all recognize that God is holy and his standard is perfection. We human beings are sinful and cannot reach God's standards. The Bible says that in Romans 3:23. It also says in Romans 6:23: "The wages of sin is death, but the gift of God is eternal life in Christ Jesus our Lord." The wonderful thing is, God didn't leave us to flounder but provided a way that we might be in his family. Romans 5:8 tells us that "God demonstrates his own love for us in this: While we were still sinners, Christ died for us." Jesus provided the way of salvation. He said, "I am the way and the truth and the life. No one comes to the Father except through me."
>
> Knowing these verses is not enough. You must follow through by receiving Jesus Christ as your Savior. John 1:12 says, "Yet to all who received him [Jesus Christ], to those who believed in his name, he gave the right to become children of God." One more thing—you can't get to heaven by good works. It's not a reward for the good things we have done. Ephesians 2:8–9 tells us that salvation is by grace through faith—we can't do it ourselves. It's a gift God wants to give us if we receive Jesus Christ.
>
> If you are ready to take this step, why don't you bow your head right now and thank God for sending his Son, Jesus Christ, to die on the cross for your sins. Then tell Jesus you want him to be your Savior.

It had been good for me to concentrate on someone else's need. I was perfectly at peace, just knowing that God had given me a work to do. In the midst of my anxiety about Paul, God drew my attention away from my own fears.

I went to the desk, handed the young woman my note, and said, "When we get to Florida, I'll send you a copy of my book *What Do You Say When* . . . Perhaps it will help reinforce what I have just written. The book contains stories of people just like you. I once met a woman in a swimming pool who didn't know how to pray. I met another woman on the tennis court who asked, 'Nellie, what makes you tick?' Another woman told me, 'I wish I knew God better.'"

"Thank you so much," the registrar said. "I really appreciate what you've done. It means a lot to me. By the way, my name is Maria. I would appreciate it if you would pray for me—that is, if you ever think of me."

"I've already prayed for you and will continue to do so. Now, is there some way I can find out about my husband's condition?" I asked.

"Ordinarily we don't allow anyone except hospital personnel in the treatment area, but go ahead. I'll call and tell them you're coming."

I appreciated her kindness. I walked through the double doors and greeted the nurse at the desk. "Has the doctor discovered the cause of my husband's problem? Is he going to be all right? Is he still in a lot of pain?"

The nurse gave me a big smile. "Yes, he's going to be fine. But first he has to get rid of the kidney stone that is causing the pain. We've sedated him and taken some X-rays. Let's see if he's awake yet.

"Mr. Pickard, your wife's here to see you," the nurse said, as we entered his cubicle. Paul was groggy and had a hard time opening his eyes.

"What's wrong with me?" he asked.

"You're going to be okay. You have a kidney stone," I said. "They are going to help you get rid of it. But I want you to know your pain hasn't been wasted. I had a chance to share the gospel with the woman at the front desk. She seems very responsive and would like a copy of my book. Is there any way I can get hold of one?"

Paul managed to say, "Underneath the clothes in the backseat is an open box. Lift up the clothes and. . . ." Then he went back to sleep.

I returned to the lobby and watched as a policeman brought in a gunshot victim. The young man's friends filled the room. Their faces appeared somber and tense. No one spoke.

Since it was two o'clock in the morning, I wasn't exactly eager to go to the parking lot alone. But I *had* to get the book! As I walked toward the door, I noticed the sheriff and a policeman standing in a corner. I approached them and asked whether one of them would be willing to go with me to my car so I could get a book I wanted to give to the registrar.

Southern hospitality rose to the occasion. "I think we can help you," the sheriff said. He motioned for the policeman to go with me after the two of them checked out at the desk.

When I opened the car door and reached under the clothing that was hanging up in the back, I had no trouble finding my book.

The policeman walked beside me as we went back to the hospital. "May I see your book?" he asked. I handed it to him and he browsed through it in the lobby.

"Lady, now I understand. You want her to know the Lord, right? My father is a minister and so was my grandfather. I like what you're doing."

I went to the desk and gave Maria the book. She thanked me and said, "I really appreciate your willingness to talk to me. I wish we could spend some time together, but I know that's impossible."

I encouraged her to start reading the Bible. "Start in the Book of John. It will tell you who Jesus Christ is. You need to get to know him better," I said.

At four o'clock that morning, the hospital released Paul, with the condition that he see a doctor as soon as we got to Boca Raton. The doctor handed him a prescription for pain. "Stop at a drugstore in the morning and get it filled," he said. "You have to do it while you're in Georgia; otherwise it won't be honored. But if the pain gets intense as you travel, you had better stop at the nearest hospital."

We had about three hours of sleep and soon after dawn stopped at four drugstores. It was Sunday, so all were closed until noon.

"Let's keep going," Paul said. "We don't want to stay here another four hours."

Though I was concerned that Paul get his medicine, I took his suggestion and began driving. I drove from eight in the morning until two in the afternoon. Paul slept most of the way. I prayed, "Help us reach our destination without incident. Please keep Paul safe until we arrive."

When Paul awoke, he said, "I feel better. I feel like driving."

We reached Boca Raton at six that evening. Paul took our luggage upstairs and sat down to rest. All of a sudden the pain returned. I hurried to the drugstore and explained the situation to the pharmacist. I asked if he could possibly honor the prescription. He said, "Ordinarily we don't, because it's from out of state—but under the circumstances, I'll help you out. That is, if you promise to see a doctor the first thing in the morning."

God saw us through. Six days later, Paul passed the stone!

Reflection

Paul and I believe in God's divine appointments. They are always surprises, though we also know that we won't be exempt from life's difficulties. The Bible says, "Yet man is born to trouble as surely as sparks fly upward" (Job 5:7). But Hebrews 13:5 reminds us that God has said, "Never will I leave you; never will I forsake you." Sometimes God combines the two truths, so blessings often come out of hardships.

For Maria, Paul's medical problem meant an introduction into God's family and an answer she had been seeking. We would not have met her if God had not provided a reason for us to be at that hospital at that particular time.

Pain is never fun, but we praise God that Paul's pain wasn't wasted. And even the stones rose up to praise God!

43

In Need of Exercise

For bodily exercise profiteth little: but godliness is profitable unto all things, having promise of the life that now is, and of that which is to come.

1 Timothy 4:8 KJV

"I've finally finished my manuscript," I told Paul. "Sitting at the word processor for hours at a time is taking its toll on my body, not to mention those delicious desserts at the retreats and seminars where I'm invited to speak. I'm gaining weight and feeling logy.

"Joan tells me the mall opens two hours early every morning just for walkers. I think I'll join her. Maybe that will get me back in shape. Besides, I think I deserve some time for myself, don't you?" I said with a hint of silliness.

"I agree," Paul said. "You do need some exercise. You're still going to be available to share your faith, aren't you?" he teased.

"Of course, but I even need a break from that once in a while."

Walking was invigorating. I often met Joan and other people from church and walked with them. One morning I noticed a young woman reading a newspaper at a table in the eating area of the mall. As I passed by, she looked up and smiled, so I asked, "What are you reading?" Before she could answer, I noticed it was one of those tabloids seen at the supermarket checkout counters.

"Do you believe that stuff?" I asked.

"No, not really, but I enjoy reading about it. I buy this paper every week and come here to read before I start work."

"I read something a lot more exciting than that. Something that gives direction to my life and shows me how to have real fulfillment. I just love it," I said.

"And what's that?" she asked.

"I read the Bible every morning. It's a great way to start the day."

"You know, my mother says the same thing. Maybe I'll ask her to give me a Bible for Christmas."

"That's a great idea. It will do a lot more for you than the paper you're reading." I introduced myself and she told me her name was Sarah.

The week after Christmas I passed by the counter where Sarah was working. "I got my Bible for Christmas," she said as she held it up for me to see.

"Wonderful! I remember that you used to read the tabloid at the table over there. Do you have enough courage to read your Bible instead?" I teased.

"I . . . think so," she answered with some hesitation.

Early the following day I saw Sarah reading her Bible at her usual table. I walked a little longer, then sat down beside her and asked, "Do you know anything about Jesus Christ?"

"I used to go to Sunday school a long time ago, and I remember a few things. I need to know more about God, though," she admitted wistfully.

"The way to know God is through Jesus Christ," I said. "He came to earth to show us what the Father is like. Jesus said, 'I am the way and the truth and the life. No one comes to the Father except through me.'

"Sarah, when you went to Sunday school, did you ever hear the verse that says, 'For God so loved the world that he gave his one and only Son, that whoever believes in him shall not perish but have eternal life'? That's John 3:16."

"Yes, I've heard that before," Sarah answered. "But I'm not sure what it means."

I continued to share with her from Scripture. "It also says in Romans 3:23, 'For all have sinned and fall short of the glory of God.' That means that no one can reach God's standards, that the whole world stands guilty before God. Now let me tell you what it says in Romans 5:8: 'But God demonstrates his own love for us in this: While we were still sinners, Christ died for us.'

"But Sarah, you also need to know that even though you may do nice things, heaven is not a reward for good behavior. That's what it says in Ephesians 2:8–9. The solution is found in John 1:12, which says, 'Yet to all who received him'—Jesus, that is—'to those who believed in his name, he gave the right to become children of God.'"

After giving Sarah time to think about what I had said, I finally asked her, "Do you believe God when he says you are a sinner?"

"Yes, I know I am," she replied.

"Would you like to experience his love and forgiveness by receiving Christ as your Savior?"

"I surely would," she answered.

I helped Sarah pray. Right then and there she confessed she was a sinner and received Jesus Christ as her Savior.

"Even though I've heard some of these Bible verses before," she said, "I never made them personal, that is, meant just for me. I hope you will teach me more about the Bible." I promised I would.

I saw Sarah again the following week. She was excited as she told me that she and her boyfriend had gone to church on New Year's Eve. "I really enjoyed it," she said, "now that I know more about what it all means."

I gave her a Bible-study booklet, "The Uniqueness of Jesus," published by Campus Crusade for Christ. I asked her to look it over and said I would help her with her questions when she was ready.

The next time I saw Sarah, she looked troubled. "My brother died in his sleep last night," she told me. "He was only twenty-seven. I feel just awful. He was so young. I will have to be gone for several days. The funeral will be in Indiana."

I assured her of my prayers, knowing we would have to put the Bible study on hold for the time being.

Soon after that, as I was walking the mall with my friend Joan, she pointed to a woman walking across the aisle from us. "Roger is having a Bible study with that woman's husband this morning," she told me.

"What about her—is she a believer?" I asked Joan.

"I'm not really sure about Jane," she answered.

The following day Joan had a hair appointment, so I walked alone. When I noticed Jane walking ahead of me, I caught up to her and asked with a smile, "Do you know Joan Van Noord?"

"Yes, and I know Roger, her husband, too," she said. "They are such fine people."

"They attend our church," I said. Jane told me the name of her church and we got better acquainted as we walked together. When we passed the counter where Sarah usually worked, I told Jane the story of how we had met. "I hope to start a Bible study with her soon," I added.

To my delight and surprise, Jane asked in a hesitant voice, "Could I join your Bible study? I've been wanting to attend one for a long time. When I asked my pastor if he was interested in having Bible classes at the church, he said no."

"I would be delighted to get together with you. How about next Monday, before we walk?"

Before we started our study, I asked Jane if she had ever committed her life to Jesus Christ. "I'm not sure, but I'd like to" was her response. We prayed together, and she told the Lord she wanted him to be in control of her life. It was a moving moment for both of us.

Five days later, we met again and Jane said, "Last Monday was the highlight of my week. If I hadn't committed my life to Christ, I wouldn't have made it through the past few days."

"Tell me about it," I prodded.

"Well, it's been a very rough week. One of my relatives committed suicide. My daughter's husband left her and their eight children. And my cousin's husband has been diagnosed as having cancer. I was overwhelmed by all this news, but I am so grateful for the experience I had on Monday. With the strength that God is giving me, I am doing what I can to help my daughter and to encourage the others in their grief."

We've gotten together several times since, and Jane says, "I need this study. I want to learn more. I appreciate your help."

Because of my walks I was also able to witness to a young man from the bakery department at the mall. When he told me his name was Christopher, I said, "I like your name—especially the first part."

"You mean Chris?" he asked.

"Well, no, I mean Christ."

He smiled and then surprised me by saying, "Interesting you should say that. I've been thinking about Christ lately and wish I knew more about him. They don't teach much about him in church these days, do they?"

"They do in the church I attend," I said. "I'd like to give you a booklet I have in my purse. It will give you the basics of what Christianity is all about. Why don't you read it and see if it makes sense to you?"

"Thanks, I'd like to do that."

When I saw Chris later that week he said, "Thanks for giving me the booklet. It did make sense to me. I also prayed the prayer on page ten. And I received Christ as my Savior."

I was delighted and encouraged him to start reading the Scriptures. The next day he told me he had started to read the Bible from the beginning and had just finished the creation passages.

"I'd encourage you to start reading the Book of John first. It's important that you learn more about Jesus Christ."

"I'll do that," Chris said.

When I saw Chris the following morning, he showed me a book he had picked up at a local bookstore. It was about the science of the mind. One quick look convinced me that the authors had distorted the Scriptures. They were false teachers. I told Chris the book was man-centered, not God-centered.

"I wondered about that," he said. "They write as though man, not Jesus, is the true vine."

"You've got it," I said. "I have plenty of books for you to read. You've started well, but you've got to stay on track."

Reflection

I also met a security guard at the mall. Her name is Linda. She is a fine Christian who has been involved in Bible-study groups for several years. Linda is willing to disciple Sarah and has already encouraged her to dig deeply into the Word.

Christopher is desirous of learning more about God and the Bible. Since I can only talk to him briefly over the counter and give him books to read, I asked him if he would be interested in a weekly Bible study.

"I'd be very interested," he said.

I called my friend Roger Van Noord, who is on staff with "The Navigators." He contacted Chris and they have made arrangements to get together regularly.

I'm very conscious of the networking that goes on in God's work. Some sow, some water, but only God can give the increase.

My actual walking time is sometimes shortened because I can never let witnessing opportunities slip by. But that's all right. I do have a stationary bicycle at home that I can use to make up for my lack of exercise! And somehow I think I've shown that even bodily exercise can be profitable in terms of soul winning!

44

Hotel Encounters

[Jesus said:] "What good is it for a man to gain the whole world, yet forfeit his soul? Or what can a man give in exchange for his soul?"

Mark 8:36–37

Are the two men seated across from us speaking French?" I asked my husband as I glanced around the restaurant.

"I'm not sure," Paul answered. "But they sound like Frenchmen."

Our young waiter was standing nearby, waiting to take our order. He heard my question and said, "Actually they're speaking Italian."

"Is *your* background Italian?" I asked.

"No, Mexican. My parents live in Texas. I've been in this city only a few months."

"I should have known—I see your name is Juan, and that certainly isn't Italian."

"Juan is a Spanish name."

"I find this hotel fascinating," I said. "There are so many different nationalities represented here. They even have clocks on the wall behind the front desk that show the time in London, Tokyo, Singapore, and Moscow. You must serve a lot of businessmen from these countries."

"Yes, we take care of people from all over the world. Where do you live?" Juan asked.

"We're from Birmingham, Michigan. I'm here speaking at a women's retreat sponsored by radio station WBCL. It's connected with Summit Christian College."

"What do you speak about?" Juan asked.

"I'm here encouraging Christians to share the gospel of Jesus Christ. The world is a mess, and Jesus is the only hope for its confused and frightened people. Do you have a church background?" I asked.

"I was raised as a Roman Catholic," he answered. "But I'm not attending church at the present."

"I would like to give you a booklet that will give you an idea of what I talk about at these seminars. Would you read it and then—when I come back for another meal—tell me what you think? I'd like to know if it makes sense to you."

Juan took the booklet and said, "I'd love to read it, and I'll let you know what I think of it."

Paul and I ordered our meal. I made a point of telling Juan to serve me decaffeinated coffee so I would be able to get a good night's sleep.

The meal was excellent but I did have a hard time sleeping that night. I was sure Juan had forgotten my request and given me regular coffee.

The following evening we again visited the hotel's dining room. Some of the workshop leaders at the retreat were also there. When I saw Juan, I asked, "Did you get a chance to read the booklet?"

"Yes, I did," he said with great enthusiasm. "The best part was about receiving Jesus Christ."

I had often given someone this booklet (*The Four Spiritual Laws*), but never had I received such an energetic response. It was as though something had been settled in this young man's life. I wanted to be sure he understood, so I asked, "Did you pray and agree with God that you are a sinner and need Jesus Christ to save you?"

"I sure did. It felt good to receive Jesus as my Savior," he repeated.

"That's the best decision you'll ever make in your life, Juan. Now I'd like you to meet some of the new friends I met at the retreat." I brought him over to their table and said, "Juan, I want you to meet my friends. Each one has received Christ as Savior. Because their lives have been transformed, they are at the retreat encouraging other believers to be their best for God."

"Mrs. Pickard gave me a booklet explaining Christianity," Juan said. "The best part was receiving Jesus Christ. I'm happy to say, 'I did that.'"

"I'm so glad, Juan. But, by the way," I said teasingly, "I'm sure the last time I ate here, you gave me regular coffee instead of decaffeinated. I know because I didn't sleep. But I've forgiven you."

"It *was* decaffeinated, Mrs. Pickard. Perhaps you didn't sleep because you got so excited telling me about Jesus Christ."

Everyone had a good laugh, and I finally gave in and said, "You may be right."

Juan promised he would start reading in the Book of John. He appeared to be very sincere about his new commitment.

The following morning we had breakfast in the coffee shop. I told the waiter to be sure to give me decaffeinated coffee. "I'm still sure I was given regular the other night, because I couldn't sleep," I said to Paul.

"Why don't you sue the hotel? That seems to be part of the American way," joked the man sitting a few tables away.

I smiled and answered, "I don't believe in suing people." It was early in the morning and very few people were in the restaurant. My husband commented on the man's crisp accent and asked if he was from England.

"Yes, as a matter of fact I am. I'm on business here for Lloyd's of London. I travel all around the world. Sometimes my wife comes with me."

"Why don't you come over and join us?" I suggested.

"Thanks, but I'm used to dining alone."

The Englishman and my husband kept talking across the room, so I once again urged him to sit with us, adding, "Maybe we can learn from each other."

"I think I'd like that." Since his order had already been taken, he hailed his waiter and told him he had changed his seat.

We had a good time getting acquainted. Paul and our new friend talked about world conditions. We enjoyed hearing him speak. His accent was delightful, and he seemed to be full of knowledge in many areas of life.

"What is the spiritual tone in England these days?" I asked.

"Not very good. Our people aren't very inclined toward religion, and the church doesn't seem to meet their need."

"What sort of impact did Billy Graham's crusade have on the English?" I asked.

"I think it was a dud," he answered.

"That surprises me. I heard all kinds of good reports."

"Well, I didn't go for it," he replied.

"What about you?" I asked. "What is your religious background?"

"I was raised in the Church of England. Though I don't attend church regularly, I *am* a Christian. But I have problems concerning the way God runs things," he went on.

"What do you mean?" I asked.

"I don't think God is fair. He took my mother when she was only thirty-four years old. She was a good woman. It seems as though God takes the good people and rewards the bad ones. I just don't understand it. And what about the wicked rulers? Why does he allow them to live?" The Englishman then put his head in his hands and said, "I just don't understand. I can't figure out God's ways. I think he should let good people live and get rid of evil." He appeared very upset.

"Have you ever read the Bible?" I asked.

"Oh, I read it now and then."

"You remind me of a verse in the Bible that says, 'You turn things upside down, as if the potter were thought to be like the clay! . . . Can the pot say of the potter, "He knows nothing"?' That's from Isaiah 29:16. You are criticizing a God you don't know. The Bible is God's Word. Why not start reading it regularly?"

"Well, I'm not sure the Bible is true."

"You really surprise me. You are a well-educated and intelligent man. You are knowledgeable in so many things except the most important thing of all—God's Word."

Paul said, "You say you are a Christian. On what basis do you say that?" The Englishman didn't answer, but instead went on arguing the authenticity of the Bible.

"On what basis, then, do you think you are a Christian?" Paul persisted.

Our new friend bowed his head and quietly said, "Because I believe there has to be more to life than what I see in the world. I do believe—I just don't *know*."

Then I said, "I have written a couple of books about people who discovered God through the Bible. They put their trust in him and made him Lord of their lives. I'd like to give you my books if you promise to read them."

"Thank you very much. I know my wife will read them right away. Let me give you my card," he continued. "I would be pleased if you would call us if you ever get to London."

We all rode up on the elevator together. We pushed the button for the third floor. Our English friend, who took out a key for the penthouse suite, said, "Now *I* probably won't sleep tonight. You've given me a lot to think about."

Reflection

Such chance encounters as these provide an endless seedbed for sowing the Good News—the universal message of salvation that transcends cultural and national boundaries.

Juan, the young Hispanic waiter, was eager to receive Christ. All he needed was to know how. On the other hand, the English businessman was hurt and angry. He wanted to tell the Creator how to run his universe. As far as the world is concerned, this man is successful, but he is spiritually impoverished. He left a crack in the door, however, when he admitted that he probably wouldn't sleep that night! He accepted my books, knowing what the subject would be. Then he issued an invitation for us to call him if we get to England. The seed was cast. Now we pray that God will send someone to water it.

45

All in the Family

A man is not a Jew if he is only one outwardly, nor is circumcision merely outward and physical. No, a man is a Jew if he is one inwardly; and circumcision is circumcision of the heart, by the Spirit, not by the written code. Such a man's praise is not from men, but from God.

Romans 2:28–29

"We got some more mail from the College of Jewish Studies today," my husband said. "Ever since I attended the mini-course in Hebrew they keep sending invitations to other programs."

"What are they offering now?" I asked.

"They have a four-session course on the meaning of the Passover. Would you like to go?" Paul asked. "Besides learning something new, maybe we can even contribute to the discussions."

"I'd like that," I answered. "We wouldn't want to offend anyone, but I wonder if we'll be allowed to ask questions. The Jewish people I've met seem to know so little about the Bible. Maybe this rabbi will be different."

We eagerly anticipated our first class. The rabbi, a young man with a pleasant personality, talked about the Seder, the Passover feast commemorating the exodus of the Jews from Egypt. First he explained the significance of preparing for it properly.

The cleaning of the house and the food and dishes to be used are all of utmost importance, but Passover is also a learning experience for the children. There are questions to be asked and answered pertaining to the deliverance of the Israelites from their slavery in Egypt. It is a time to joyfully thank God for intervening in history and freeing them from bondage.

The rabbi emphasized over and over that all leaven (yeast) was to be removed from the home and that no leavened products were to be eaten during this holiday period. This restriction referred to products made from wheat, barley, rye, or oats, such as bread and cake. When the Israelites fled from Egypt, there was no time to wait for bread to rise. Eating unleavened bread (matzos) at Passover was to serve as a reminder to the Jewish people of their escape.

Although our first session was very informative, I noticed that nothing was mentioned about how the death angel "passed over" the Israelites' homes—sparing those who obeyed God's command to put some of the blood of a lamb "without defect" on the top and side of the doorposts. This sign was crucial to the survival of their firstborn (Exodus 12:1–30). When the meeting was opened for questions I asked about this.

"We don't talk much about the blood," the rabbi said. "You see, the Jews have been accused of killing Jesus. And some Jewish children even claim they have been told that Jews make matzos from the blood of Christians."

I was shocked at this statement and began shaking my head.

"You don't agree?" the rabbi questioned.

"I've never heard of such a thing."

When he looked at me, I sensed he had already known we weren't Jewish. I'm sure all doubt was removed after that exchange.

I went to the rabbi later and said, "My husband and I are Christians. We came to learn more about our Jewish neighbors. I want you to know we are very happy that the United States has sided with Israel. For God said, 'I will bless those who bless you [Abraham and his offspring], and whoever curses you I will curse . . .' [Gen. 12:3]. But if it offends you to have us here, we won't continue to come."

"Not at all. Please continue to attend," he answered graciously.

"You talked about getting rid of the leaven in the house," I said. "Does that perhaps also refer to the sin in our lives?"

"Well, we don't call it sin. We call it missing the mark," he said.

"Yes," I said, "sin is 'missing the mark,' and the Bible says a lot about that subject. I think it's important to discuss the Bible and learn about God's ways." I then looked at the rabbi and said, "I have several Jewish friends and neighbors with whom I would love to discuss the Bible. But I find they don't know the Scriptures very well, not even the five Books of Moses. That is very disappointing."

"You are right," the rabbi said. "And it's too bad."

On the way home, Paul and I talked about our new experience. We both felt it was worthwhile, for we were beginning to better understand the Jewish people.

I decided to bring my Bible with me the following week. The rabbi referred to the Book of Exodus several times, and I wrote down the passages he mentioned. I kept my Bible on my lap, not wanting to make a big deal about it. One of the men in the group came over to where I was sitting. He noticed my Bible and asked, "Is that a Thompson's Chain Reference Bible you have?"

I looked up in surprise and said, "Why, yes. How did you know?"

"I own one. It's very helpful." He then went back to his seat.

I must talk to that man afterward, I thought.

The group members also talked about inviting poor people and college students who would be away from home to their Seder observances. "You need to encourage people to ask questions, especially the children," the rabbi said. "Tell them the reason for the celebration: that God brought the Jews out of their slavery in Egypt. Emphasize that it is a time of gratefulness to God."

After the meeting, I asked the man who owned the Thompson's Bible how he happened to have it.

"I was traveling on an airplane," he said. "The man sitting next to me was reading the Bible. We got talking about it and he sent me a copy. I really enjoy reading it. By the way, I'm a cantor at a local synagogue, though I'm also involved with a family business. My name is Isidore."

I introduced myself and said, "How about reading Isaiah 53 this week? I'd like to discuss it with you next time." He wrote it down and said he would do it. Then he smiled and we parted.

I was eager to talk to the young cantor, but I never saw him again, for he didn't show up for the final two meetings. I'm praying that

God will give him a hunger for his Word. I also pray that God will open his eyes and heart so he can receive the truth.

Our third session was held in the auditorium, where we were joined by the women's auxiliary. When I arrived, I noticed a young black man in his early twenties. He was preparing the coffee and tea and had arranged some delicious-looking cakes on the table. He smiled as I took my plate. "Are you Jewish?" I asked.

"No, I'm not."

"Are you a Christian?" I asked.

"I don't know. I belong to the sanctified church."

I wasn't sure what he meant, so I said, "Well, I'm saved and sanctified; 'sanctified' means set apart to God. But what does that word mean to you?"

"I'm confused about a lot of things," the young man admitted. "Our church worships on Saturdays and we follow God's law. I've asked three rabbis here how I can find God, but they tell me they don't know. I really need to find God. Nobody seems to know how."

I smiled and said, "The only way you can find God is through Jesus Christ. He died for our sins and was buried and rose again. Christ paid the penalty for our sins. Though he was sinless, he took our sin upon himself. When we confess to God that we are sinners and receive Jesus Christ as our Savior, we are saved from the penalty of our sinfulness. We then have a new and wonderful life in him."

The young man beamed as he said, "A light just turned on in my head. Somehow I know what you're saying is the truth."

"I'll bring you something to read next week," I said. "I have to leave now. Class is ready to start. Think about our conversation, and maybe next week we can talk a little more."

"I'll look forward to it," he said. "By the way, my name's Darica."

"I'm Mrs. Pickard. See you next week."

I prayed for my new friend all that week. I prayed for an opportunity to make the way of salvation clear to him.

I was delighted to see Darica walking down the hall as I entered the building the following week. "I have something for you to read," I said. "It explains how you can have a personal relationship with Jesus Christ. Maybe we can talk after the meeting."

"I'd like that. You see, I'm afraid of going to hell. I've got to find the way to God." Then shyly he added, "My cousin died recently. He had AIDS. It scares me to death."

"Have you been fooling around with sex?" I asked.

"No," he answered. "And I don't want to."

"Well, you won't have to worry about going to hell if you know Jesus Christ as your Savior," I told him. "I'll see you in about an hour."

The rabbi seemed eager to start our final meeting. "We have a lot to cover today," he said. He then looked at me and asked, "Did you bring your Bible today?"

"I meant to, but I forgot to put it in my bag," I said. I was surprised at his question. I didn't realize he knew I had brought it the week before.

"Well," he said, "I'm going to read from 1 Kings 18 today. Then we're going to talk about Elijah. Can anyone tell me about Elijah?" he asked. No one answered. "How did Elijah die?" the rabbi asked. Again no one responded, so I said, "He didn't die. God took him to heaven."

"According to 2 Kings 2:11, he was taken up in a whirlwind," my husband added.

"I figured you'd know," the rabbi said. Then he asked the rest of the group to read the story of Elijah at their Seder. "Don't read it from any book but the Bible. Read it from the Bible," he repeated.

I was happy to hear the rabbi emphasize reading the Bible. I was also glad I had talked to him previously about the Jewish people not being knowledgeable about the Scriptures.

When the meeting was over, both Paul and I thanked the rabbi for welcoming us into the group. Then I said, "At the first session you said that Christians blame the Jews for killing Jesus. You also said that Jews have been accused of making matzos from Christian blood. That hurt me. You see, I believe it was my sin and your sin that put Jesus on the cross. And I have never heard the untrue connection between matzos and the blood of Christians. A lot of people call themselves Christians, but that doesn't mean they are true believers. Anyone who honors Christ would never deliberately hurt a Jew."

"I could tell you were hurt that first week," he said. "I'm sorry."

Then we shook hands and I told him we felt attending the course had been worthwhile.

I found my new friend, Darica, eating his lunch in one of the classrooms. He grinned broadly when he saw me. "I received Christ as my Savior a few days ago," he said. "I'm so glad we met and that you could help me find the way to God."

"This is just the beginning of your new life. Do you have a Bible?" I asked. When he told me he did, I said, "It's important that you read a portion of it every day. The Bible is God's Word. It's food for your soul. It will help you grow in the Christian life. I suggest you start reading in the Book of John. It will help you to know Jesus better. And I know you attend church, but if you'd like to visit ours sometime, we'd love to have you." I told him our location and the time of our service. He thanked me and I left.

A few months after we visited the Jewish Center, our pastor, Len Crowley, gave a series on the "The Last Act," which pertained to the promises God had given Israel. He did such an excellent job, that I decided to give the rabbi a tape of one of the messages. He received it well and thanked me. We had a good talk. I told him I planned to give him the rest of the tapes and hoped he wouldn't be offended.

While at the Jewish Center that day, I saw Darica again and asked him whether he was still reading the Bible.

"Every night," he answered. "A strange thing has happened since I've accepted Christ. Some of my old friends don't come around anymore."

"That's normal," I answered. "Not everyone will be happy about your commitment to Christ."

"That's all right with me," Darica smiled. "The most important thing is, I now know God through Jesus Christ. Thanks for your help."

Reflection

Paul and I felt we understood our Jewish friends a little better after attending these meetings. If we are to lead them to Christ, we need to be interested in their traditions. It is a great help to be aware of the Scriptures pertaining to their observances, because it's a good opener for a discussion. Although the Bible is the only source of truth, if we are to witness effectively to people, we must first show that we love them.

46

For Such a Time As This

For it is by grace you have been saved, through faith—and
this not from yourselves, it is the gift of God—not by works,
so that no one can boast.

Ephesians 2:8–9

Our mail delivery has been spasmodic of late. This can be
irritating, especially if I'm looking for an important piece
of mail. I sometimes make several trips to the letter box,
only to be disappointed.

We live in a townhouse, and our mailboxes are situated around
the corner from our home. One nice thing about this is that we often
meet neighbors and chat as we wait for the postman. One day I met
a woman pushing a pretty little girl in a stroller. This child smiled
brightly and said, "Hello."

"Hello there," I responded. "And what is your name?"

"Al—sandra."

"Is this nice lady your mommy?" I asked.

"She's my nanny," she answered proudly.

"Her name is really Alexandra," the woman said. "She's not quite
three years old. That's a big name for such a little girl, isn't it?"

"Maybe someday she'll shorten it to Alex or Sandra," I commented. "But Alexandra is a pretty name; it sounds sort of musical."

I introduced myself and the woman told me her name was Eve.

"Are you new in the neighborhood?" I asked. "I haven't seen you
before."

"Yes, I am. I started to work for Alexandra's mother two weeks ago. I'm from Vermont. I work for an agency and asked to be transferred out of state because I just had to get away. I'm trying to sort things out in my life. This has been a very hard year for me," Eve said sadly.

"You sound like you're hurting. I know I'm a stranger to you, but would it make you feel better if you talked about it?" I asked.

"I usually don't talk about my problems. But you seem so kind, and I need to talk to someone. It would be a welcome relief," she said with a smile.

"If I can help you in any way, I'd like to be available."

"I have no one but this child to talk to all day long," Eve told me. "Alexandra's mother and father both work. After dinner I go to my room so the parents can be alone. They are very nice to me, but I spend most of my evenings that way, even though they gave me the use of a car and told me I could have the evenings off. Of course, when they go out to dinner I have to baby-sit."

"Where do you go on your evenings off?" I asked.

"I don't go anywhere. I don't know my way around, so I wouldn't dare go out at night. I'd never find my way back home."

"Do you have a family?" I asked.

"Yes, I have four children in Vermont. My youngest daughter is with my mother right now. I thought getting away for a while would help me. I need to straighten things out in my mind. My troubles started when I discovered my husband had cheated on me. Then he began physically abusing me. He is a big man and very strong. He has hurt me many times, which is why I came out here to Michigan. I was afraid of him, but now I'm so lonesome I can hardly stand it," she added.

"Do you have a church background?" I asked her.

"Yes, I do," Eve said. "But I'm very disappointed in the church I've attended most of my life. Recently they started playing rock and roll music. I don't think that belongs in a church. And I saw my pastor buying liquor. I don't understand that. I don't want to go back, but I don't know where else to go."

"I attend a very fine church," I said. "It is probably not your denomination, but I'd love to have you come with my husband and me on Sunday. You'll meet a lot of wonderful people."

"I'd love to go, but I have to work Sunday morning," she said.

"Well, we have an evening service."

"I'll go anyplace," she laughed. "I need to get out of the house."

When we picked up Eve the following Sunday evening, she appeared entirely different from our first encounter. She had obviously dressed very carefully and had a refreshing radiance about her.

I introduced Eve to many of my friends at church. She was charming and outgoing. For the moment she seemed to have forgotten the pain she was carrying.

"I enjoyed the service very much," she said afterward. "I'd like to come again." I told her we'd be happy to pick her up for church anytime.

On the way home, I asked Eve whether she had visited any of the malls in our area. "No, I haven't," she replied. "I'd like to get some shoes, but I don't know where to go."

"I have time this week," I said. "I'd love to take you shopping and show you some of my favorite places." Eve seemed excited about the prospect, so we made a date to visit a couple of malls and several stores. She found the shoes she wanted and bought a couple of gifts for her friends back home. We had a good time and were becoming better acquainted.

Eve took Alexandra for a walk every day, usually ending up in the picnic area of our subdivision. It's a beautiful place, located in a ravine with a stream running through it.

"I love to sit and look at the water," Eve mentioned one day. "It's so peaceful. Why don't you come down sometime and we can talk?"

"I'm free tomorrow," I told her. "I'll meet you after lunch."

I liked Eve. She had high standards and we had fun together. I wanted very much to present the claims of Christ to her. *Tomorrow will be a good time to find out where she stands,* I thought.

The following day was beautiful. The sun was shining and I was looking forward to seeing my new friend. I prayed for wisdom, as I didn't want to offend her in any way. I knew Jesus Christ could meet her needs. He would see her through the hurt and pain in her life.

Eve and Alexandra were sitting at a picnic table by the stream when I arrived. "Isn't this a wonderful place?" Eve said. "Vermont is beautiful, but this part of the country is lovely, too."

As I sat down, she said, "You told me you were going to speak in Grand Rapids next week. Tell me all about it. What are you going to talk about?"

"Well, I speak about our relationship to God. A lot of people have gone to church for years but don't know how to be a part of his family. I tell them what the Bible says. It's the only authority we have about God. Tell me, Eve, have you received Jesus Christ as your personal Savior? Do you believe he died for you *personally?*"

"I'm not sure, but I've tried to live a good life and be kind to people. I do my best," she said.

"Those are fine qualities," I said, "but that is not enough. You see, God sent his only Son, Jesus Christ, to die for our sins. Since the Bible says, 'For all have sinned and fall short of the glory of God,' we know that none of us can make the grade. Only Jesus is perfect. That puts us in a dilemma. Let me show you a little booklet. I'd like to read it to you and then I'll let you keep it." Then I showed her *The Four Spiritual Laws.*

We talked about the fact that we are separated from God because of our sin. And that "the wages of sin is death"—spiritual separation from God. I told her that the wonderful thing is: "God demonstrates his own love for us in this: While we were still sinners, Christ died for us" (Rom. 5:8). But he was buried and raised on the third day; Peter and the other disciples saw him, and more than five hundred people were witnesses to his life after the resurrection (1 Cor. 15:3–6).

"Eve," I continued, "Jesus said, 'I am the way and the truth and the life. No one comes to the Father except through me.' That's in John 14:6. He didn't say, 'I'll show you the way.' He said, 'I *am* the way.' But it isn't enough to know these facts. We must each receive Jesus Christ as our Savior. John 1:12 says, 'Yet to all who received him, to those who believed in his name, he gave the right to become children of God.'

"Another verse you need to know is Revelation 3:20. Jesus says, 'Here I am! I stand at the door and knock. If anyone hears my voice and opens the door, I will come in and eat with him, and he with me.' Jesus wants to be in your life, Eve. He wants you to trust him and have fellowship with him. He wants you to depend on him and accept his guidance. You don't have to bear your burdens and problems alone. He is waiting for your answer. Do you want him to be Lord of your life?" I asked.

Eve bowed her head and said, "Yes, I do want Christ in my life."

I helped her pray, and she received Christ as her Savior. What a beautiful time we had together.

"Strange how we met, isn't it?" Eve commented happily.

"God works in mysterious ways. You came all the way to Michigan so you could be introduced to the Savior! I believe God brought you here for such a time as this."

I gave Eve some Christian literature to read and told her to start reading the Book of John.

"I'm invited to a baby shower for one of my missionary friends. Would you like to come with me?" I asked.

"Are you sure it will be all right?"

"I'm sure it will be fine. But I'll call and double-check. Inell, the expectant mother, is a good friend. She's home on furlough from Africa and will be returning when the baby is ready to travel. Meeting people is her specialty, so she'll love getting acquainted with you."

Later I called to make sure the hostess would be prepared to have an extra guest. "No problem," she said. I explained that Eve was a brand-new babe in Christ. It would be good for her to be with other believers.

The shower was lovely and we had lots of fun. Several women came to our table and wanted to be introduced to Eve. I was delighted when Debbie, Inell's sister-in-law, who is also a missionary, showed special interest in Eve. She spent considerable time talking to her, making her feel welcomed and accepted.

Even though I had told Eve she didn't have to bring a gift, she had gone shopping with Alexandra and her mom and found some lovely embroidered bibs for the baby. This helped her feel more a part of the group, and Inell was touched.

Reflection

Eventually Eve felt ready to go back to Vermont. She missed her children, other family members, and old friends. She was stronger and ready to face whatever problems were ahead—because she now had the Lord as her guide.

Eve has been gone for several months now, but I've talked to her on the phone a few times. Her husband is back home again. "There are still problems," she said. "But if you want a home bad enough, you will be willing to bear the pain as you work them through with God's help." She also told me that she and her mother had visited four different churches. They liked a particular Baptist church very much. I pray they will get established in a Bible-believing church and have fellowship with other believers.

I constantly marvel at God's grace and his love for humankind. It's interesting how I met Eve. The mailbox is a friendly place and provides an easy way to get acquainted. Ephesians 5:16 speaks of "making the most of every opportunity, because the days are evil."

Opportunities for witnessing are everywhere. If you tell God you are available to him, he will show you where they are.

47

Salt and Light

[Jesus said:] "You are the salt of the earth. . . . You are the light of the world. . . . let your light shine before men, that they may see your good deeds and praise your Father in heaven."
Matthew 5:13–14, 16

J called the health-food store's manager to inquire about their sale on vitamins. "I notice you are advertising bee pollen. What is that supposed to do for a person?" I asked.

The man hesitated for a second, then said in a laughing voice, "You'll live forever; yep, you'll live forever."

"I know you're joking," I said. "But I *know* I'm going to live forever, and not because I buy your bee pollen. I plan to come to your store tomorrow and I'll tell you why I'm so sure."

"I'd like to hear about it," he said. "I'm really interested in why you think you're going to live forever. I'm going to be in and out of the store tomorrow. If I miss you, please leave your message with one of the clerks."

The man seemed congenial. *I'll go in the store tomorrow and tell it like it is,* I thought.

The following day, I went to the health-food store. I asked for the manager but was told he wasn't in. "Do you want to leave a message?" the clerk asked.

"Well, yes," I answered. "Please tell him that the woman who said she was going to live forever came in to see him. Tell him it isn't because of any vitamin or food product I eat. I know he was teasing when he said that eating bee pollen would make a person live for-ever. But I want you to tell him that *I* was serious."

The clerk looked at me skeptically. "I'm interested, too," he said. "How do you know you're going to live forever?"

"I know because I've accepted Jesus Christ as my personal Sav-ior. There's a verse in the Bible that describes Jesus' prayer to the Father shortly before his crucifixion. This is what he said: 'Now this is eternal life: that they may know you, the only true God, and Jesus Christ, whom you have sent.' Those words are in John 17:3."

"You'd sure shock the manager if you told him that," the clerk said.

"It's God's truth," I said. "People need to know that God made a provision for their sin. If you confess you are a sinner and accept Jesus Christ as your Savior, God will let you into his heaven. Then you'll live forever with him. That's the Good News I want you to tell your boss."

The clerk tried to change the subject by saying, "I don't believe in God. I'm my own god, the only one in charge of my life."

"I can't believe what you're saying," I commented. "How can you say such a thing?"

"Well, whether I'm godly or ungodly, I make my own choices."

There was a young girl standing nearby. She also worked in the store and was listening to our conversation. I turned to her and asked, "What do you think about this man's statement? He thinks he's the god of his life."

"Well," she said, "if he *was* God, he'd never get sick—and he does. He has problems with his legs and other ailments, too. So it doesn't make much sense for him to say he's God. He obviously doesn't understand about *our* God."

What a perfect answer, I thought. *She sounds like a Christian.*

"Are you a believer in Jesus Christ?" I asked.

With a radiant smile she said, "I certainly am. Jesus is my Savior."

The male clerk then said, "I know I'm going to hell when I die. I really don't mind, because I'll be there with my friends."

"But in hell there is utter darkness," I said. "You won't be having a good time or living it up with your friends. You won't even see your friends. You'll be miserable. You'd better make things right with God before you die. If you die without knowing Jesus Christ, you're lost.

You need to have him forgive your sins and must know him as your Savior before it's too late."

He shrugged his shoulders and said, "I'll take my chances."

As I walked out of the store, I thought, *How sad.* Later I prayed that the Spirit of God would remind him of our conversation and that it would trouble him. I continue to pray that he will ask the Christian girl in the store more about the true and living God. And I plan to visit the store again!

A couple of months after this incident, I met my friend Connie.

"I heard you just got back from visiting your fiancé in California. How was your trip?" I asked.

"I had a wonderful time. I'd like to tell you what happened on the way home. I was in a good mood when I got on the plane, full of good will toward everyone. As I sat down, my seat partner said, 'I just discovered that an old friend of mine is on the plane. We haven't seen each other in years. Would you mind trading seats with her?'

"'Not at all,' I said. 'I hope you have a wonderful visit catching up on old times.'

"As I approached the section where I was to be seated, I had second thoughts. I discovered that my new seat was in the smoking section. The air was blue with smoke, as though everyone had decided to light up at once."

"That would be hard for me to handle," I interrupted. "I get a coughing spell every time I'm around anyone who smokes. What did you do?"

"Though I wasn't happy about it, I decided to make the best of the situation. Then I prayed, 'Lord you know how much smoking bothers me. If you have some purpose in this setup, I'm available to you.' I began to feel better.

"I sat down and introduced myself to my new seatmate. She in turn said, 'I'd like you to meet my husband, George. My name's Hilda.'

"I told them that I wasn't supposed to be sitting in that section and explained why I had traded seats. When I commented, 'Isn't the Lord good to give us such wonderful weather?' the woman looked at me strangely as though she didn't know what I was talking about. She told me she didn't know anything about the Lord and that her husband was an atheist.

"'Changing seats couldn't have been a mistake after all,' I said. 'I'm sure God meant for me to sit next to you. I'd like to tell you something about God and how you can know him as I do.'"

"How did the woman respond?" I asked Connie.

"She was polite as I began telling her that God loved us so much he sent his only Son to die on the cross for our sins. She seemed interested, so I continued with our conversation. I said, 'I believe this situation was an appointment arranged by God.'

"'Do you really think so?' she answered. She seemed surprised but touched.

"'You mean that God would care enough that he'd arrange for us to have conversation together?'

"'Absolutely,' I said. Time went quickly as I continued to talk about God's love for all mankind. When we landed, I said, 'I hope we'll meet again. And I hope your last flight will be to heaven.'

"'Well,' the woman smiled, 'I don't think it's fair to come to God when I'm in a jam. If I haven't trusted him up until now, I don't think it would be right. I don't want to be rude.'

"I looked at her and said, 'But God wants us to come to him anytime—even if we're crying for help. He's waiting for you to call on him. He's always there. I'm praying that you will come to know God as I have.'"

"Connie," I said, "you took what might have been an unpleasant experience and turned it into a blessing. I'm sure that pleased the Lord."

Reflection

There are confused and needy people all over the world. Opportunities to spread the light of the gospel are everywhere. We just need to open our eyes and ears to the possibilities of sowing the seed of God's Word. He will give the increase.

Witnessing is a mind-set. God has provided every believer with spiritual antennas so that we can pick up on a person's remarks and respond with a biblical truth.

48

Christmas Coffees

Do not be anxious about anything, but in everything, by prayer and petition, with thanksgiving, present your requests to God. And the peace of God, which transcends all understanding, will guard your hearts and your minds in Christ Jesus.

Philippians 4:6–7

"Would you be willing to be one of the speakers at our Christmas Coffees?" my friend Lauren asked.

"Christmas Coffees? I don't know anything about them," I said. "I've been speaking on the East Coast for the past few weeks. I've probably missed a lot. Tell me about them."

"The women of the church have been encouraged to invite their neighbors to their homes during the holidays," she said. "It will be an opportunity to share the real meaning of Christmas and show love to those who live near us. Someone will also present an inspirational message, and the people attending will be given an opportunity to receive Christ. Your name came up as a possible speaker. Would you be willing to help?"

"I'd love to be involved," I said. "I think it's a great opportunity to reach our neighbors for Christ. Was this your idea, Lauren?" I asked.

"Actually, my friend Jeanie read about a church in Minnesota that's been having Christmas Coffees for several years. Their church members host about two hundred such gatherings every year. The results have been astounding. We decided to present the idea to the ladies of our church. Even though some of the women are timid about inviting their neighbors, they're willing to get involved. I'll give you the telephone numbers of your hostesses so you can call and get directions to their homes."

When I called Pam, one of my hostesses, to confirm my commitment, I reminded her that I would be giving the guests an opportunity to receive Christ as Savior at the end of my talk. "We'll trust the Lord for the results," I said.

There was dead silence. I thought we'd been disconnected. "Are you still there?" I asked.

"Yeah," she said hesitatingly. "It's just that I'm not comfortable having you give an invitation. You see my mother is coming and she said, 'If it gets too heavy, I'll leave right in the middle of the program.' That makes me very nervous, so I'd prefer you didn't give an invitation."

"Pam," I answered, "I didn't set up the program. If I'm to do this, I'll have to follow the planned format. Don't worry, I won't collar anyone. I'll just share how I began to understand the real meaning of Christmas. Perhaps some will identify with my experience."

The following day I got a call from Pam's co-hostess, Becky, who said, "Pam would like us to meet for coffee and discuss the meeting. She's concerned about her mother and is still hesitant about your giving an invitation. I think it will be just fine, but for her peace of mind perhaps we'd better get together."

"Why don't you come here on Wednesday?" I offered. "It will be better than going to a noisy restaurant."

Wednesday morning I got a call from Pam. "I won't be able to meet with you. Mother is having some chest pains and I have to bring her to the doctor. But Becky will come."

"We'll be praying for your mother," I said. "God can use this to remind her that earthly life is short and we need to prepare for the hereafter. Remember, Pam, God's in control. We need to trust him."

I didn't know Becky well. I had met her briefly at an autographing party. She had recently moved into Pam's neighborhood and the two of them were just getting to know each other. They had become acquainted through carpooling their children to the same Christian school. Becky's husband was the new president of Tyndale Bible College. I had heard him speak and was impressed by his interest in evangelism. He told us that his wife had been involved with Campus Crusade and had a heart for sharing the gospel. I was looking forward to spending time with her.

Becky and I had a good time getting acquainted. She was excited about the Christmas Coffees and felt we should give the women an opportunity to receive Christ, as originally planned. "We'll pray that the Spirit of God will work in Pam's mother's heart," I said. "By the way, Pam told me that her mom's bringing a friend with her. She said both of them will walk out if they don't like the message. I mentioned the problem to the pastor. He suggested we seat the two women near the door. 'If they're not happy with the program they can slip out, but I really think they're just bluffing,' he said."

Becky and I spent some time in prayer and reassured each other that we were pleasing God in our endeavors.

The morning of the Coffee at Pam's house, I arrived with a sense of peace, remembering the words of my former pastor, Joe Stowell: "If we do the possible, God will do the impossible." I had experienced that many times and knew I had nothing to fear.

Besides Pam, Becky, and myself, four other women came. Pam's mom, Jean, and her friend Lou were delightful. We had a good time talking as we sipped our coffee. They didn't seem at all intimidated. Pam was the one who seemed nervous.

Finally we were asked to come into the living room and Pam introduced me: "Nellie will give us a brief message. It will be a good preparation for the holidays."

This was what I said:

Christmas is the time of year when there seems to be unity in the community. [The women nodded and smiled.] There's an excitement and joy in the air as we talk to our neighbors about our plans for the holidays. But in the busyness of the season, it's easy to forget the real meaning of Christmas.

I'm reminded of the time we spent Christmas in Florida. When I went to a department store to do some shopping, I noticed a sign in the window that said, "Shopping at——is the real meaning of Christmas." I couldn't believe it. *Does Christmas only mean spending a few dollars on gifts?* I thought.

I walked into the store and politely asked one of the saleswomen to call the manager so I might speak to him. He appeared concerned and asked whether something was wrong.

"Definitely," I answered. "I'm greatly offended by the sign in your window. The real meaning of Christmas is *not* shopping at your store. Jesus Christ is what Christmas is all about. He was born to die so that he might save us from our sins. It really hurts me to see your sign."

"I agree with you," he said. "We both know the real meaning of Christmas. But my boss told me to put the sign in the window."

"I would appreciate it if you would give your boss a message from me," I said kindly. "Tell him if he doesn't remove the sign, I will try to influence my friends not to shop at your store. I might also sue him for false advertising."

That kind of commercialism has crept in and blurred the reason we celebrate Christ's birthday. There was a time when I, too, looked forward to Christmas mainly because of the gifts I would receive. But now that I've made Jesus Christ Lord of my life, I anticipate the season with a new appreciation and awe. God gave us his Son, the best gift of all.

I'm overwhelmed when I think that Jesus Christ, who knew no sin, took the burden of my sin upon himself. He opted to be my substitute. I deserved to die, but he took my place. I have received God's gift of salvation by confessing my sin and acknowledging Jesus as my Savior. The greatest sin anyone can commit is to reject Jesus Christ. He is God's only provision for our sin.

There are usually people in a gathering such as this who have never received Jesus Christ as their Savior. I would like to give you an opportunity to do that today. If you would like to receive Christ, I will pray out loud and you can pray silently after me. It isn't so much the words you say that are important to God, but the attitude of your heart.

At that point Pam left the room. I knew she was still struggling, afraid that her mother and her friend would leave.

Then I began to pray: "Dear heavenly Father, I thank you for sending your Son, Jesus Christ, to die on the cross for me. I confess I have sinned and gone my own independent way. I now receive Jesus Christ as my Savior and Lord. Thank you for accepting me into your family. Guide me and direct me in your way. In Jesus' name I pray. *Amen.*"

I gave all the women a piece of paper, asking each to write her name on it. "This is the first time we've had a Christmas Coffee," I said. "I'd appreciate it if you would let us know if you enjoyed it and would like to do it again. If you prayed to receive Christ, please put a check mark by your name. When I see that, I will pray for you."

Three of the four guests put a check mark by their name. The note from Pam's mom was a thank-you for delivering God's message. Her friend Lou said the message was especially important to her this Christmas. The third came from Mary Lou, who wrote: "My son has received Christ. Even though he has had great sorrow in his life, he finds God's strength sufficient. I want that kind of faith. Thank you for taking time to talk to us today. I received Jesus Christ today."

The fourth woman, Christine, got up to leave. She seemed to be in a hurry. When she got to the door, she turned and said, "You sounded so serious when you spoke."

"Yes, our relationship to Christ is serious business," I replied.

"I'll talk to you about it—sometime," she said.

Just then, Pam came out of the kitchen to say goodbye to Christine as she hurried out the door. After she left I asked Pam, "What happened to you? Are you all right?"

"I had butterflies in my stomach," she said. "I was so nervous about my mother and her friend, I actually got sick. But I want you to know that I did pray while you were talking. I desperately wanted my mom to accept Christ. I'm really surprised that she and her friend stayed."

"Pam, both your mom and Lou prayed to receive Christ today. Your fears were in vain. Isn't God good?"

"I can't believe it. I just can't believe it!" she exclaimed. "The whole neighborhood could have been here and I wouldn't have been nervous. It's just that my mother. . . ."

"I know," I said. "It's normal to become fearful over what someone close to you may do. It's also a time of testing—a time to hand over our fears to the Lord and put our trust in him."

Before Pam's mom left she said, "Nellie, would you be willing to have lunch with us after the holidays? It would be nice if you could tell us more about the Bible."

Of course I said, "I'd love to."

Reflection

Fear saps us of our energy and is never productive. It also robs us of our peace. But Jesus said, "Peace I leave with you; my peace I give you. I do not give to you as the world gives. Do not let your hearts be troubled and do not be afraid" (John 14:27).

Pam is a different person today because she is learning that God is in control of all things. She has witnessed a miracle, a change of mind and heart in her mother. It's a beginning. Philippians 1:6 says, "Being confident of this, that he who began a good work in you will carry it on to completion until the day of Christ Jesus."

Christine left early and seemed uncomfortable with my message. I didn't know if I would ever see her again, but I knew that Pam and Becky would have contact with her.

The following week, Becky came to me and said, "Jessica, my six-year-old, spent the evening with Christine's daughter, Gabrielle. An interesting thing happened. Gabrielle read some Bible verses that her grandmother had written down before she died. Then she asked Jessica if she could explain how to become a Christian. Even though my daughter is only six, she knows the Lord and can explain the way of salvation. She simply told Gabrielle she would have to confess that she had sinned against God and then receive Jesus as her Savior.

"'I'd like to do that,' Gabrielle said. Then Jessica prayed and helped her eight-year-old friend pray to receive Christ. At that point the bedroom door opened and Christine asked, 'What are you girls doing?'

"'We're reading verses from the Bible,' her daughter answered.

"'Oh,' she said as she closed the door."

The Christmas Coffees are over until next year. Only God knows the far-reaching results. Perhaps he will see to it that Christine opens the door to Jesus Christ.

49

Healed in Prison

If we confess our sins, he is faithful and just and will forgive
us our sins and purify us from all unrighteousness.

1 John 1:9

As Ed was finishing out the last few days of his prison sentence, his heart was full of praise and thanksgiving to God. Though keenly aware of the arthritic pain in his back, he looked at his steel cot and thin mattress and prayed, "Thank you, Lord, that I wasn't made to sleep on the floor." When he looked through the iron bars on his cell window, he was filled with the wonder of God's creation. Later he told us the rest of his prayer:

Thank you, Lord, for the birds and flowers, the trees, the sky, and water. You've given them all for us to enjoy. I never want to take your works for granted again. And, Lord, I didn't think I could ever say this to you, but thank you for allowing me to go to prison. You had to hit me hard, but you got my attention. You have taught me about priorities, so the rest of my life is yours. You will be first, my family second, and business third. Thank you for forgiving me. I will always want and need your guidance.

Ed was far from a hardened criminal. He was a highly skilled sales-and-marketing expert who had received many awards. Ed had lectured at Michigan State and Cornell and been invited to the White House to represent the hotel industry. For fifteen years, he was vice-president of sales and marketing at a posh thousand-room hotel and club in Florida. Under his tenure at the resort, sales rose tenfold. By the world's standards, Ed lived extremely well. Most people would say, "He had it made." So how did Ed land in prison—this man who at one point in his life mortgaged his home to help build a church?

My husband and I had occasion to have lunch with Ed and his wife, Jeanne, whom we knew as members of the church we attended in Florida. Since we were just winter visitors, we had not read any of the newspaper articles connected with his incarceration. "Tell me, Ed," I asked, "why were you in prison?"

"I unwisely got involved in a kickback scheme," he said ruefully. "An associate of mine for over thirty years, a man I trusted, came up with the idea. Although I said no at the beginning, later he told me there would be ten other participants and convinced me there was nothing wrong."

"Being a Christian, didn't that bother you?" I asked.

"You bet it did, but this happened at a time when I had taken my eyes off the Lord. That's a dangerous situation! I understand now what Peter was talking about when he said, 'Your enemy the devil prowls around like a roaring lion looking for someone to devour' [1 Peter 5:8b]. It's the weak Christian the devil is looking for. That was me. It didn't seem so bad at first. I was busy working and making money. But, even though I wasn't close to the Lord at the time, God never left me. The Holy Spirit kept after me, convicting me that I should come clean. Soon I was miserable with guilt."

"What did you do about it?" I asked.

"Since I knew the day would come when I would have to pay everything back, I didn't touch the money except to put it in a special fund. But I became a recluse. I was depressed and ashamed and didn't want to speak to people at church. When I came home I went to my room and pulled the shades. Since my guilt was more than I could bear, my health began to fail."

"Did Jeanne notice your change?" I asked.

"Oh, I knew she was concerned about me. She asked a lot of questions about why I was so glum and wanted to know what was wrong. I kept telling her I was just tired.

"Finally I couldn't keep it to myself any longer. 'I have defrauded my customers,' I told Jeanne. 'I have sinned against God, and I've let you down. I want to make restitution. Can you find it in your heart to forgive me and help me make things right?'"

"Were you able to forgive Ed right away?" I asked Jeanne.

"I was angry and hurt, of course. Then Ed got angry because I was angry, so I said, 'Now wait a minute. How do you expect me to react? Give me a minute to catch my breath.' When I realized the load of guilt he'd been carrying, it explained everything. I put my arms around him and assured him of my love. I told him, 'I'll stick with you no matter what. With God's help we'll work it out.'"

Ed, with tears in his eyes, turned to me and said, "I was overwhelmed with Jeanne's love and forgiveness. I couldn't have made it without her support."

"Perhaps this is what our wedding vows mean when we promise to stay together for better or for worse," I said. "But what about your children? Did you tell them right away?"

"The thought of telling them was agony," Ed said, "but I knew it had to be done, even though I might lose their love and respect. I had to give myself up to the authorities and I didn't want the children to hear it from anyone else. Of course they were shocked. But they put their arms around me and said, 'Dad, we love you. We'll pray for you and support you through this.'

"Next I went to my pastor and told him I had a problem. He could tell I was distraught but I was too ashamed to tell him the complete story."

"Then what did you do?" I asked.

"I went to my lawyer, who advised me not to turn myself in. 'It would be like waving a red flag,' he said. 'You haven't been accused yet and may never be.' I found another lawyer, who gave me the same advice. I was especially concerned about Jeanne and what would happen to her financially. But I was shocked when this lawyer suggested that we divide our joint property and then get a divorce. 'That way they can't touch her money, and you can always remarry later,' he said.

"At Jeanne's urging, we went to a third lawyer. He gave me the same advice as the other two. 'What about my conscience?' I asked. 'How do I correct my wrongs? This whole thing goes against my Christian beliefs. What do I do with the money? I haven't spent a cent.'

"'This is a joke,' the lawyer laughed. 'You take the money, but you don't spend it. If it will alleviate some of your guilt, give *me* the money and I'll give it to charity.'

"I left his office heartsick. Even after seeing a Christian psychologist, I found no relief. The guilt was tearing me apart. I resigned my job, hoping that would settle matters.

"I finally decided to visit a longtime trusted minister who had once been a prison chaplain. After telling him my story, I asked whether he knew of a good lawyer who would agree that I should turn myself in and would represent me in court. Fortunately he did, and an appointment was set up immediately.

"This attorney was very kind. He said that because of my age and general background I would probably be put on probation or, at worst, under house arrest. He then made arrangements to see the prosecutor. At that point I decided to tell my pastor the whole story."

"What was his reaction?" I asked.

"He had had no idea of the reason for my distraught condition. I told him I had confessed my sin to God and planned to resign from the church office I held. Jeanne offered to resign from the women's ministries, too.

"Pastor said, 'There's no reason why Jeanne should resign. She hasn't done anything wrong.' He then said, 'God has forgiven you, and I forgive you.'

"'But,' I told him, 'I just can't forgive myself.'

"My pastor helped me understand that lack of self-forgiveness is pride, whereby we put ourselves above God. It reveals a failure to trust the One who has offered us unconditional love and forgiveness."

"Why were you eventually sent to prison?" I asked. "That wasn't what your lawyer expected."

"That was quite a surprise," Ed replied. "The prosecutor was not as sympathetic as my lawyer. He told me I could get anywhere from nine to seventeen years. The lawyer and prosecutor went back and forth. My lawyer argued that it was my first offense, but the prosecutor was determined that white-collar crime must stop and that I should be made the example. I was sentenced to two and a half years.

"Of course, I was shocked and depressed at the sentence. They took me to the county jail overnight, then to South Florida Reception Center. I thought I was on my way to a minimum-security prison, but I was placed in maximum security—with hardened criminals. I was there for two weeks. Then, because of my deep depression, I was temporarily put in the medical center for another two weeks.

"My stay in maximum security was a humiliating experience. I was stripped of any remaining dignity. At first my depression got worse and I didn't want to live. I had disappointed God, my family, and my church. I was a failure. One of the inmates had told me he could get me anything I wanted. Since I just wanted to die, I asked him if he could get me a pill so I could end it all.

"But God wouldn't let me do it. Suddenly a verse from the Bible flooded my mind. It was 1 Corinthians 6:19–20: 'Do you not know that your body is a temple of the Holy Spirit. . . . ? You are not your own; you were bought at a price. Therefore honor God with your body.' I realized that suicide was no answer. All I could do was cast myself on God and plead for mercy."

"Did that give you relief?" I asked Ed.

"That was the beginning of the healing process. I began to devour Scripture. I read Psalm 51 over and over again. With David, who had also sinned greatly, I prayed, 'Have mercy on me, O God, according to your unfailing love; according to your great compassion blot out my transgressions. Wash away all my iniquity and cleanse me from my sin. . . . Against you, you only, have I sinned and done what is evil in your sight.'

"I knew my greatest sin was against God. He created me and formed me. Because I had received Jesus Christ as my Savior, knowing 1 John 1:9 was a comfort: 'If we confess our sins, he is faithful and just and will forgive us our sins and purify us from all unrighteousness.'"

"Ed, did you do anything constructive while in prison?" I asked.

"While in maximum security I was given a job as a clerk in the tool room. *This place needs some improving,* I thought. The prison authorities liked my ideas and I was able to use my business experience. I was allowed to redesign the tool room, develop a new job description, and compile an inventory. I got satisfaction out of being useful.

"After a few weeks I was moved to Dade Correctional Center, which was a minimum-security facility. That was a great improvement. I spent a lot of time in chapel and joined a Bible study group. Soon I began to witness to other inmates and share with them about

God's love and forgiveness. When I saw that God could use me even in prison, I could praise him for this experience.

"One day I received over four hundred cards from the church. My pastor had encouraged the congregation to continue praying for me and to let me know they still cared. I was overwhelmed, and so were the prison officials. The chaplain announced the news at the service and read some of the cards. 'We are looking forward to your homecoming,' some said.

"Because of my good behavior, and prison overcrowding, my sentence was reduced to a little over five months. I finished my prison term on a Tuesday. Sunday morning I went to church with Jeanne and sat near the front. That wasn't easy. *How will I be received?* I wondered. But I prayed, 'Whatever happens, Lord, I'm going to serve you the rest of my life.'"

Paul and I were there in church that Sunday. After the opening hymn, the pastor said, "I want to tell you all that Ed came home on Tuesday and is with us this morning." There was a joyful clapping of hands! He came home to his church family and they received him. There had been repentance and forgiveness. Ed had met God's requirements and could once again enjoy fellowship with other believers.

At the end of the service, when the invitation was given for rededication of our lives to Christ, Ed and Jeanne walked the aisle as a testimony to God's grace. Ed was indicating to all of us that he wanted to serve the Lord the rest of his life.

My husband and I went up to stand beside them. What a joy it was to talk to them in the counseling room. Tears flowed freely as Ed thanked the Lord for his mercy, his love, and forgiveness.

It was then that I had suggested the lunch meeting at which Ed later told us how he was healed in prison.

"Yes, I would like that," he said. "I want to tell you what God has done in my life."

Reflection

It's been over a year since Ed's incarceration. He is now working for a Christian organization. God is using him to be a witness. God did not forsake Ed in prison and he never will.

50

Witnessing Starts at Home

> But when the chief priests and the teachers of the law saw the wonderful things he [Jesus] did and the children shouting in the temple area, "Hosanna to the Son of David," they were indignant.
>
> "Do you hear what these children are saying?" they asked him.
>
> "Yes," replied Jesus, "have you never read, 'From the lips of children and infants you have ordained praise'?"
>
> Matthew 21:15–16

When Easter services were over, Emily had a big question for her parents: "Why did Jesus have to die?"

"He died for our sins," her mother, Sandy, answered. "We are all sinners, and Jesus was the only one who could pay the penalty for our sins. He was the perfect sacrifice."

"What's a sacrifice?" the little girl asked.

"In the Old Testament, before Jesus' time, an animal was slain to take the place of the person who sinned. It had to be a spotless lamb, goat, or bull—an animal without defect. This offering was to cover the sin until Jesus came. Only Jesus could truly substitute for our sins, and he sacrificed his life for us."

"Why was Jesus the perfect sacrifice?" Emily persisted.

"Because, even though he was human, he never sinned. When Jesus died on the cross, God was giving his Son to pay the penalty for *our* sins."

"But if Jesus died, God did, too, because they're the same. Right?"

"God the *Son* died on the cross and then arose from the dead. God the *Father* is up in heaven. When we receive Jesus as our Savior, God accepts us because of what his Son did on the cross for us. That's what John 3:16 means. 'For God so loved the world that he gave his one and only Son, that whoever believes in him shall not perish but have eternal life.'"

Sandy was ready with those answers because Jesus Christ was a reality in her own life. She had known the time would come when her daughter would have some questions about the Lord.

When Sandy shared this story with me, her eyes sparkled. She knew that Emily had listened carefully and learned the wonderful truths about Jesus Christ. What greater joy can a mother and father receive than to give their children the answer to eternal life!

Our friend Dale came to me at church one Sunday and said, "I really feel all stressed-out. Between my business, preparing to move, and the kids underfoot, I wonder if I'm going to make it. Please pray for me. I'm so impatient with the children, and I really don't want to be that kind of father."

"I know four children can be a trial at times," I said. "I had three, and now I look back and all I can think of was the fun we had together. You'll make it. We parents all survive."

Dale said, "Let me tell you what happened yesterday. Because I wanted the house to look presentable for prospective buyers, I've been painting and fixing up the place. I noticed that someone had written on the freshly painted wall. I was sure Debbie was the culprit. So I called her and asked whether she had written on the wall.

"'No, Daddy,' our six-year-old replied.

"'Yes, you did,' I said. Of course, she broke out in tears, and afterwards I felt badly because I was really hard on her. But I knew she was the one who did it. How would you have handled the situation, Nellie?"

"It's easy to say *now* what I would have done. Although I've made mistakes and certainly wasn't a perfect parent, I'm older now and have learned from experience. It takes a lot of wisdom to raise children. Dale, you want to be a godly role model, right?"

"I sure do."

"If you think Debbie is having a problem with lying, why don't you say, 'Do you know who wrote on the wall?' If she says, 'No, Daddy,' say, 'Let's ask God to show us who did. We need to take care of this situation.' Ask her to pray, too. If she's guilty, she'll probably cry. But you must be gentle with her so she feels safe in telling you the truth."

"That's a good idea," Dale said. "I'll try to remember that."

Dale shared our conversation with his wife, Suzi, who called me a couple of days later and said, "I need to tell you what happened next. Debbie came downstairs with a cut on the sleeve of her T-shirt. She'd obviously used the scissors on it, but I asked, 'Debbie, how did your sleeve get cut?'

"'I don't know, Mommy.'

"'You have no idea who did it?'

"'No, Mommy,' she said very softly.

"'Then I said, 'Let's pray and ask God to show us who did it. We can't have anyone cutting up your clothes. I'll pray and then you pray.' Debbie prayed and went on her way, apparently not bothered at all. After dinner that night she came to me and said, 'I need to tell you something, Mommy. It has to be a secret.'

"'Oh, you've got a secret to tell me? Great,' I said.

"'Mom, I know who cut my T-shirt.'

"'You do? Tell me about it.'

"Debbie hung her head and struggled to speak. 'I did it, Mom.' She couldn't stand it. She had lied before, but this time she had asked God to point out the guilty one and the pressure was too much. I told her, 'I'm glad you told me the truth. That's what God wants you to do. It also shows that the Spirit of God is working in your life. That's what happens when you receive Jesus as your Savior. God's Spirit lives in you and helps you to do what's right. I think it's important that we tell Daddy about this.'

"'Oh, Mom, do I have to tell him?' Debbie pleaded.

"'I'll go with you. It will be okay.' We went upstairs and Debbie told her dad what she had done.

"Dale said, 'It was wrong of you to do that, Debbie, but I'm glad you came and told me. You must always tell the truth. Tell me, Debbie, why did you cut your T-shirt?'

"'I wanted to be like you, Daddy. When you go running in the morning you put your black T-shirt on, and it has no sleeves. I want to look like you.'"

Suzi told me that Dale's heart melted. He took his daughter in his arms and said, "I think we can fix that. Mommy will take you shopping tomorrow. Maybe she can find a T-shirt just like mine. But please don't use the scissors on your clothes. You ruin them and I work hard to buy them for you." Debbie said she was very sorry and promised not to do it again.

"Debbie and I went shopping," Suzi told me. "We found a black sleeveless T-shirt just like Dale's."

Both Suzi and Dale were excited to see the change in their little girl. They thanked God that night for the working of the Holy Spirit in Debbie's heart.

Reflection

Jesus said, "Let the little children come to me, and do not hinder them, for the kingdom of heaven belongs to such as these" (Matt. 19:14). What a privilege it is to train up a child in the nurture and admonition of the Lord!

Young mothers often come to me and say, "I don't get out of the house very often. How can I be a witness for the Lord? I go around with guilt because I know God wants me to share my faith."

What I tell them is that teaching their children about Jesus Christ *is* being a faithful witness. It is also the most important thing a Christian can do as far as his or her training is concerned. Living a life consistent with what we teach is of equal importance. God wants parents to "train a child in the way he should go" (Prov. 22:6). That is God's will, and he is pleased when we heed his command.

51

The Truth
Will Come Out

For all have sinned and fall short of the glory of God, and are justified freely by his grace through the redemption that came by Christ Jesus.

Romans 3:23–24

[Jesus said:] "I tell you the truth, no one can see the kingdom of God unless he is born again."

John 3:3

Nellie, our women's society is having a series of talks on the religions of the world," Anne, my neighbor, phoned and said. "You're a religious person. How about attending a session or two? We meet on Tuesday mornings from nine to eleven. Are you free next Tuesday, and would you like to come?"

"It sounds interesting," I answered. "Excuse me while I check my calendar. . . . Yes, I'll be able to attend."

I looked forward to the meeting. The little Community Church was only a few blocks away. I had heard it was liberal in doctrine and felt this might be a chance to find out for myself. I had attended a wedding there once, but that was the only connection I had with this church.

Anne introduced me to several of her friends. We chatted while sipping coffee before the meeting started. They were friendly and made me feel welcome.

"Today," the moderator said with enthusiasm, "we'll be studying about our own religion, Christianity. Cynthia Adams our speaker, teaches in our children's department. We're looking forward to hearing what she has to say."

Cynthia was an articulate speaker who talked to us simply and to the point. I was delighted to hear her say, "Even though we can't all be missionaries, we can all share our faith. Because we're all born into the world as sinners, the Bible says that we must be born again."

At that point a woman raised her hand and said, "But we've never been taught that at *this* church. I'm not a sinner—and I don't agree with what you're saying."

"We are studying the religions of the world," Cynthia said patiently to the woman. "Today I'm speaking about the Christian faith. I'm telling you what the Bible says. That's my source of information and my authority."

Although Cynthia's remarks caused quite an uproar, she kept her composure and continued in a gracious manner.

After the meeting was over, I waited to talk to her. "Have you been born again?" I asked.

"Yes, I have," she answered.

"I'm a born-again Christian, too," I said.

Cynthia beamed. "I thought I was the only believer here. God must have sent you here today for my encouragement," she said. "Let's meet for lunch next week."

On the way home, my neighbor Anne asked me how I liked the meeting.

I told her I agreed with the speaker: "She was right on target. I'm sorry the woman in the audience gave her a hard time. Cynthia knew what she was talking about. The Bible was her reference book. What other source is there for truth?"

"Well, I guess we don't know much about that," Anne dismissed the matter.

I went to that church with Anne several times after that, but found it to be cold and lifeless. They did not seem to really welcome the gospel.

Anne's parents lived a few blocks away. When Anne's father died suddenly at home, her mother was devastated and inconsolable.

Anne called me and said, "I don't know what to do about my mother. Will you come over and talk to her? Maybe you can help her."

When I went to the house, I found Anne's mother in bed. She was usually a very dignified woman, but today she was weeping uncontrollably and still in shock.

I sat down beside her bed, took her hand, and said, "I'm going to pray for you." She squeezed my hand tightly. While I prayed, she cried but still hung on to my hand. I stayed with her for several hours. Before I left, I shared the gospel with her and said, "God is your only source of help. When you feel better, perhaps we can talk again."

Later Anne and her family thanked me repeatedly for taking the time to talk and pray with her mother.

Several other neighbors have asked me to pray when an emergency arose in their families. "We know you get through to God," one woman said. But when things got better, most of them weren't interested in knowing more about God—which I find very sad.

When I met Cynthia for lunch, I asked her how she got involved in the church at which I had heard her speak.

"We moved to this area from the east side of the city and wanted to attend a church near our home. We thought the Community Church would be the answer. I now have my doubts, but I'll continue to teach my Sunday school class and see if I can be an influence in the children's lives."

"How did you become a Christian?" I asked.

"I accepted Christ when I was twelve years old, at a church on the other side of town. It took a long time before I grew spiritually, however. An interesting thing happened one day when I was on my way to work. On the bus I noticed the lady next to me reading some shorthand notes. I knew shorthand well, and my eyes caught the Scripture references she had written on a pad. I didn't say anything at first, but we both got off at the same stop. Since it was raining, she offered to share her umbrella.

"'I noticed you were reading Scripture,' I said to her.

"'Yes, I'm memorizing them for my class,' she told me. 'I attend a Bible class and we have a wonderful teacher.'

"When I told her I was a Christian and wanted to learn more about the Bible, she said I was welcome to come. That was God's provision for me," Cynthia said. "I had a hunger for the Word and I was satisfied. The teacher knew the Bible well and I ate it up, much like a starving child. That's how I began to grow as a Christian. Oh, the teacher's name was David Gillespie. Have you ever heard of him, Nellie?"

"Of course. He came to our church after he retired," I answered. "I loved hearing him speak from time to time. He's now with the Lord."

Cynthia and I had a good time getting better acquainted. When it was time to get back to our families, we promised to keep in touch. "Before we leave may I ask you to pray for my husband?" Cynthia asked me. "I'm concerned about him. Bob's a wonderful man, but he doesn't know the Lord."

We prayed together and I promised that Paul and I would continue to remember Bob in prayer.

It was a sad day when, sometime after that, Cynthia called and said, "I won't be teaching my Sunday school class any longer."

"What happened?" I wanted to know.

"One of the officers in the church stood outside my classroom and heard me talking about confessing our sins and our need to receive Christ as our Savior. He reported it to the elders and I was told I could not talk about sin to the children because 'We don't believe in teaching our children such things.'

"'Then I resign,' I told him. 'If I can't teach Bible truth, I don't belong here.' Then I went home and told Bob that we no longer were members of that church and would have to find another place to worship. Bob took it well. 'It's up to you to find another church,' he said."

"I'd love to have you come to our church," I said.

"Nellie, your church is so big, but I've heard about a small evangelical group I'd like to try. Perhaps Bob can get acquainted with some of the men. It would help him to know some real Christians on a personal basis."

Paul and I continued to pray for Bob. One day Cynthia called and said, "Bob came to Christ last night. It's wonderful! He already wants to get busy for the Lord. He has seen such a difference in the two churches. God has opened his heart and his eyes. I'm so happy and grateful to the Lord."

Cynthia and I continued to see and encourage each other. One day she said, "I love our little fellowship group, but there's nothing for my son. There are no boys his age. We've decided to come to your church so he can get into a young people's group." Of course I was delighted.

Even though we now attend the same church, we rarely get together. Cynthia and Bob are busy people, and I spend a lot of my time speaking and writing. But when Cynthia and I do see each other, we are reminded of how God brought us together—and we are thankful.

Reflection

It is dangerous to attend a church where the Bible is not honored as the authoritative Word of God. Such a church is preaching "a different gospel" (Gal. 1:6). Many churches do not want to talk about sin. It makes them feel uncomfortable, so they pretend there is no such thing. When my rabbi friend said to me, "We don't talk about sin—only 'missing the mark'"—I realized that "missing the mark" feels more comfortable. People say, "We all make mistakes," as if to excuse their wrongdoing. For many Christians, church has become nothing more than a social gathering place.

How blessed we are when we confess our sins and experience God's cleansing and forgiveness. Then we are free of sin's burden—free to do what is right.

One day, when we see Christ, we will be without sin. Until then, when we do become aware that we have sinned we can and must confess it.

If we claim to be without sin, we deceive ourselves and the truth is not in us. If we confess our sins, he is faithful and just and will forgive us our sins and purify us from all unrighteousness. If we claim we have not sinned, we make him out to be a liar and his word has no place in our lives.

1 John 1:8–10

Blessed Assurance

If we confess our sins, he is faithful and just and will forgive
us our sins and purify us from all unrighteousness.

1 John 1:9

My friend Casey asked me to comment on people who believe they can be saved but worry that if they sin they are lost again. "I visit a man in a nursing home who has no peace," he said. "He says he's never sure from one day to the next if he's really saved. Nellie, have you had any experience with people who are insecure about their salvation?"

"Yes, I have," I said. "And it's certainly important for a believer's peace of mind to feel secure in Christ."

Then I told Casey about my favorite aunt, who—like the man in the nursing home—once believed that even after accepting Christ as Savior, salvation could be lost if a person sinned.

For quite some time, my aunt had been in a continuous state of misery because she didn't know for sure if she was going to heaven when she died. We had many discussions about it. I loved my aunt, but it grieved me to see her in such a state. I had to be careful and wanted to be respectful. I'm sorry to say, I did argue with her once in a while, but she was a sweet person and never got angry.

What this situation did for me was cause me to search the Scriptures for answers. I was rather young at the time, so I'm afraid that even though I wanted to help my aunt, I also wanted to prove to her that I was right. That was pride on my part, and God calls that sin.

Yes, I sinned by my attitude, but God didn't erase my name from the Book of Life. Instead he gently taught me the better way.

My aunt later moved to California and I didn't see her for many years. When she came back for a visit we had a long talk. The first thing I said to her was, "Auntie, I want to apologize to you for trying to prove you wrong about the security of the believer. I really didn't have a right attitude."

"I don't remember that at all," she said. "But I now know that when I die I'm going to be with the Lord. I am sure of that. I've been attending 'Bible Study Fellowship' in California. We compare Scripture with Scripture to find the answer for our hope. I now understand what it means to have eternal life. Jesus paid for my salvation, and I'm truly secure in him. He went to prepare a place for me. I'm no longer worried about my future. I believe—just like you." She beamed and gave me a hug.

She was a different person after that. I could see that she had real peace. My aunt has since passed away, and I know she's with the Lord.

I have found some verses that are helpful to Christians who, like my aunt, are not sure about their salvation. John 10:27–30 is a beautiful passage to read and remember. Jesus said:

> "My sheep listen to my voice; I know them, and they follow me. I give them eternal life, and they shall never perish; no one can snatch them out of my hand. My Father, who has given them to me, is greater than all; no one can snatch them out of my Father's hand. I and the Father are one."

Jesus is the Good Shepherd. He is in control. I believe a person who *claims* to have accepted Christ, yet continually lives in a state of sin, thereby rebelling against God, probably isn't saved. The difference between a truly born-again believer and an unbeliever is that the believer runs away from sin and the unbeliever runs *after* it. When the believer does fall into sin and the Spirit of God convicts him, God has made a provision for that: "If we confess our sins, he is faithful and just and will forgive us our sins and purify us from all unrighteousness" (1 John 1:9).

That was written to Christians. None of us is perfect, but our goal is to fulfill God's requirements. We press on toward that goal, as Paul says in Philippians 3:14. We don't give up, because we know we are God's children and must take one step after another, growing in knowledge of his will and his loving grace. He is perfect and we are not, but we come to God through the perfection of our Savior. He is our righteousness, and God the Father looks at us through Jesus Christ to see if we are covered by his blood.

Hebrews 12 says this so well that we should read the entire chapter often and especially keep verses 4 through 8 in our hearts:

In your struggle against sin, you have not yet resisted to the point of shedding your blood. And you have forgotten that word of encouragement that addresses you as sons:

"My son, do not make light of the Lord's discipline,
and do not lose heart when he rebukes you,
because the Lord disciplines those he loves,
and he punishes everyone he accepts as a son."

Endure hardship as discipline; God is treating you as sons. For what son is not disciplined by his father? If you are not disciplined (and everyone undergoes discipline), then you are illegitimate children and not true sons.

A person may be confused as to whether or not he or she is saved or lost. If that is the case, it is best to check to see if that person is truly born again. Ask, "Have you received Jesus Christ as your sacrifice for sin? Have you told him you want to live for him and have him guide and direct your life?" If the answer is "yes," you might double-check by asking, "Do you have a desire to read the Bible and obey his commands?" If the answer again is "yes," it is a good indication that this person is in the family of God.

Reflection

The apostle John said: "My dear children, I write this to you so that you will not sin. But if anybody does sin, we have one who speaks to the Father in our defense—Jesus Christ, the Righteous One. He is the atoning sacrifice for our sins, and not only for ours but also for the sins of the whole world" (1 John 2:1–2).

All of us as believers must accept the fact that we will not be perfect until we are with our perfect Redeemer in heaven. Until then, we need to keep growing in Christ and press on toward that goal.

May you enjoy the abundant life that Christ came to give all who confess their sinfulness, accept him as Savior, and dedicate their lives to serving the Lord.